A Short

JAZZ

A Short History of

JAZZ

Bob Yurochko
Kean College of New Jersey

Note from Wynton Marsalis

Nelson-Hall Publishers/Chicago

Project Editor: Rachel Schick
Illustrations: Corasue Nicholas
Cover Painting: *Jazzman* by Mary Selfridge

Library of Congress Cataloging-in-Publication Data

Yurochko, Bob
   A short history of jazz / Bob Yurochko.
     p.   cm.
   Includes bibliographical references (p. 297) and index.
   Discography: p. 299
   Videography: p. 303
   ISBN 0-8304-1331-6
   1. Jazz—History and criticism. I. Title.
  ML3506.Y87   1993
  781.65'09—dc20   92-2738
                           CIP
                          MN

Manufactured in the United States of America.

10 9 8 7 6 5 4 3 2 1

CONTENTS

NOTE FROM

WYNTON MARSALIS

Bob Yurochko's book, *A Short History of Jazz*, is comprehensive. It is written to address specifically the gaps in the education of the newer students of jazz. Of particular importance is the inclusion of suggested videos, which give the students a chance to come into contact with significant information from the history of jazz as presented by the artists themselves. This will be a welcome addition to readers worldwide and is something that is sorely needed for the modern student.

—Wynton Marsalis

ACKNOWLEDGMENTS

Many people have been very generous with their time and efforts in making this monograph possible. I am indebted to Vincent Pelote, librarian at the Institute of Jazz Studies at Rutgers in Newark, New Jersey, for his expertise concerning recordings and many suggestions for the manuscript. Extensive research materials were provided in New Orleans by the curators of the Research Center at the Historic New Orleans Collection, and the Jazz Museum and Archives of the Louisiana State Museum. Bruce Boyd Raeburn provided some very interesting insights at the William Ransom Hogan Jazz Archive at Tulane University. John Litweiler, author and former director of the Jazz Institute of Chicago from 1977 to 1988, is to be commended for his incisive comments and historical knowledge. Also, Assistant Editor Rachel Schick helped give the book life with many stylistic suggestions. I am grateful to Robert Santelli, writer and professor of music at Monmouth College in New Jersey for his advice and encouragement, which was immeasurable. The rationale for this book was suggested in part by Dr. Mark Lender, author and grants officer at Kean College, New Jersey, where we spent many hours of organizational planning. Much of the biographical data, particularly of the earlier jazz musicians, is attributed to Leonard Feather's scholarly volume, *The Encyclopedia of Jazz*. There were many publishers, recording companies, musicians and photographers who generously supplied me with necessary materials and I hope that this trend will continue for the sake of all writers. Finally, I am eternally grateful to my wife, Trisha, who was a great source of encouragement throughout this long project. Our son, Michael the computer wiz, spent many hours helping me organize the manuscript, which seemed at times quite hopeless. This book is dedicated in large measure to my many jazz students who were inspirational for its need.

—Bob Yurochko

PREFACE

This book is intended for both beginning and advanced students of jazz. The format lends itself to the further development of those with musical skills as well as providing a solid foundation for laypersons. The reader will find a chronological history of jazz from early West African roots to contemporary times. Each phase of development is presented with brief stylistic introductions which focus on major performers and the music. A Study Guide that accompanies each part includes important recordings and videotapes, as well as selected readings. One of the most important innovations of this book is the use of videotapes, which have become increasingly available. Through the use of videotapes students are able to recognize performers, instruments, and the music. Visual impressions reinforce the aural experiences of form and musical elements. Many of the videos also include interviews with the performers, who add valuable insights into their music. It is *strongly recommended* that all efforts are made to upgrade the sound system of the television monitors being used. Adding a tuner or amplifier and larger speakers of quality to television sets with stereophonic sound offers the best reproduction of the music. At the end of the book is a list of jazz video producers and distributors. There are a great variety of jazz videos now available, and those chosen for this book best represent each jazz style as presented chronologically in the text. In most cases catalogs are available upon request from these companies, while others charge a small fee. By using both recordings and videos, the instructor or student gains a great deal of flexibility when examining each style.

Suggestions

Using this book as a classroom text provides many options and avenues to the study of jazz. Since the main activity should be listening, recordings and videos that are suggested will enhance the jazz experience if approached properly. The videotapes, like the recordings, should be carefully previewed because the videos need not be viewed from beginning to end to be effective. The instructor is encouraged to use live music for greatest effect when possible. I would suggest that material from the study guides could be readily adapted for this purpose. Written tests and long lectures, which are hallmarks of traditional learning, *should not* be emphasized. Imaginative activities such as live music, demonstrations, selected readings, and informal discussions are some very effective ways of approaching meaningful teaching and learning. Reports written by students that are informal but basically structured are an excellent way of setting up a one-on-one dialogue and tracking learning effectiveness. The videos should be presented with limited but necessary narration by the instructor to focus on instrument, performer, and style identification. The videos have an ameliorating effect on the minds of students that becomes indelible.

The material in this book is intended for a single semester study; however, it will easily provide enough material for a full-year course. It is recommended that every style be covered in a semester course and that the instructor or student carefully choose recordings or videotapes to supplement the study. In some cases availability will dictate the proper medium. Instructors should make every attempt to build a comprehensive jazz video library along with compact disc, LP, and cassette recordings. Offering this study or course over a full year can be accomplished easily with an in-depth approach using both recordings and videos for each style, with supplemental readings of suggested books. The student should be able to recognize audibly the various styles and instruments used in jazz by the end of the course and the instructor should maintain a balance of visual and purely audible experiences.

The *Listener's Guide* in chapter 26 presents some very interesting options for the student and should be used to structure informal written reports or oral reports on listening assignments. Understanding the elements of jazz music in the Listener's Guide will provide the student with a foundation in basic recognition. This section should be used as a cross-reference when approaching each style, and as a reference point for each of the various activities throughout the entire study period. It is imperative that the student have some basic understanding of melody, rhythm, harmony, form, improvisation, and the other elements before and during all phases of jazz study. These elements can be taught or learned by using the various exercises that are suggested. Exercises and examples are crucial to comprehension. Using the language of jazz will be accelerated by referring frequently to the *Glossary*, which explains jazz terms as they are to be used and understood. There are currently a number of jazz radio stations, which can be a great source of inexpensive jazz experience. Many libraries offer listening labs with a cross section of jazz styles, along with interesting books on jazz.

The *Smithsonian Collection of Classic Jazz (SCCJ)* in its revised edition of 1987 is referred to throughout much of the book because of its availability in all three formats—CD, LP, and cassette. It is an excellent collection of selected recordings with incisive historical annotations by Martin Williams. Another feature of the collection is the biographical index of jazz musicians by Ira Gitler. This collection is highly recommended. The recording industry is currently experiencing massive changes as vinyl LPs are being phased out in favor of digital compact discs and cassette tapes; consequently, many fine examples of jazz styles and performers are no longer accessible on vinyl recordings. One such example is the early music of Don Ellis. Selected lists of recordings and videos are included in the book, with an extended discography and videography. The bibliography provides some very interesting reading and additional insights. Again, it is recommended that the student study the Listener's Guide and become familiar with the Glossary before proceeding with Part I.

PART I

Early Background

CHAPTER ONE

WEST AFRICAN AND EUROPEAN HISTORY

Since the music we call jazz is essentially the black man's art, it makes sense to trace African Americans through slavery. The autobiography written by Fredrick Douglass in 1845, *Narrative of The Life of Frederick Douglass: An American Slave* adequately describes the complete subjugation of the human spirit in slavery. The novel by Harriet Beecher Stowe, *Uncle Tom's Cabin*, written before the Civil War in 1852, depicts this human tragedy with its passionate indictment of slavery. This powerful novel sold 300,000 copies in the first year, was translated into thirty-seven languages, and has never gone out of print. Its political impact was immense, with heartrending emotional influence. The characters of Uncle Tom, Topsy, Sambo, Simon Legree, and Little Eva became impressed on the minds of Americans for generations. Slavery was first introduced in Virginia about 1619 and continued over two hundred years. The *Middle Passage*, which was in fact the Atlantic slave trade route to the southern territories of the New World, was one of several routes which also included South America and the Caribbean. It is estimated that between fifteen and twenty million slaves were captured by West African kings and sold to European merchants. This incredible number of people represents one of the largest depletions of a population from a single continent throughout the history of the world.

English, Dutch, Portugese, French, and Spanish trading companies sold these captured slaves mostly in southern climates for field work. Entire families and villages were cruelly and indiscriminately dispersed in the slaveholds of large ships. During the long ocean voyage, countless numbers of men, women and children bound in leg irons perished from disease and starvation. The exact number that died on these passages is difficult to estimate from the total number who eventually reached their destinations. These once proud African citizens arrived in the New World naked, exhausted, and starved to face a life of deprivation and inhumane cruelty. It was ironic that the sole possession of these people was their cultural heritage, expressed in religious activities and worship, through chanting, danc-

3

Figure 1.1: Many of the slaves that were shipped to the Louisiana Territory from the Slave Coast of West Africa were natives of Dahomey, which is now the Republic of Benin, and Yorubaland, which is Nigeria today.

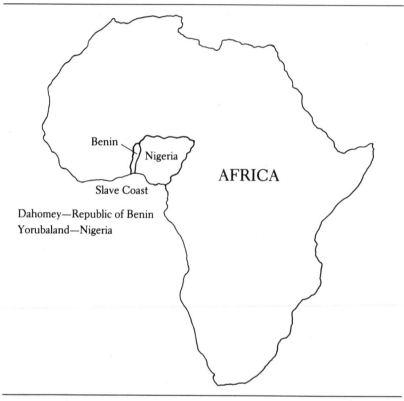

ing, and drumming. Rhythms became one of the most important elements of this rich cultural expression that would find its way into the folk and religious music of white European colonists. The unlikely mixture of such diverse cultural activities between black and white people produced the basic elements for jazz music in terms of rhythm and harmony.

Many more had come directly from West Africa, and a variety of tribes could be identified in New Orleans. Writer G.W. Cable, who lived in New Orleans, gave the following description:

> See them . . . tall, well-knit Sengalese from Cape Verde, black as ebony, with intelligent, kindly eyes and long, straight shapely noses; Mandingoes, from the Gambia River, lighter of color, of cruder form, and a cunning that shows in their countenance; whose enslavement seems specially a shame, their nation the 'merchants of Africa', dwelling in towns, industrious, thrifty, skilled in commerce and husbandry; and Foulahs

playfully miscalled 'Poulards'—fat chickens—of goodly stature, and a perceptible rose tint in their cheeks; and Sosos, famous warriors, dexterous with the African targe; and in contrast to these, with small ears, flat upturned noses, shining skin, wide mouths and white teeth, the negroes of Guinea, true and unmixed, from the Gold Coast, the Slave Coast, and the Cape of Palms.*

Although slaves were forbidden to practice their religion and culture in New Orleans, *Place Congo*, or Congo Square, was established in the late 1700s as a place for slaves to congregate on Sundays. Place Congo is located in present-day Louis Armstrong Park. Slaves would gather in large circles, singing and dancing in West African rituals. These large circles were referred to as *ring shouts*. Jerah Johnson recounts the arrival of the first professional American architect, Benjamin Latrobe, in New Orleans in January of 1819. Latrobe characterized the dances at Place Congo as brutally savage dancing to the beat of African "bamboulas" and "banzas." Although the dances were outlawed by the legislature in 1835, dancing continued on a less grandiose scale until it gradually ceased in 1856. The early years of Place Congo saw various African tribes dance

Figure 1.2: The Figa, which is a clenched fist with the upward thumb placed between the index and second finger of the hand, represents a symbol to ward off evil spirits.

---

*"The Dance In Place Congo," *Century Magazine* (February/April 1886), reprinted by Farouk von Turk, 1974.

Congo Square (*Courtesy of author*)

Louis Armstrong Park (*Courtesy of author*)

Daughter Marie Laveau's tombstone at the St. Louis Cemetery No. 1 New Orleans, LA (*Courtesy of author*)

Voodoo "gris-gris" at the Voodoo Museum of New Orleans (*Courtesy of author*)

West African/Roman Catholic Altar at the Voodoo Museum of New Orleans (*Courtesy of author*)

separately. In later years, the tribes began to blend and the instruments improved, including the addition of instruments like the tambourine.* The type of music permitted by the white masters was strictly controlled because of the fear of Yoruba and Dahomean practices of *vodun* or voodoo. Voodoo, which means "spirit world," was originally an African religion from central West Africa called "Eudon." It arrived with the slaves to the French West Indies four hundred years ago, where the ancient African beliefs were combined with Catholicism. The French term "Vaudon" became Americanized to "Voodoo." Dumballah is the most powerful spirit and god in voodoo, represented by the snake that is used to bring female spirits from the earth and male spirits from the heavens together. The ritual includes a young nude female dancing with a snake held above her head to entice the spirits. Gris-gris is French for gray-gray. Gris-gris causes a spiritual reaction when bad black magic is mixed with good white magic. Another ritual is to insert pins on the right side of voodoo dolls to produce spiritual reactions. It is a chief religion of the West African tribes of Ibos, Magos, and Dahomeans and teaches faith, love and joy as virtues.

Private vodun ceremonies and the public performances at Place Congo were important West African influences that eventually contributed to the birth of jazz. Particularly important in these performances was the use of simple drum rhythms with the leg bones of large birds. The tone of these *talking drums* communicated the tribal vocabulary; the drums expressed language through music, and masks worn by dancers created a spiritual image. Voodoo was at the core of tribal beliefs and was expressed through music and dance rituals. These rituals as followed by the Yorubas centered around the living, the dead, and the unborn. The most famous voodoo queen was Marie Laveau, who cast spells with powder and pins in voodoo dolls. Her daughter, also named Marie, carried on the tradition with exotic ceremonies and wild sex orgies, as reported by writer Jason Berry. Daughter Marie Laveau's tomb is marked in the St. Louis Cemetery No. 1 and the period of early voodoo in New Orleans is commemorated in the Voodoo Museum in the French Quarter. Although many of the voodoo customs are subjects of novels and movies today, countries such as Brazil in South America still reflect voodoo worship in popular culture. Santeria is a folk religion brought by African slaves to the Carribean in the 1700s that has spread to the United States during this century. Animal sacrifices and supernatural forces are an essential part of this religion. The root of Santeria is Yoruba, originating in Nigeria. The Brazilian form of Santeria is

*Jerah Johnson, "New Orleans' Congo Square: An Urban Setting for Early Afro-American Culture Formation," *The Journal of the Louisiana Historical Association* (Spring 1991), Vol. XXXII, No. 2.

called Macumba or Candomble and is a mixture of Iberian Catholicism and Yoruba religion. Its main god is Chango, god of fire and stone. It is found throughout most of Latin America.

New Orleans

The Louisiana Territory was annexed to the United States in 1803 through the Louisiana Purchase, bought by President Jefferson from Napoleon, who himself had reacquired it from Spain, at a cost of $15 million. Louisiana became a state in 1812, and the population soared from 25,000 to over 100,000 by 1840. About half of the population was either black or Creole. The golden age of New Orleans lasted through the antebellum period until the Reconstruction, from 1862 to 1877. After the Reconstruction, constitutional rights for all African-American people were suspended by southern governments. By the 1900s New Orleans as a port city had doubled its population to over 200,000, making it the largest city in the South despite its reputation for political and social upheavals. The deep southern climate and its location near swamps and marshes made New Orleans a very unhealthful city, with additional perils of floods and hurricanes. Otto L. Bettmann, in his book *The Good Old Days—They Were Terrible*, reports that during the yellow fever epidemic of the South in 1853, some 7,848 lives were claimed in New Orleans. The disease was finally stamped out in 1900 by Dr. Walter Reed, an army surgeon who traced the source to a virus carried by mosquitoes.

Since New Orleans had been a province of both Spain and France, many of the European customs and cultural influences were present in the city. Colorful military and brass bands paraded in full European tradition throughout most southern cities for a variety of social occasions. One of the earliest major white influences was Jack "Papa" Laine (1873–1966). He was a drummer and leader of several bands in 1900 in New Orleans under the name of Reliance Band. He is known as "The Father of White Jazz" by musicians. Many trained musicians from his bands went on to make jazz history with bands such as the Original Dixieland Jazz Band and the New Orleans Rhythm Kings. These musicians included George Brunies, Joseph "Sharkey" Bonano, and Norman Brownlee. Creoles, who were Africans with mixed French or Spanish ancestry, were among the first colored people to gain access to the study and practice of music. They were referred to as *Creoles of Color* and musicians like Jelly Roll Morton, Alphonse Picou, Sidney Bechet, and Kid Ory were among the most famous. The Creoles attained a very high social status, with strong ties to European education and music. After the Reconstruction period, they fell to the same fate as the black slaves but made great contributions to the birth of jazz with their trained musical knowledge in opera and classical music. The blending of Creole culture and the poorer slave culture, which had no experience with

European music, produced the roots of jazz. The Creoles of Color had emerged from the Black Code of 1724 which made provision to free part Africans. By the 1800s, some Creoles had amassed large fortunes with the passing of their masters and sent their children to France for education. With deep roots in reading music, the Creoles had great difficulty in playing an early jazz style without written music. The Creoles were treated as a separate class distinct from the darker-skinned slaves and pure Negroes. In New Orleans, most Creoles lived downtown and were well-educated, with highly respectable positions before Reconstruction. Some Creoles held slaves, received large property holdings through the Black Code, and had early access to musical training. The Creoles held operatic training in high esteem, establishing their own opera house in New Orleans with class distinctions prevalent in reserved seating. The Negroes, on the other hand, lived in the rough, unruly uptown areas of the city and being very poor, were generally house servants and performed unskilled labor, as described by Louis Armstrong in his autobiography *Satchmo: My Life in New Orleans.*

The collision of West African and European cultures was largely responsible for the music that was yet to be named. The slaves had simple wind instruments and primitive drums, which reflected their communicative spirits in folklore and worship. The *call-and-response pattern,* in which a leader's singing or incantations were answered by followers or the congregation, has become one of the main characteristics of jazz. Folk songs, work songs, and spirituals were also contributions of African Americans. Ring shouts and cakewalks, which were European dances and forerunners of ragtime, were exhibited through minstrelsy after the Civil War. Though insurance was unavailable to blacks and Creoles, many belonged to secret societies or lodges that paid family benefits and created colorful parades by brass bands in elaborate funerals. The great importance and intense appeal of secret societies was documented by one lodge member, Sister Johnson:

> A woman's got to belong to at least seven secret societies if she 'spects to get buried with any style . . . and the more lodges you belongs to, the more music you gits when you go to meet your maker. I belongs to enough now to have shoes on my feets. I knows right now what I'm gonna have at my wake. I already done checked off chicken salad and coffee. They is wakin' me for four nights and I is gonna have the biggest funeral the Church ever had. That's why everything I makes goes to the church and them societies.*

Gumbo Ya-Ya, edited by Lyle Saxon, Dryer and Tallant. Copyright 1945 and © renewed 1973 by the Louisiana State Library. Reprinted by permission of Houghton Mifflin Company. All rights reserved.

As the custom prevails to this day, mournful dirges are played by the band on the slow march to the cemetery with the *second line* accompanying the body. The second line is the group of mourners and passersby who fall in behind or alongside the band during the procession. Upon returning from the cemetery, these mourners and band would break out in joyous celebration to tunes like "When the Saints Go Marching In" or "Didn't He Ramble." With the European bands providing discarded instruments, African Americans were able to perform as the popularity of the military band peaked in the middle of the 1800s. It might be said that West Africans provided heavy doses of rhythm while the Europeans contributed harmony. All that was left would be melody with improvisation to complete the early style of *Jass*. It is truly remarkable that the impact of two such diverse cultures as African and European would give birth to a pure American art form. This great trade-off of musical influences continued long after the Civil War period. The funeral of clarinetist Alphonse Picou, an early New Orleans music pioneer, was one of the largest on record. An estimated 10,000 people viewed the procession on February 9, 1961. One recent dixie jazz funeral was that of New Orleans' first black mayor, Dutch Morial, in January of 1990. As reported in an Associated Press article carried by the local newspapers:

> Morial had done much to bring equal rights to the black citizens of New Orleans. A mass was held at St. Louis Cathedral and proceeded to a jubilant and mournful jazz procession with about 1000 people at the service. The procession was led afterwards to St. Louis Cemetery No. 1 by members of the Olympia Brass Band and members of the Zulu Social Aid and Pleasure Club, the city's all-black Mardi Gras club. The musicians played "Nearer My God to Thee" and "Battle Hymn of the Republic," then a spirited "Gloryland" that sparked dancing and clapping. Wynton Marsalis played "Just a Closer Walk" as the coffin was moved to the hearse at the end of the cemetery. Outside, the band including tuba, trumpet, bass drum and wailing clarinet picked up the mournful tune but switched quickly to "Down by the Riverside" as people held aloft gaily decorated umbrellas and pictures of Morial as they danced.

The colorful parades, picnic ground concerts and rich Creole influences paved the way for the melting pot of jazz. Diverse cultures rich in tradition sprung up in an otherwise rough and hard life. Most of the musicians who paraded by day played in the local dives at night. Wages were so low for the uptown Negroes that they also held jobs of menial labor to survive in an otherwise destitute and impoverished background. It was highly inconceivable that such culturally rich elements would not only survive but flourish in the midst of an environment that provided many hardships for its citizens, including yellow fever and cholera epidemics in the colonial era. Today, New Orleans is known as the Crescent City and more recently as the Big Easy. Its rich historical mystique has captured the imaginations of tourists and generations of writers and musicians in this country much as Venice has done in Europe.

Today, this tradition of parades and balls by various organizations in New Orleans is Carnival, which begins on January 6th with an elegant ball and culminates in a citywide party with Mardi Gras (Fat Tuesday) before Ash Wednesday. Mardi Gras is the final day of Carnival and is marked by a colorful parade of the most prestigious organizations, with colorful bands, dancers in masks and costumes, and is an official holiday. During Carnival there are at least fifty parades with twice as many balls. The final day is presided over by the king, Rex, who is an outstanding luminary and citizen. French-Canadian explorer Pierre Le Moyne landed near the mouth of the Mississippi River on Mardi Gras in March of 1699 and named it Pointe du Mardi Gras. In the mid–1800s the Mardi Gras celebrations began as we see them today. Robert E. Lee's daughter, Mildred Lee, was crowned its first queen in 1884. Louis Armstrong was King of the Zulus in 1949.

Study Guide

Recordings

World Library of Folk and Primitive Music, Vol. II.
Alan Lomax (Columbia KL-205).
This collection of African music from the French Colonies exhibits some of the cultural traits of slave music. The examples from Nigeria or Niger Territory, as well as other West African nations, reveal musical characteristics of the call-and-response patterns and intricate drumming.

Musical Characteristics
Notice that all of the instruments used in the music are fairly simple and primitive. Flutes made by hand produce a limited number of pitches. The vocal and instrumental patterns are often characterized by a continuous repetition of rhythm or beat. Modern jazz still uses much repetition as a musical device in melodic, rhythmic, and harmonic elements, but provides variation and sequence for sustained musical interest. African rhythms remain quite intricate to assimilate in modern jazz. The call-and-response patterns are heard in work songs, religious songs, and virtually every phase of African life. The annotations in this collection provide a useful guide to the recordings with an interesting variety of vocal and instrumental primitive songs.

Musical Form
Side One, Band 1:
1. "Music for a Camel Tournament I"—Tuareg women singing with drumming by an instrument called the *Tindi.*

2. "Song of Exile"—Voice bends sung by a woman of the Orfela tribe.
3. "Song from Salah"—Part singing by Harratin women accompanied by a large frame drum.
4. "Music for a Camel Tournament II"—Tremolo voice style sung by Tuareg tribesmen.

Band 2:
5. "A Muezzin Call to Prayer"—Leader chant and response.
6. "Wedding Song"—Sung by the Dankali tribe with Moslem influence.
7. "Song to Make the Camels Drink"—An example of call and response in a work song.

Band 3:
8. "Song of Tobaski"—Singers are of the Sonray tribe, Niger Territory, with drums.
9. "Flute Players"—Played by Dogon tribe on transverse flutes with simple primitive polyphony.
10. "Bardic Song"—Members of the Dogon tribe sing and play primitive harps.
11. "The Hunt"—Primitive violin playing by the Jerma tribe.
12. "Song of Religious Procession"—Jerma tribe with violin and drum playing.
13. "Drum Duet"—Malinke tribe plays drums in a contest.
14. "Song of Praise"—Malinke tribe sings a bardic song with harp accompaniment.

Band 4:
15. "Funeral Song"—Sung by the Gwin tribe with call and response in an ode to their dead village chief.
16. "Whistle Band"—Wara tribe.
17. "Work Song"—Gwin tribe sings an agricultural work song.
18. "Song for Rain"—Gwin tribe sings this with an orchestra of rattles, harps with bells, and a male chorus.
19. "Festival Dance"—Gwin tribe plays drums and rhythm is kept by large harps.

The Origins and Development of Jazz.
Follett Educational Corp. (Columbia L25; two records).

Musical Form
Record One, Side A
1. "African Chant"—This is a characteristic call and response in African songs.

2. "Yoruba Drumming"—The Nigerian drumming is an ethnic style with jazz characteristics.

3. "A Kumba Ci"—With Robert Le House and chorus, this is a more updated version of African culture with many jazz stylings like the call and response in a riff style, altered scale tones, and basic improvisation.

4. "Early American Jazz Drums"—This shows the transition of early African drumming to the early New Orleans dixieland school, with a solo by Warren "Baby" Dodds on the full drum set. Dodds was born in 1898 in New Orleans and died in Chicago in 1959. He is considered to be one of the first great drummers of the early school, performing with Louis Armstrong, Papa Celestin, and King Oliver.

Readings

Marshall W. Stearns, *The Story of Jazz*
Oxford University Press, 1962.
Part One, "The Pre-History of Jazz"
Part Two, "New Orleans"
Readings on the early history and background of jazz are highly recommended because virtually no recordings are available of the music, and more importantly, to develop an understanding of the cultural, social, and environmental circumstances that were so vital to the development of the music. Dr. Stearns' book is a most important historical treatise of these early days. As we have only eyewitness accounts for actual documentation, this book must be used in reference as it provides much vivid detail and color of the period.

Frederick Douglass, *Narrative of the Life of Frederick Douglass: An American Slave. 1845.*
Signet, New York: 1968.
Born into slavery, Douglass was self-taught in reading and writing. This narrative offers a first-hand indictment of the inhumanity of slavery with all of its social injustices. Frederick Douglass, an African American, became a famous orator, U.S. Minister, and one of the first great leaders of his people. This dramatic biography was first published in 1845.

Paul Bohamnan and Philip Curtin, "The Era of the Slave Trade"
Chapter 15 in *Africa and Africans.*
Natural History Press, 1971
"The Era of the Slave Trade" includes the origins of black slavery, the slave trade in Africa, the growth and incidence of the slave trade with astonishing statistics, a detailed map with sources of eighteenth-century slave trade from 1711 to 1810, and the impact of the slave trade on Africa.

CHAPTER TWO

JAZZ ROOTS
(1896–1917)

New Orleans

The first legendary music figure to emerge after the closing of Place Congo was Charles "Buddy" Bolden. Born in 1868, he operated near a barbershop in the uptown section of New Orleans, and was a powerful cornet player. Bolden was easily the most popular figure in the early days of pre-jazz, until he became deranged during a parade in 1907 and died in the East Louisiana State Hospital in 1931. Since his performances took place before jazz was recorded, all that is left are eyewitness accounts of his "live fast, die young" exploits. A youthful Louis Armstrong recalled hearing Buddy play with a rough and powerful tone, using a very unorthodox embouchure. He was one of the first in a mold of great jazzmen, and was characterized as a sharp dresser, big drinker, and ladies' man. Bolden's music was highly influenced by the blues and religious Negro music, and was described as having a hot and raggy sound.

The riverboats of the Mississippi River provided easy access for early men of music to travel northward to cities like St. Louis, where ragtime music was thriving. The early jazz players assimilated many of the ragtime tunes, blending them with their own environmental influences. Bolden and other musicians were able to memorize these early tunes and give them special interpretations that were more loosely transcribed for the night life in cabarets and clubs of early New Orleans. The early musicians reflected the West African folklore and cultural traditions in the European forms of ragtime. Parades, brass bands, voodoo ceremonies, slave life, secret societies, and wandering Delta bluesmen all contributed to this rich mixture of music that found its way into the sporting houses and clubs. Work songs, spirituals, and country blues provided strong rural elements in the deep Delta country and eventually were blended in the night life culture of the city.

The *spiritual* was a religious song of the early American blacks, influenced by white Protestant church music in the South. African-American church singing evolved gradually into the *call-and-response* styles of sermons and gospel songs. Spirituals represent the crowning achievement in characterizing the Negro soul through hymns of European influences. Spirituals such as "Swing Low, Sweet Chariot" and "Nobody Knows the Trouble I've Seen" are typical of this kind of influence. The call-and-response patterns of gospel songs probably had the greatest effect on the emergence of jazz and were a pure African contribution.

Instruments

European military bands and brass bands played instruments that were eventually adopted for jazz use. Portable instruments that could be used on the march became the early traditional choice with eventual modifications for indoor use. See figures 2.1 to 2.6.

It is recommended that a live classroom demonstration be used for each instrument.

Study Guide: New Orleans

Video

New Orleans—Til the Butcher Cuts Him Down—Kid Punch Miller (Film by Philip Spaulding). Rhapsody Films, Inc.; 53 min.
This video captures the heyday in New Orleans of old-time cornet player Kid Punch Miller. He had played with all the early greats, including King Oliver, Kid Ory, Jelly Roll Morton, and Louis Armstrong. Particularly interesting is the old time New Orleans funeral parade featuring Dejan's Olympia Brass Band playing "Oh, Didn't He Ramble," with the accompanying crowd following as the *second line*. Try to identify the instruments as they pass by the camera. Notice the atmosphere and tradition throughout the film that was the glory of New Orleans. Also, it is interesting to observe the cornet playing style of Kid Punch Miller. Many of the early musicians did not have the benefit of lessons from renowned teachers, and were largely self-taught on instruments that were not as technically advanced as those manufactured today. Modern instrument technology and instruction have greatly improved the intonation and technical facilities of wind instruments. In the film Miller also composes a piece of music, transcribing it from his horn to the written page. Today, by contrast, virtually all composers and arrangers use the piano to write music. *Til the Butcher Cuts Him Down* reveals much of the basic, early, quite informal, approach to the performance of jazz. This video definitely reflects the ambience of the early days of jazz in New Orleans.

Figure 2.1: The Cornet—A brass instrument that eventually was replaced by the trumpet. It was capable of carrying the melody and supporting countermelodies that could be heard outdoors.

Figure 2.2: The Tuba (*left*), Sousaphone—Provided the bass line and foundation in the outdoor setting. It is a brass instrument, and modern marching bands in the United States often use the Sousaphone, created by John Philip Sousa, which is easier to carry over the shoulder.

Figure 2.3: The Guitar (*left*), Banjo (*middle*)—Stringed instruments which provided the chordal changes or harmonic structure as portable outdoor instruments. The piano began to come into strong favor for indoor use, although the guitar or banjo often supplemented the rhythm section.

Figure 2.4: The Clarinet (*above right*)—A woodwind instrument that usually played a countermelody for contrast to the melody of the cornet. Its higher notes could be used effectively for bending notes and adding color.

Figure 2.5: The Snare Drum (*opposite page, top*), Bass Drum—Percussion instruments that provided the beat or time, giving the music its rhythmic characteristics. The snare drum is the smaller drum carried with a shoulder strap and snare strings made of gut or metal on the bottom head. The bottom head is called the snare head and the top head is called the batter head. The bass drum is the larger drum that provided the strong beats as the snare drum provided the weak beats, giving a steady rhythm. Modern marching bands often use four bass drums of varying size for tonal effects. Drum sets were used for indoor performances with one player playing the bass drum, snare drum, tomtoms, hi-hat cymbals, ride cymbal, and crash cymbal.

Figure 2.6: The Trombone—A brass instrument that provided countermelodies and fortified the harmonic structure. A *glissando*, which is the long slurred note affected by the slide in a downward or upward motion of the pitch, was highly audible and colorful, adding excitement. One of the most famous trombone glisses is that used on the tune "Tiger Rag."

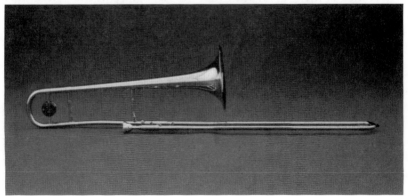

Blues

One of the most important musical forms in jazz is the *blues*. Perhaps
no other style has been more confused in its musical structure and form.
The term has been used rather loosely to describe many contemporary
groups defying true identification. Unlike simple folk songs and work
songs which are simple song forms in two parts with a question and answer in the lyrics, the blues is structured with *three phrases* in each verse.
Each phrase is marked by a chord change to identify the chord structure. The *first phrase* is marked by the key tonic chord, which states a
question in the lyrics. The *second phrase* restates the lyrics to a different
chord for added emphasis. A final, *third phrase* states the answer with
yet another chord that resolves the verse or stanza back to the key
chord. The lyrics of folk songs, work songs, and blues state much of the
human condition of love, suffering, and joy through highly expressive
singing.

Example of blues lyrics:

> "Hey wicked woman, don't wanna see you no more"
> "Hey wicked woman, don't wanna see you no more"
> "Tired of your cheatin', gonna show you the door."

Blue notes illustrated in the *blues scale* (see figure 2.7) are particularly
emphasized by blues singers.

Figure 2.7: F Blues Scale

Notice in the F blues scale that the A♭ represents the flatted third
note of the scale and the E♭ represents the flatted seventh of the scale;
these are referred to as blue notes. The B, or C♭ is the flatted fifth, which
came into later use in the 1920s and is frequently used since the 1950s to
complete the scale.

The *chord structure* for each complete verse was usually played by a
guitar or some other portable instrument in early country blues. Words
and chords were sometimes improvised in a very informal manner. Bending the voice on blue notes was influenced by field hollers by which slaves
could identify each other as a means of communication. Voice bending
was also heard at the ring shouts with bursts of jubilation in Place Congo.
The musical effects of spirituals and gospel songs also characterized blues
styling.

F Blues Chord Structure (one chord per measure):

First Phrase:	F	F	F	F
Second Phrase:	Bb	Bb	F	F
Third Phrase:	C	Bb	F	F

This is the chord structure of a basic blues in the key of F. Each phrase has four chords which contains four beats, or one measure, for a total of twelve measures in each verse. The important chords at the beginning of each phrase or stanza are the three main chordal accents for each verse. There are many options and variations to this basic blues structure regarding the other chords; however, most blues have a total of three main chords accented in the harmony. The blues scale provides a basis for the melody to be sung over each chord. See figure 2.8.

Figure 2.8: Example of Blues Chord Structure

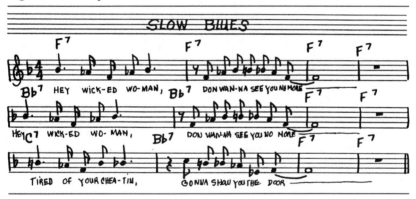

The harmony supplied by the chords was usually played by the guitar. Eventually the piano greatly expanded the expressive blues form by being able to play the melody and harmony with a variety of rhythms and tempi. The blues form can be used without the blues scale and can be heard through the music of great musicians like Charlie Parker, who recorded a great variety of blues.

Country Blues

Early blues which were, again, an outdoor activity in the earliest stage were called rural or country blues. There is no exact date for the earliest blues, but this is one of the oldest forms of American vocal music that relates directly to jazz. Many of these early blues singers like Blind Lemon

Jefferson, Robert Johnson, and folk singer Huddie Ledbetter, who was better known as Leadbelly, were traveling American minstrels who rambled throughout the South and Delta country. Leadbelly was the most famous of these singers and, according to Marshall Stearns, learned the blues from Blind Lemon Jefferson. Leadbelly was a convicted prisoner, leader of a chain gang, and conveyed much of the rustic South through his folk songs and work songs. He was also a guitar player, born in Louisiana in 1888, and died in New York City in 1949. Much has been written about his musical exploits, and he remains a true American legend.

Robert Johnson, another very important blues singer and guitarist, was born in Mississippi in 1898 and died there in 1937. He was murdered shortly after his last recordings, and is considered one of the greatest of all the old-time Delta bluesmen. Johnson is characterized in legend as a shiftless drifter who walked side by side with the devil. Some of his most famous blues are "Cross Road Blues," "Me and the Devil Blues," and "Hellhound on My Trail."

Study Guide: The Blues

Recordings

"Cross Road Blues"—Robert Johnson.
***King of the Delta Blues Singers* (Columbia 1654). Recorded in 1936.**

Musical Characteristics
"Cross Road" is one of the famous blues by Robert Johnson. The informal structure of adding beats and measures to accommodate the lyrics sometimes resulted in irregularities. These irregular structures were characteristic of many early blues singers. The instruments were sometimes out of tune and the singers would extend the phrases until they remembered the lyrics or improvised new ones. Despite all of these rough edges, the most important ingredient is the highly colorful and expressive lyrics.

Musical Form
1. Begins with guitar strumming the introduction with an irregular 4 bars.
2. Both first phrases of each stanza or verse begin with 2 bars of lyrics followed by 3 bars of guitar accompaniment, a total of 5 bars instead of 4. (question or call)
3. Both second phrases of each stanza or verse follow the same pattern as the first. (question or call)
4. Both third phrases begin with 2 bars of lyrics followed by 2 bars of accompaniment for a traditional 4 bars. (answer or response)

After listening to "Cross Road Blues," compare and contrast "Me and the Devil Blues" and "Hellhound on My Trail." Robert Johnson's recordings are available in complete form on Columbia.

The South, Vol. I. (Folkways Records FJ 2801)
Edited by Frederick Ramsey, Jr.

1. "Ol' Hanna"—Doc Reese
   A field holler that has deep inroads to the blues. The title refers to the sun: "Well, well, don' you rise no more." This is a prison work song.
2. "Juliana Johnson"—Leadbelly
   The opening monologue describes this piece as an axe-cutting work song. The actual log chopping is emphasized by grunting voice inflections and is a fine example of the early folk song.
3. "John Henry"—Leadbelly, Sonny Terry, Brownie McGhee
   This is a great African-American folk ballad that describes John Henry as a strong steel-drivin' man who worked on the railroads until he met the girl, Polly Ann.

Readings

Albert Murray, *Stomping the Blues*
McGraw-Hill, 1976.
A very informal, high-spirited book about jazz and blues. Over 250 interesting pictures of musicians and vocalists, with their respective recording labels. Many anecdotes about the blues.

The New York Times, Sunday, October 13, 1991
Arts and Leisure, Section 2.

1. "The Blues in Black and White" by Studs Terkel.
   Terkel asks, "Can a white man really understand a black man's blues?" He discusses Robert Johnson, Big Bill Broonzy, Sonny Terry and Brownie McGhee and questions whether new devotees actually feel the despair and dreams of the music as they hear it.
2. "Two Generations, Two Revivals of the Blues" by Jon Pareles
   This article deals with the revival of the blues through Robert Johnson in the 1960s and the 1990s. The author discusses the recordings of B.B. King and John Lee Hooker.
3. "Blues in the '90s: Toward Twilight or a New Dawn?" by Cornell West
   Here, West focuses on the music's revival outside the black community.

Video

Blues Like Showers of Rain (Directed by John Jeremy).
Jazzland; 30 min.
This is one of the best videos on early country blues, with historic photographs and field recordings. Featured are the voices and songs of Otis Spann, J.B. Lenoir, Little Brother Montgomery, Willie Thomas, Sunnyland Slim, Robert Lockwood, Lightning Hopkins, James Brewer, and Speckled Red. This classic film captures the down-home aspect of the blues from its early days of destitution to great joy and exhilaration although some of the scenes of early Southern prejudice are extremely graphic.

Midwest—Ragtime Music

The European style that merged with West African styles was ragtime music. Ragtime was characterized by:

1. Stress on form and harmony
2. Stress on reading music
3. Highly syncopated rhythms

Although ragtime is not considered jazz, as a forerunner of jazz this style merged with great popularity from 1896 to 1917. It evolved from European dances, marches like the cakewalk, and was originally performed on piano. Ragtime melodies, unlike the blues, were written and were to be played precisely, demanding ability of the pianist, who had to coordinate a fast-moving right hand with an accompanying left hand that moved in great leaps. Ragtime style was developed mostly by black, schooled musicians. This original American music was pioneered by Midwestern composers such as Tom Turpin, James Scott, Joseph Lamb, and the greatest of them all, Scott Joplin. Ragtime music was a precursor of the later-emerging stride style of jazz piano. The center of this activity was in the Missouri cities of St. Louis, Sedalia, and Kansas City, although orchestra leader James Reese Europe was highly active in the Northeast. See figure 2.9.

Scott Joplin

Scott Joplin was born in Texas in 1868, grew up in a poor black family, and received music lessons at an early age. He moved to St. Louis in 1890, and then to the hotbed of ragtime, Sedalia, Missouri, in 1897. Joplin became friends with publisher John Stark, who helped him launch his career with the famous "Maple Leaf Rag." He wrote many other famous rags such as "Easy Winners" and "The Entertainer," as well as an opera, *Treemonisha*.

Figure 2.9: Centers of Jazz Activity

Joplin died in 1917 in New York City from syphilis, which he had contracted at an early age. Soon after his death ragtime fell in a great state of decline because of expensive publishing costs and the demanding musicianship that was characteristic of the music. In the Northeast James Reese Europe, who was not considered a jazz figure, gave a ragtime concert in 1912 at Carnegie Hall with the Club Clef Orchestra. The orchestra consisted of 125 men featuring mandolins, banjos, guitars, 'cellos, and basses, plus ten pianos. More recently, Gunther Schuller has led ragtime revivals with a recording of the *Red Back Book* collection of Scott Joplin, as published by John Stark, with the New England Conservatory Ragtime Orchestra for Angel Records. Schuller has most recently led a second revival of these recordings in 1990. Joshua Rifkin is considered to be one of the foremost modern interpreters of ragtime music on piano.

One of the earliest blues compositions written in a ragtime style for piano was "I Got The Blues," which was written by A. Maggio for the Cable Piano Company, New Orleans, in 1908. It was billed as a characteristic ragtime two step and was "respectfully dedicated to all those who have the blues." "I Got The Blues" was clearly written in a ragtime style, featuring a blues in the key of G.

Study Guide: Ragtime Music

Recordings

"Maple Leaf Rag"—Scott Joplin.
SCCJ (record side 1, cassette side A, CD I.) Recorded in 1986 from a roll made by Joplin in 1916.

Musical Characteristics
Ragtime music lacked much of the expressiveness of the blues. This music is very structured and formal, with virtually no liberties in tempi or melodic interpretation. It is played exactly as it is written.

Musical Form
"Maple Leaf Rag" consists of four different tunes, called *strains*. Each strain is sixteen bars long and forms a pattern in which each melody is repeated: AABBACCDD

This form is based on the march form.

    1st strain— AA
    2nd strain—BB
    3rd strain— CC (also called the "trio" strain)
    4th strain— DD

Notice the frequent use of *syncopation*, which is accenting the normally weak beat. Compare this version to that of Jelly Roll Morton.

"Maple Leaf Rag"—Jelly Roll Morton.
SCCJ (record side 1, band 2; cassette side A; CD I.) Recorded in 1938.

Musical Characteristics
Jelly Roll's interpretation of "Maple Leaf Rag" reveals a heavy-handed New Orleans touch. Much of the rhythm and melody are improvised. Much more feeling is evident in this version and it becomes more of a jazz composition than ragtime.

Musical Form
1. Morton uses the introduction in a highly swinging manner.
2. Musical form as follows: ABACCDD
3. A tango, or Spanish tinge, is used in the first D section.
4. A big New Orleans-style stomp is in the second D section.

Also recommended is a collection of sixteen piano rolls from 1915 to 1931 by Eubie Blake, Jimmy Blythe, James P. Johnson, Jelly Roll Morton, and Fats Waller, available on *The Greatest Ragtime of the Century* (Biograph BCD-103).

CHAPTER THREE

BIRTH OF JAZZ
(1917)

Although no actual date has been generally agreed upon for the birth of jazz, there were many events in and around the year 1917 that provide historical support for this date:

A. The closing of Storyville caused a mass exodus of musicians from New Orleans to the Midwest, led by Joe "King" Oliver to seek work in 1919.
B. The first recording by the Original Dixieland Jazz Band.
C. The death of Scott Joplin signalled the virtual end of the ragtime craze.
D. W. C. Handy's "St. Louis Blues," although published earlier, became popular.
E. The word *Jass* began to appear as *Jazz* in Chicago.

There can be no doubt that the early formation of jazz took place in New Orleans, but the sad fact that the music industry didn't record jazz until 1917 leaves us with no evidence of the music played prior to this date. It is also ironic that the jazz created in Chicago was primarily played by transplanted New Orleans men who took their hometown style into a new geographical setting. The trail of jazz activity began in the South in New Orleans and flowed upward to Chicago in the Midwest, then Northeast to the final great hub of jazz activity, New York City. There were many other highly influential pockets of jazz creativity in this geographical transition, like the *territory bands* of the Southwest around Kansas City. Great recording companies began to dominate the industry in New York City.

Storyville

The cradle of jazz appears to be Storyville in New Orleans, although the revolutionary rhythms and tempos had been set in motion by countless New Orleans brass bands earlier. This was a red-light district north of the French Quarter legislated by New Orleans, led by Alderman Sidney

Story, in 1897. The early Storyville location stretched from the downtown side of Iberville Street to the uptown side of St. Louis Street; and from the lake side of Basin Street to the river side of Robertson Street. This Tenderloin District, as it was sometimes called, provided fancy bordellos, cabarets, and legalized prostitution. It was here that many musicians found work and were able to fashion a music that was so highly influenced by both African and European cultures. One of the most famous of these sporting house mansions was Mahogany Hall, operated by Madame Lu Lu White on Basin Street. The personal guidebook of new Mahogany Hall includes an introduction by Lu Lu White. The cover of this guide pictures the building, erected at the cost of $40,000. It was built of marble, with mahogany staircases. Mahogany Hall was four stories high, with five parlors and fifteen bedrooms. The guide also featured the profiles (complete with pictures and introductions) of twenty-one girls who worked there. Another was Tom Anderson's Cafe, located just a few doors away. So-called "mayor of Storyville," Tom Anderson was the kingpin of vice and politics in Storyville. He was elected to the state legislature and was a political boss who mixed business with pleasure. A guide to the District called the *Blue Book* was available to patrons as a directory to the many sporting houses in Storyville:

Miss LuLu White—Corner Basin and Bienville Streets

Nowhere in this country will you find a more popular personage than Madame White, who is noted as being the handsomest octoroon in America, and aside from her beauty, she has the distinction of possessing the largest collection of diamonds, pearls and other rare gems in this country.

To see her at night, is like witnessing the electrical display on the Cascade at the late St. Louis Exposition.

Aside from her handsome women, her mansion possesses some of the most costly oil paintings in the Southern country. Her mirror-parlor is also a dream.

There is always something new at LuLu White's that will interest you. "Good time" is her motto.

Study Guide: Storyville

Reading

Al Rose, *Storyville, New Orleans.*
The University of Alabama Press, 1974.
Al Rose's book captures Storyville in its heyday with an extremely colorful history of the district. Featured are many exotic photos of the mad-

ames and prostitutes by the official Storyville photographer, Ernest Bellocq. The early ambience is presented through interviews of actual participants. A very engaging book and very highly recommended.

"Jelly Roll" Morton

Famous pianist-composer Ferdinand Joseph "Jelly Roll" Morton was the house pianist at Mahogany Hall as well as many other sporting houses in the district and fashioned a rich mixture of new music from ragtime and blues. Jelly Roll was born in 1890 in Louisiana and played piano in Storyville bordellos until 1917. He was a Creole with access to early musical training, and later became somewhat of a braggart who claimed to have invented jazz. He is one of the most controversial figures in jazz history, but there can be no doubt as to his musical genius and jazz legacy. His famous recordings, made for Victor Records from 1926 to 1930 with a band entitled Morton's Red Hot Peppers, assured his success as a performer and composer. He died in Los Angeles in 1941. Storyville was closed by the U.S. Navy in 1917, and many musicians traveled up the Mississippi to seek employment and new opportunities. W. C. Handy had written one of the first published blues, "Memphis Blues," in 1912; his more famous "St. Louis Blues" appeared in 1917.

The book *Mister Jelly Roll* by Alan Lomax, first published in 1950, was based on extended recorded conversations with Morton at the Library of Congress in 1938, during which he sang and played the piano, illustrating his claim to be the founder and creator of jazz. He attests that he despised jam sessions and began to write down a peculiar form of mathematics and harmonics that would form the basis of his arrangements. Jelly Roll recalled his experiences in St. Louis with ragtime music and light classics, and claimed to have arranged jazz as early as 1912. He then proceeded to Chicago with his "hot style" interpretations of ragtime in theater bands. His tune "Jelly Roll Blues" became "The Chicago Blues," and was a hit with brass bands throughout the country. Morton joined Freddie Keppard's Olympia Band and rated Keppard, a fellow Creole, as the greatest of all dixieland trumpet players, even greater than Armstrong. Jelly Roll, who was the self-proclaimed Inventor of Jazz, bitterly disputed W. C. Handy's reputation as the Father of the Blues.

Study Guide: "Jelly Roll" Morton

Recordings

"Black Bottom Stomp"—Jelly Roll Morton's Red Hot Peppers.
SCCJ **(record side 1, band 6; cassette A; CD I). Recorded in 1926.**

Personnel
Jelly Roll Morton—piano, George Mitchell—trumpet,
Edward "Kid" Ory—trombone, Omer Simeon—clarinet,
Johnny St. Cyr—banjo, John Lindsay—bass,
Andrew Hilaire—drums

Musical Characteristics
This is a fine example of the New Orleans style that shows Morton's ability as a composer and arranger as well as performer. The black bottom
stomp is a rhythm which closely resembles a popular dance *the Charleston.* "Black Bottom" is skillfully arranged with a well-planned musical format that overflows with musical exuberance.

Musical Form
Style—fast New Orleans dixieland flat-fours (see Glossary).

1. Introduction—8 bars
2. Opening Theme—16 bars with clarinet and ensemble.
3. Second Chorus—trumpet trades 4s with the ensemble.
4. Third Chorus—clarinet solos with banjo accompaniment.
5. Interlude—change of key, 4 bars.
6. Second Theme—unusual 20 bars with stop or break time in measures 7–8.
7. Second Chorus—clarinet solo in low register with the Charleston
   stomp rhythm.
8. Third Chorus—unaccompanied piano solo.
9. Fourth Chorus—muted trumpet solo over stop time.
10. Fifth Chorus—banjo solo with the bass alternating rhythm in beats 2
    and 4 of each measure.
11. Sixth Chorus—full ensemble in collective improvisation with trum-
    pet lead.
12. Final Chorus—full ensemble plays very strongly with fills by bass and
    drums; trombone plays glisses, or rips, in a tailgate style.

"Dead Man Blues"—Jelly Roll Morton's Red Hot Peppers.
SCCJ (record side 1, band 7, cassette side A, CD I). Recorded in 1926.

Personnel
Same as "Black Bottom Stomp," plus Barney Bigard, Darnell Howard—
clarinets

Musical Characteristics
This is a slower-paced dixieland piece, with Morton's arranging for a clarinet trio that would later influence Duke Ellington. "Dead Man Blues"

reveals some fine polyphonic writing with the typical lead trumpet. The mood shift of the opening funeral march to the happier musical treatment demonstrates the marching brass band traditions. There are many other New Orleans dixieland style pieces that begin with a funeral march before breaking into a joyful polyphonic structure, and some end with a sad, mournful tag.

Musical Form
Style—slow 12-bar blues.

1. Introduction—funeral march
2. Opening Theme—ensemble in slow polyphonic style.
3. Second Chorus—clarinet solo in high register.
4. Second Theme—trumpet solo plays 2 choruses.
5. Third Theme—clarinet trio plays 2 choruses with trombone counter-theme and cymbal back crashes.
6. Final Chorus—full ensemble in collective improvisation by the trumpet, clarinet, and trombone.
7. Tag—clarinet trio plays 2 bars from the third theme.

The student should also listen to Morton's "Grandpa's Spells" and "King Porter Stomp," which are included in the *SCCJ*. Jelly Roll Morton's music, although recorded at a relatively late date (1926), clearly shows his mastery and formation of the New Orleans style. He is to be regarded as one of the first masters who gave definition to the music, as one of the earliest composers. Morton's understanding of the instruments is shown by his ability to arrange for them effectively. He certainly had a thorough knowledge of the style and left a rich legacy. "King Porter Stomp," recorded in 1939 as a solo, is a culmination of his pianistic skill, and became a jazz hit throughout the swing era with musicians like Benny Goodman.

Another outstanding recording of the early period is that of the Red Onion Jazz Babies playing "Cake Walking Babies from Home." This early 1924 piece is also included in the *SCCJ*, revealing the early talents of Louis Armstrong on cornet and Sidney Bechet on soprano saxophone. Bechet, originally a clarinetist, was one of the few early New Orleans musicians who was on an equal footing with Armstrong in improvisational technique. Both men were unusually inventive and imaginative in this early period of improvisational development, and display amazing breaks in the recording. Bechet was like Armstrong, a truly superlative musician who was clearly ahead of his time and perhaps gained greater appreciation in Paris during the dixieland revival of the mid–'50s.

The Original Dixieland Jass Band

The first jazz recording was launched by the Original Dixieland Jass Band in 1917. The term *jass*, used to describe this music, was considered to be vulgar, with sexual overtones, by the general public. The ODJB was a group of white musicians from New Orleans led by cornetist Nick Larocca that had great influence in making Chicago, and later, New York City as new hubs of jazz activity. It was paradoxical that a white group would be the first to record music that was created and fashioned by the great Creole masters of New Orleans; soon another white group, the New Orleans Rhythm Kings (NORK), came into prominence.

The ODJB was one of the first groups to bring this music northeast, making a sensational debut at Reisenweber's at Columbus Circle in New York City. *Original Dixieland Jass Band, Vol. I.*, recorded by Victor on February 26, 1917, produced two early pieces, "Dixie Jass Band One-step" and "Livery Stable Blues" that featured a ragged style of syncopation. The striding effect of 4/4 (four strong downbeats called flat-fours) clearly depicted the early New Orleans marching style and was overdone with "cat-call" and "barnyard" effects supplied by the clarinet and trombone. Their later recordings of these same pieces became much smoother and more musically sophisticated. This controversial group became a great success story in early jazz. Many jazzmen accused them of stealing their sound from the early generation of New Orleans black masters, which was then freely admitted by NORK.

Study Guide: Original Dixieland Jass Band

Recordings

"Livery Stable Blues," "Dixie Jass Band One-Step"—Original Dixieland Jass Band.
The 75th Anniversary, 1992. (BMG Bluebird 610982-2. Reissued in 1982).

Personnel
Nick Larocca—cornet, Eddie Edwards—trombone,
Larry Shields—clarinet, Henry Ragas—piano,
Tony Spargo—drums

Musical Characteristics
These two pieces were recorded on the same date and represent the first two recorded tunes in the history of jazz. The early versions of the New Orleans dixieland style are somewhat exaggerated, with boisterous musical effects. "Livery Stable Blues" is a slower flat-four in a 12-bar blues

style, also with three themes. Again, aside from the clarinet, cornet and trombone "catcalls" and "wailing," there are no solos. "Livery Stable Blues" was used as an opening to the famous Paul Whiteman Concert on Feb. 12, 1924 in Aeolian Hall, New York City, to show the early clamorous style of jazz. "Dixie Jass Band One-Step" represents the early New Orleans model of a fast flat four with three separate themes in collective improvisational style, and there are no solos.

Musical Form
"Livery Stable Blues"
Style—New Orleans slow flat-four blues.

1. Introduction—4 bars
2. A theme—full ensemble, 12 bars repeated.
3. B theme—full ensemble punctuated by bass drum, 12 bars repeated.
4. C theme—trombone leads ensemble to "animal calls" by clarinet, cornet and trombone again in break time, 12 bars repeated.
5. A theme, B theme repeated.
6. C theme—repeated as before
7. Tag—1 bar

"Dixie Jass Band One-Step"
Style—New Orleans fast flat-four blues.

1. A theme—full ensemble with break time, 8 bars repeated.
2. B theme—clarinet takes lead first 2 bars of a repeated 8-bar melody.
3. A theme—same as in first A theme.
4. B theme—same as in first B theme.
5. C theme—full ensemble in collective improvisation with severe clarinet bends, trombone glissando, wood blocks, and cowbell, 16 bars repeated.
6. C theme—same as previous strain.
7. Tag—1 bar.

New Orleans Dixieland

King Oliver, another Storyville veteran, was a very talented cornetist, who as a soloist and sideman in New Orleans, helped fashion the music that would be called dixieland jazz in the '20s. He and a host of other first-generation musicians, including Kid Ory on trombone and trumpeters Freddie Keppard and ex-Buddy Bolden sideman Bunk Johnson began to create this new improvising style. Oliver worked with many of the musicians who later became members of his band in Chicago, the Creole Jazz Band. Other first generation New Orleans musicians were trumpeters

Kid Rena and Buddy Petit, who like many other early pre–jazz men were not recorded in their early years.

Early dixieland jazz in New Orleans was performed on instruments that were used in parades. Until the turn of the century most of the parade and brass bands played marches and music without improvisation. The earliest influential style on the formation of jazz was the blues, which encouraged an improvisational approach. As the ragtime men met the blues men, a trade-off between written and improvised, or "faked," music had much to do with jazz's evolution.

Early improvisation was approximated by *ragging a tune* in a hot style. This transitional form of improvisation in jazz developed into a paraphrase style, in which the performer stayed relatively close to the melody. It wasn't until the first great improviser of jazz, Louis Armstrong, began to develop this technique that improvisation became an art in itself. Edward "Kid" Ory was one of the early New Orleans hot jazz legends on trombone. The term "tailgate trombone" is attributed to Kid Ory and others who played in wagons with bands to advertise musical and other social events in New Orleans. Since the trombone player was seated near the tailgate of the wagon to provide room for his long trombone slide, the term took effect. These are some of the characteristics of New Orleans dixieland music:

1. *Collective improvisation*—The clarinet, cornet and trombone would alternate playing the improvised melody while the other instruments would provide support melodies. The clarinet was the highest in pitch, with the cornet in the middle and the trombone playing the lower melodies.
2. A *flat-four rhythm*—The 4/4 rhythm was supplied by the banjo, drums, and tuba. This was highly characteristic of New Orleans dixieland because of the early marching influence. It was easier to march to four beats per measure.
3. *Great feeling and emotion*—These were added to ragtime tunes, conveying a loose feeling that would be characterized as *swing*. Hot jazz was the ideal, with joyous swing through improvisation.

Joe "King" Oliver

King Oliver was born in New Orleans in 1885 and grew up playing cornet in marching bands and cabarets. After Storyville closed he moved to Chicago in 1919, and in 1922 led his famous Creole Jazz Band at Lincoln Gardens with Johnny Dodds on clarinet, Honore Dutrey on trombone, Lil Hardin on piano, Bill Johnson on banjo, Baby Dodds on drums, and the very famous Louis Armstrong on cornet. Louis Armstrong recalled the call he received from the King to come to Chicago as being one of the most exciting events in his life. The Creole Jazz Band, unlike the ODJB, is considered the seminal group in the early New Orleans dixieland style. Oliver had a profound influence on Louis Armstrong, and the two played with great musical empathy. This can be heard on "Dippermouth Blues."

Study Guide: King Oliver

Recordings

"Dippermouth Blues"—King Oliver's Creole Jazz Band.
SCCJ (record side 1 band 5, cassette A, CD I). Recorded in 1923.

Personnel
Joe "King" Oliver—cornet, Louis Armstrong—cornet,
Honore Dutrey—trombone, Johnny Dodds—clarinet,
Lil Hardin—piano, Bill Johnson—banjo, vocals,
Warren "Baby" Dodds—drums

Musical Characteristics
This is one of the earliest and finest examples of the early New Orleans dixieland style. The musical rapport that each musician brought to this group resulted in spontaneous and balanced control of the collective improvisational style. The solos by Johnny Dodds and Oliver are models of this early style. Also, Baby Dodds was considered to be the first great drummer of this period.

Musical Form
Style is an instrumental blues.

1. Collective improvisation—muted cornet in the middle range with trombone in the lower range and the clarinet playing the upper range. The banjo plays a flat 4.
2. Clarinet solo; note the *stop time* accompaniments by the rhythm.
3. Balanced collective improvisation, with Louis Armstrong playing lead cornet.
4. Oliver cornet solo, with contrapuntal ensemble responses.
5. Vocal break, collective improvisation, and tag.

PART II

The Jazz Age

CHAPTER FOUR

CHICAGO

The jazz scene shifted to the Midwest and Chicago, in particular because of the recording studios there. New York City in the Northeast also boasted some early recording studios. The Original Dixieland Jass Band had recorded for RCA Victor in 1917, revealing a very rough and almost mawkish interpretation of the dixieland style. With so many great transitional New Orleans sidemen now finding work in the North, the geographical relocation of jazz was set in place.

The flurry of jazz activity in Chicago during the Roaring '20s was set into high gear with the arrival of the New Orleans Rhythm Kings at the downtown Friars Inn, and on the South Side where Joe "King" Oliver held forth. White musicians were greatly affected by the music of the black New Orleans musicians and began to fashion it into a Chicago style. Musicians like Bix Beiderbecke, Hoagy Carmichael, Paul Mares, Frank Teschemacher, and the others of the Austin High gang thoroughly absorbed the New Orleans style, with many younger musicians like Benny Goodman waiting in the wings. This brisk musical activity, combined with the night life in Chicago, provided a favorable environment for the evolution of New Orleans dixieland to Chicago dixieland. Louis Armstrong realized his lifelong dream when the call came from King Oliver in 1922; Louis became the dominant force in jazz, a great soloist and improviser.

Louis "Satchmo" Armstrong

Louis Armstrong was born in the shadows of poverty in New Orleans. The birthday he himself gave was July 4, 1900; however, the records substantiate his correct birth date as August 4, 1901. The reason for this disparity is because accurate birth and death certificates were often not properly kept or filed. He was sent to the Colored Waifs Home in New Orleans in 1913 for firing a blank gun during a street celebration. He had

Louis Armstrong (*Photo courtesy of RCA/Bluebird*)

begun his musical upbringing as a singer and was introduced to the cornet in the orphanage band. His early days in the city are vividly recol-
lected in his autobiography.

> When I was born in 1900 my father, Willie Armstrong, and my mother,
> May Ann or Mayann as she was called—were living on a little street
> called James Alley. Only one block long, James Alley is located in the
> crowded section of New Orleans known as Back O' Town. It is one of
> the four great sections into which the city is divided. The others are Up-
> town, Downtown and Front O' Town, and each of these quarters has its
> own little traits.
>   James Alley—not Jane Alley as some people call it—lies in the very
> heart of what is called the Battlefield because the toughest characters in
> town used to live there, and would shoot and fight so much. In that one
> block between Gravier and Perdido Streets more people were crowded
> than you ever saw in your life. There were churchpeople, gamblers, hus-
> tlers, cheap pimps, thieves, prostitutes and lots of children. There were

bars, honky-tonks and saloons, and lots of women walking the streets for
tricks to take to their "pads" as they called their rooms.*

Armstrong was befriended by Joe "King" Oliver, who was a great influence in his early career before leaving New Orleans. Young Louis was
given several nicknames such as Satchmo, short for Satchelmouth, which
captured his broad smile early in his career, and Dippermouth, which referred to the broad formation of his lips when playing. Later he was simply called Pops. After joining Oliver in Chicago, Armstrong began to gain
a formidable reputation. He received an offer from Fletcher Henderson
in New York City in 1924, and left Oliver at the behest of Lil Hardin, who
had become his wife. Later he switched to the trumpet and became one
of the first true ambassadors of jazz. He was greatly admired and loved by
the American public until his death in 1971. Although many African
Americans considered him to be a clown detracting from this proud race,
he spoke out vehemently during the Civil Rights Movement in the '60s,
refusing to go on a State Department tour. Given his circumstances in
the early South, Armstrong was a survivor; due to his strong, admirable
personality, he was able to turn social circumstances in his favor.

His studio recordings in Chicago with the Hot Five and Hot Seven
clearly placed him at the pinnacle of the jazz world, as its greatest improviser. All of these recordings have been reissued by Columbia in four volumes: *The Hot Fives, Vol. I* (44409); *The Hot Fives and Hot Sevens, Vol. II*
(44253); *The Hot Fives and Hot Sevens, Vol. III* (44422); and *Louis Armstrong and Earl Hines, Vol. IV* (45142).

Gunther Schuller, in *Early Jazz*, points out the distinguishing qualities and features of Armstrong's solos that set him apart from all the rest:

1. His superior choice of notes and the resultant shape of his lines.
2. His incomparable basic quality of tone.
3. His equally incomparable sense of swing with attacks and releases in
   his phrasing.
4. His subtle and varied repertory of vibratos and shakes in his phrasing.†

Armstrong was simply far ahead of any of the soloists during the period.
Fletcher Henderson's band was greatly influenced by the arrival of young
Armstrong, and Henderson's soloists began to play with much more
imagination. Louis Armstrong is to be regarded as the first truly great improviser in the history of jazz, and ranks as a genius.

---

*From Louis Armstrong, *Satchmo: My Life in New Orleans,* © 1982, 1954. Used by permission
of the publisher, Prentice Hall/A division of Simon & Schuster, Englewood Cliffs, N.J.
†Source: Gunther Schuller, *Early Jazz.* New York: Oxford University Press, 1968.

Study Guide: Louis Armstrong

Recordings

"Struttin' with Some Barbecue"—Louis Armstrong and His Hot Five.
SCCJ (record side 2, band 6, cassette side B, CD I). Recorded in 1927.

Personnel
Louis Armstrong—cornet, Edward "Kid" Ory—trombone,
Johnny Dodds—clarinet, Lil Hardin Armstrong—piano,
Johnny St. Cyr—banjo

Musical Characteristics
Even though Armstrong was such a strong jazz influence in the Chicago
area, his preference for the New Orleans flat-four style continued
throughout his career. This recording is a classic that reveals his rapid development with improvisation in creating dazzling and daring melodic
lines. Armstrong's gift of melodic invention clearly outshines the solos of
Dodds on clarinet and Ory on trombone. Perhaps the only New Orleans
contemporary able to match his creativity was Sidney Bechet, a clarinet
and soprano saxophone player who eventually finished his career in
Paris. Listen to Bechet's clarinet solo on "Blue Horizon," *SCCJ* (record
side 2, CD I cassette side A).

Musical Form
1. Opens with cornet lead and group collective improvisation in the introduction.
2. First chorus with the same format as the introduction. The rhythm is
   a flat-four.
3. Clarinet solo in the low register, with banjo in flat-fours.
4. Trombone solo with banjo and piano off-beats.
5. Cornet solo with off-beat accompaniment. Note how Armstrong's
   construction of melody is a jubilant display of technique from bottom to top ranges of the cornet.
6. Ensemble in break time before restating the melody as in the opening chorus. Stop time is used playing the first beat every two bars at
   the end.

"West End Blues"—Louis Armstrong and His Hot Five.
SCCJ (record side 2, band 8, cassette side B, CD I). Recorded in 1928.

Personnel
Louis Armstrong—trumpet/vocals, Fred Robinson—trombone,
Jimmy Strong—clarinet, Earl Hines—piano,
Mancy Cara—banjo, Zutty Singleton—drums

Musical Characteristics
Here is one of the most famous Armstrong recordings, which placed him above all others in improvisational style. His opening free solo (cadenza) has been the object of much analysis by succeeding trumpet men. Armstrong began his switch to trumpet from cornet and exploited its brilliance particularly in the upper register. His dazzling introduction, in which he doubles the tempo (twice as fast) was highly innovative, soaring up and down the register of the horn with marvelous phrasing.

Musical Form
1. Opens with a free trumpet solo in double-time.
2. Ensemble plays a slow flat-four with trumpet lead.
3. Trombone solo with drummer playing wood blocks.
4. Wordless vocals with call and response from the clarinet.
5. Piano solo in double time.
6. Horns sustain long chords with piano and banjo in flat fours.
7. Trumpet solo in double time.
8. Short piano interlude and out.

Video

Louis Armstrong—Satchmo
CBS; 90 min.
An excellent portrait of Satchmo, with clips from movies and live performances. Very intimate and personal view of the man and his music spanning his entire career as one of the most popular jazz figures in America. Also featured are Dizzy Gillespie, Jack Teagarden, Billie Holiday, and the 1958 African Tour. This is extensive documentation of the first true genius in jazz. Highly recommended!

Reading

Louis Armstrong, *Satchmo: My Life in New Orleans*
Da Capo, 1986.
This book is a very vivid autobiography by Armstrong, detailing his early life in New Orleans until his call from King Oliver in 1922. It includes many recollections of his youth of poverty and deprivation during the waning years of Storyville. His upbeat spirit and great love of humanity are revealed in both his life and music. The 1986 edition features a new introduction by Dan Morgenstern. Very interesting reading.

Bix Beiderbecke

Leon Bix Beiderbecke was born in 1903 in Davenport, Iowa. Unlike Armstrong, he was raised in a comfortable environment, and he exhibited an early interest in music on the piano. Bix was introduced to Louis Armstrong during one of Armstrong's paddle-steamer performing trips to Davenport, and fell in love with the cornet. A white musician, he became a very respected cornet soloist along with Armstrong. He was largely self-taught, as were most musicians of his day, and gained valuable experience *sitting in* (see Glossary) with many New Orleans musicians in Chicago. The New Orleans Rhythm Kings played at the Friars Inn in downtown Chicago, which was a cabaret frequented by high society and gangsters. The group included leader-cornetist Paul Mares, Jack Pettis on sax, Leon Roppollo on clarinet, Arnold Loyacano on bass, Louis Black on banjo, Frank Snyder on drums, Elmer Schobel on piano, and George Brunies on trombone. Mobsters like Al Capone had moved in on the affluent night club business in Chicago until the Great Depression caused the movement to clubs in New York City.

Bix was greatly influenced by the New Orleans Rhythm Kings as a teenager. It proudly emulated the black musical heritage of New Orleans, and was considered the best of all the white groups of its time. He also learned much through early recordings of the Original Dixieland Jass Band and was able to later assimilate the New Orleans style into a Chicago brand of dixieland with other local musicians known as the Austin High Gang. These young white Chicagoans and their associates included Jimmy McPartland, Frank Teschemacher, Bud Freeman, Jim Lannigan, Dick McPartland, a young Benny Goodman, Eddie Condon, and Dave Tough.

In 1923 he performed in his first band, the Wolverines, which became an immediate success. The Wolverines made their first appearance in 1923 and their first recording in 1924, for Gennett, at Richmond, Indiana. Beiderbecke played in 1925 with Bix and His Rhythm Jugglers, which included young trombonist Tommy Dorsey and clarinetist Don Murray, two of Bix's closest friends. Bix had another close relationship with songwriter Hoagy Carmichael. He came into heavy alcohol abuse as he built his reputation. Beiderbecke joined bands led by Jean Goldkette and played in sessions with saxophonist Frankie Trumbauer, who was one of the early figures of the Chicago jazz school. He joined Paul Whiteman in New York and was a featured soloist from 1928 to 1930. Bix became hopelessly ill from his uncontrollable drinking and died from lobar pneumonia in Queens, New York in 1931.

During his brief 28 years, Bix became a true musical legend of the Jazz Age. With a gifted ear he was able to reach harmonic infrastructures with a sensitive and lyrical style. His fame as a jazz romanticist became widespread after his death much as a modern cult figure. Beiderbecke's improvisational approach provides an interesting contrast to his contemporary, Louis Armstrong, whose style was bolder with searing improvisational lines.

Study Guide: Bix Beiderbecke

Recordings

"Singin' the Blues"—Frankie Trumbauer and His Orchestra.
SCCJ (record side 3, band 4, cassette side B, CD I). Recorded in 1927.

Personnel
Bix Beiderbecke—cornet, Frankie Trumbauer—C-melody sax,
Bill Rank—trombone, Jimmy Dorsey—clarinet,
Paul Mertz—piano, Eddie Lang—guitar,
Chauncey Morehouse—drums

Musical Characteristics
Unlike New Orleans-style dixieland, this Chicago style is a bit more laid-back and lyrical. The use of C-melody saxophone and guitar replacing the banjo in a 2/4 rhythm bears some of the distinctions of the Chicago style. Compare the styles of Armstrong and Beiderbecke in 1927.

Musical Form
Slow two-beat rhythm

1. Introduction—wind instruments playing theme in two-part style.
2. Solo—C melody sax with two-beat rhythm, break, and double-time.
3. Solo—cornet with break and double time.
4. Collective improvisation.
5. Solo—clarinet with solo break.
6. Collective improvisation with cornet lead.
7. Solo—guitar with solo break, and out.

"Riverboat Shuffle"—Frankie Trumbauer and His Orchestra.
SCCJ (record side 3, band 5, cassette side B, CD I). Recorded in 1927.

Personnel
Bix Beiderbecke—cornet, Bill Rank—trombone,
Don Murray—clarinet, baritone sax,
Frankie Trumbauer—C-melody sax,
Don Ryker—alto sax, Itzy Riskin—piano,
Eddie Lang—guitar, Chauncey Morehouse—drums

Musical Characteristics
This piece shows the Chicago style. Beiderbecke's lyrical concept of playing is felt throughout his lead and imaginative solos with exciting, well-conceived breaks. Beiderbecke's playing with Trumbauer is considered his best, and this recording provides an interesting solo comparison with

those of Armstrong during the same period. "Riverboat Shuffle," written by Hoagy Carmichael, is played with the early New Orleans flat-four style, unlike the Chicago two-beat of "Singin' the Blues."

Musical Form
1. Introduction—full ensemble with guitar breaks.
2. Full ensemble with piano and clarinet breaks.
3. Solo—cornet begins with a break, continues with rhythm, another break, and full rhythm.
4. Interlude—trombone breaks.
5. Full ensemble plays with trombone breaks.
6. Solo—clarinet plays with a break.
7. Full ensemble with cornet lead and solo breaks by cornet, saxophone, guitar and saxophone again.
8. Tag.

New Orleans dixieland began as an outdoor musical activity and the instruments were portable. Later, other instruments such as the piano, string bass, and drum set were more practical for indoor use. Chicago-style dixieland was an indoor activity.

Figure 4.1: Comparison Chart
New Orleans and Chicago Style Dixieland Instrumentation

New Orleans	Chicago
cornet	cornet
clarinet	clarinet, saxophone
trombone	trombone
tuba	string bass
banjo	guitar
marching drums or drum set	drum set
Musical Style	
four-beat (4/4) meter	two-beat (2/4) meter
collective improvisation	individual improvisation
hot, raggy sound	more refined, controlled indoor activities
both outdoor and indoor activities	

CHAPTER FIVE

NEW YORK—
VOCALISTS, PIANISTS

The distressful Volstead Act, which became the Eighteenth Amendment to the U.S. Constitution on July 1, 1919, signaled the beginning of Prohibition. The new law made it illegal to sell or transport any beverage containing more than half of one percent of alcohol. Public reactions to this law promoted a number of speakeasies in which illegal bootleg liquor was readily available, accompanied by the sounds of jazz. F. Scott Fitzgerald termed the 1920s as *the Jazz Age*, and wrote several novels describing the period's night life that developed into a social frenzy with flappers, fast cars, and thrill-seekers. The Jazz Age, or Roaring Twenties, beckoned jazz back to its vulgar origins and contributed, as in the Storyville era, to disrespectful associations. Author Arnold Shaw points to Fitzgerald's novel *This Side of Paradise* as giving the Jazz Age definition. Shaw's book *The Jazz Age* says:

> Overnight, *Paradise* became the "undergraduates bible and its author the acknowledged leader of the Torrid Twenties, laureate of the Jazz Age and its excessive accent on youth." Scott having become a celebrity, the Fitzgeralds went on a roller coaster ride of glamourous Long Island partying, trips to Paris, unbuttoned high jinks, lavish entertaining, and notorious debaucheries that kept Scott emotionally and financially strapped.*

If Fitzgerald's novels such as *Tales of the Jazz Age, This Side of Paradise* and *The Great Gatsby* gave definition to the social trappings of the '20s, then it was left to some notable musicians to frame it in music. In 1920 Mamie Smith recorded the first blues record and pianist James P. Johnson recorded "Carolina Shout" in 1921. Louis Armstrong joined King Oliver in 1922 and Duke Ellington arrived in New York in 1923. In 1924, when Paul Whiteman premiered *Rhapsody in Blue*, Armstrong joined Fletcher Henderson in New York. Jelly Roll Morton recorded "Black Bottom Stomp" in 1926, the year that Ellington recorded "East

---

*Arnold Shaw, *The Jazz Age*, Oxford University Press. Reprinted with permission.

St. Louis Toodle-oo." In 1927 Ellington opened at the Cotton Club and
Frankie Trumbauer offered "Riverboat Shuffle" and "Singin' the Blues"
featuring Bix Beiderbecke, while Louis Armstrong launched his studio
recordings with the Hot Seven. Writer–musician Henry Martin has given
a very interesting chronological account of the musical and historical
events of the entire history of jazz from 1868 to 1980 in his book, *Enjoying
Jazz*, Schirmer Books, 1986, pp. 277–289.

Arnold Shaw's book offers some further unsettling characteristics of
the '20s by describing it as a lawless decade. The gangsters of the Prohibition days in Chicago committed some outrageous crimes, such as the Valentine's Day Massacre in 1929, in which seven men lined up against a
wall were shot in their backs. This was the same year that the stock market prices collapsed, with U.S. securities losing $26 billion, signalling the
first phase of the Great Depression. Other mobsters like Al Capone and
Jack "Legs" Diamond were infamous crime figures of the period, and legends were created from the gangland portraits in mid-America. The television series "The Untouchables" documented much of the prohibition
crime era.

The first motion picture with sound was "The Jazz Singer," in 1927,
starring Al Jolson; it was honored in the first Academy Awards ceremony.
The word "Jass" still had sexual connotations for most respectable Americans. Musicians unions in Chicago and Pittsburgh condemned this new
music as vulgar and immoral. It wasn't until the Paul Whiteman Concert
at Aeolian Hall in 1924, with *Rhapsody in Blue,* that jazz gained a measure
of respectibility in public eyes. Earlier, in 1920, the radio had established
its first broadcast by station KDKA in Pittsburgh, and before that the
phonograph developed by the Victor Talking Machine Company in
1916, became a fixture in most American homes. Victor distributed a
"race records" catalog in the mid–20s.

Radio stations grew into large networks such as NBC in 1926 and CBS
in 1927, and with new means of mass communication and transmission,
jazz had begun to be assimilated into popular American culture. Most radio stations played popular white versions of jazz, such as the recorded hits
of Paul Whiteman, while the real jazz that was being developed by blacks
like Fletcher Henderson went relatively unnoticed by the general public. It
was in the 1920s that the blues became a dominant force in jazz.

City Blues

A second period of early blues called *urban* or *city blues* sprang up. While
the country blues were dominated by men, 1920s city blues were sung by
women with powerful pulsating voices that characterized this transition.
They performed on the road from the South, Midwest, and finally in the
Northeast. The traveling vaudeville acts that gave way to the movies,

phonograph, and radio produced a newly sophisticated form of blues. Early city blues were performed by women in indoor settings and were accompanied by several instruments or a full orchestra rather than only a guitar. The formal blues structure was followed more closely, with more attention to the details of lyrics and instrumental arrangements. Musical performance and vocal styling was on a much higher level than the more informal country blues, and the impact on jazz was much more widespread. See figure 5.1.

Gertrude "Ma" Rainey was the first of the great classic blues singers who toured the Midwest and South in vaudeville and in the Rabbit Foot Minstrels. She discovered and tutored Bessie Smith, who was the greatest of all early blues singers, and established what writer Orrin Keepnews called a Golden Age in the 20s.

Bessie Smith

Female singers like Ma Rainey and the Empress of the Blues, Bessie Smith, expanded and refined the great blues tradition in clubs and honkytonks. Bessie Smith, who was born in 1895 in Chattanooga, Tennessee, was raised in poverty like Louis Armstrong. She learned her craft early in her career from Ma Rainey, and was brought to New York City in 1923 by Frank Walker of Columbia Records. The years of her greatest fame were from 1924 to 1927; later she became addicted to alcohol. She was involved in a car crash in 1937 and, according to reports, bled to death in route to a hospital. Her vocal style was characterized as one of expansive beauty and strength, with exquisite taste. She was one of America's greatest jazz artists.

Study Guide: Bessie Smith

Recordings

"St. Louis Blues"—Bessie Smith.
SCCJ (record side 1, cassette side A, CD I). Recorded in 1925.

Personnel
Bessie Smith—vocals,
Louis Armstrong—cornet,
Fred Longshaw—reed organ

Musical Characteristics
This is a recording of one of the earliest and most famous blues composed by W.C. Handy, who was called the Father of the Blues. Although the title suggests a blues form, the B section is 16 bars, rather than the usual

Figure 5.1: Comparison Chart
Country and City Blues

Country Blues	City Blues
Rough, sometimes irregular	Refined and well-structured
Generally outdoors	Mostly indoors
Male singers	Female singers
Accompanied by a single instrument	Accompanied by several instruments, or band
Used flatted 3rd and 7th in the blues scale	Added flatted 5th in addition to the flatted 3rd and 7th

12 bars. The support of Louis Armstrong results in a call and response in each phrase. The use of an organ was rather typical in the early stages of city blues development. Bessie's vocal style is filled with much emotion and personal expression that made her one of the greatest blues singers of all time.

Musical Form
1. Unusual form of AABC
2. Introduction is one chord.
3. A theme is a 12-bar blues that is repeated and sung with a call and response from the cornet.
4. B theme is 16 bars in a minor key.
5. C theme is a 12-bar blues in a major key.
6. Ends with a hold (fermata).

Video

The Ladies Sing the Blues
V.I.E.W., Inc.; 60 min.
Bessie is featured in this collection of famous female blues singers. It was the first appearance of a blues singer on film and is the first offering on the video. She sings the "St. Louis Blues" in a movie short filmed by Warner Bros. in 1933; in the waning years of her life, Bessie still exhibited those emotional qualities that made her famous. This video is used later in the text for examples of Billie Holiday and others. See chapter 6.

Bessie Smith and Friends, 1929–1941
Jazz Classics; 39 min.
This program features the same film clip of the "St. Louis Blues." Other artists are The Nicolas Brothers, Eubie Blake, Nina Mae McKinney, Lena Horne, Albert Ammons, Pete Johnson, and Teddy Wilson. The program also includes "Pie Pie Blackbird" and "Boogie-Woogie Dream."

Harlem Pianists

New York's Harlem was a creative center of intellectual pursuit and a haven for writers, poets, and musicians in the 20s. An ebullient Duke Ellington recalled his first visit to Harlem as a youth in the early 20s in his autobiography *Music is My Mistress*, and writer Arnold Shaw underlined the cultural development of Harlem during the period in his book *The Jazz Age*:

> In those intoxicating years, there was enchantment in the very air of Harlem. It crackled with excitement, with the anticipation of unusual experiences, and the vaulting interest to create something overwhelming. And new poetry, novels, essays and plays poured from the pens of Countee Cullen, Claude McKay, Jean Toomer, Wallace Thurman, Arna Bontemps, Aaron Douglas, Rudolph Fisher, Alain Locke, Zora Neale Hurston, among others, some inspired by the new spirit of Negro nationalism aroused by Marcus Garvey and his Universal Negro Improvement Association.*

The black and white artistic activities lured musicians to the entertainment business, and Harlem teemed with nightlife. For jazz, Harlem became the new Storyville with many clubs, theatres, and entertainment spots located between 125th and 135th streets. The Cotton Club was owned by gangsters and staged opulent floor shows that catered to the white rich clientele. Other clubs frequented by celebrities and high society were the Paradise and Connie's Inn, which also featured lavish floor shows. Duke Ellington came to the Cotton Club from the Kentucky Club on Broadway in 1927, and became America's first great jazz composer and arranger during his five years of employment. His famous compositions of the period were "East St. Louis Toodle-oo," "Black and Tan Fantasy," "Creole Love Call," and "The Mooch."

James P. Johnson, who was originally a ragtime piano player, emerged as father of the *stride piano*. The stride pianists who followed him were Willie "The Lion" Smith, Thomas "Fats" Waller, Duke Ellington, Count Basie, and Art Tatum. The main difference between ragtime and stride piano was that stride piano was usually improvised in fast tempos. While the right hand played a single melody, the left hand executed the bass and harmony in rhythms with great leaps. The left hand provided a two-beat style with the strong beat on one in the lower bass. Many of the early stride pianists earned a living by playing house parties at which all guests contributed a small amount of money to help pay the rent. Johnson was born in New Brunswick, New Jersey, in 1891. One of his early influences was Luckey

---

*Arnold Shaw, *The Jazz Age*. New York: Oxford University Press, 1987.

Roberts. He met Fats Waller in 1919, and exerted quite an influence on Waller and Ellington. Like ragtime music, stride was not blues-influenced.

Study Guide: James P. Johnson
Recordings
"Carolina Shout"—James P. Johnson, piano.
SCCJ (record side 2, cassette side A, CD I). Recorded in 1921.

Musical Characteristics
"Carolina Shout" refers to the early ring shouts such as the ones that were common in Place Congo. It was recorded on a roll that was copied by Duke Ellington as one of the first pieces he learned. Duke used this piece to show off his early talents. "Carolina Shout" uses three themes, like "St. Louis Blues."

Musical Form
  1. Introduction—Right hand begins.
  2. First theme—Right hand plays a descending melodic figure from the high register while the left hand supplies a leaping bass and harmony.
  3. Second theme—Right hand moves to middle of the keyboard with a highly syncopated left hand.
  4. Third theme—A shout-like melody is heavily ragged with a left hand roll.

Fats Waller

Thomas "Fats" Waller was born in 1904, in New York City, to deeply religious parents in Harlem. His father was a clergyman who proclaimed that jazz was the devil's music. Playing classical piano and organ he began his career at age fifteen as organist at the Lincoln Theatre on 135th street. Waller met and was taught by James P. Johnson in 1919, and became a famous attraction at the Harlem house parties. He became musically prominent during the '20s, accompanying such great artists as Bessie Smith on the organ. During the late '20s he developed as a composer for the hit show *Hot Chocolates*, with tunes including "Ain't Misbehavin'," and the show *Keep Shufflin'*. The 1988 show *Ain't Misbehavin'*, at the Ambassador Theatre in New York City, revived many of Waller's famous songs, among them his 1933 hit "I'm Gonna Sit Right Down and Write Myself a Letter." Waller became a legendary figure with his overindulgences in food, liquor, and women. He raised the art of stride piano to its highest level and was a prolific composer, comedian, and singer. He died aboard the Santa Fe Chief railroad train near Kansas City in 1943.

Study Guide: Fats Waller

Recordings

'I Ain't Got Nobody"—Fats Waller, piano.
SCCJ (record side 4, cassette side C, CD II). Recorded in 1937.

Musical Characteristics
Although this tune was not written by him, this performance shows Waller's treatment of popular material and his control of dynamics throughout the piece.

Musical Form
1. Introduction is a series of sustained chords.
2. First chorus is in 2/4, melodies shift between both hands.
3. Repeat, with more use of left hand bass, as in ragtime.
4. New theme with right hand glissando and break time.
5. Walking bass in left hand, melody in right hand.
6. Descending scale in right hand followed by descending bass pattern.
7. Both hands play together.
8. Boogie woogie style.
9. Ragtime style and ending.

Video

Fats Waller and Friends, 1941–46
Jazz Classics.
This video features Dorothy Dandridge, Bob Howard, Tiny Grimes, Mabel Lee, Cook and Brown, Dusty Brooks and His Four Tones and The Three Clefs. Program includes "Your Feet's Too Big," "Ain't Misbehavin'," "Honeysuckle Rose," "Moo Cow Boogie Woogie," "Tiny Grimes' Boogie Woogie," "She's Too Hot to Handle," "Shout Brother, Shout," "Chicken Shack Shuffle," "Breakfast in Rhythm," and "The Joint Is Jumpin'."

Art Tatum

Tatum was born in Toledo, Ohio, in 1910, with defects of vision; he remained blind in one eye, with only partial sight in the other. Art began studying violin for a brief period, but soon turned to piano playing at local clubs and radio stations. In 1932 Tatum came to New York as accompanist for singer Adelaide Hall; before long he became a musical fixture in the 52nd Street jazz club, the Onyx. After many years as a solo pianist he formed a trio, with Slam Stewart on bass and Tiny Grimes on guitar, which was very successful. He recorded extensively during his last years, displaying a gifted technique marked by speed and great facility. Tatum died of uremia in 1956. He was a highly creative improviser with marvelous imagination and technique, with complete mastery of ragtime, stride, boogie-woogie, and blues.

Study Guide: Piano Legends

Recordings

"Willow Weep For Me"—Art Tatum, piano solo.
SCCJ (record side 5, cassette side C, CD II). Recorded in 1949.

Musical Characteristics

Tatum was never afraid to cross bar lines with quick rhythmic changes and stop time changes that were musically ornamented. "Willow Weep for Me" displays his mastery of these techniques with a variety of styles. The introductory *vamp* returns, providing a musical link that gives the solo continuity and form. Also, listen to "Too Marvelous for Words" on *SCCJ* (record side 5, cassette side C, CD II), for an example of his playing shortly before his death.

Musical Form

AABA form, 32 bars with two choruses

1. Introduction—Vamp with a rolling left hand.
2. A theme—Melody in the right hand, vamp.
3. A theme—Repeated followed by vamp.
4. B theme—Minor key, stride style.
5. A theme—Repeated with vamp, double time in right hand.
6. Second chorus:
   A theme—blues, running right hand scales.
   A theme—Repeated
   B theme—Quickly paced stop-time, with scale runs in both hands.
   A theme—Returns with scale runs in both hands.
7. Coda—Vamp and ending.

Video

Piano Legends
Video Artists International, Inc.; 63 min.
Chick Corea hosts this compilation of more than twenty piano legends, including Fats Waller, Count Basie, Duke Ellington, and more modern artists such as McCoy Tyner, Thelonius Monk, and Cecil Taylor.

Reading

Arnold Shaw, *The Jazz Age: Popular Music in the 1920s*
Oxford University Press, 1987.
A very interesting book that describes important jazz figures as well as pop figures in the '20s. The most important parts of the book are the first two chapters, "The Jazz Age" and "The Harlem Renaissance."

Chapter I, "The Jazz Age," captures the excitement of the 20s with musical greats Louis Armstrong, King Oliver, Jelly Roll Morton, Bix Beiderbecke, Fletcher Henderson, and Paul Whiteman.

Chapter II, "The Harlem Renaissance," is given to the birth of the blues with Ma Rainey and Bessie Smith. Duke Ellington and the Harlem pianists are examined in the chapter "Kitten on the Keys" with literary tributes to James P. Johnson, Willie "The Lion" Smith, and Fats Waller.

CHAPTER SIX

NEW YORK—
BIG BANDS

Fletcher Henderson

One of the most important big bands to emerge during the middle 1920s was that of Fletcher Henderson. Henderson was born in Georgia in 1897 and began playing piano at age six. He was taught mainly classics because of his father's disapproval of all forms of jazz. He and his brother Horace, however, became quite famous musicians. Fletcher studied chemistry and graduated from Atlanta University in 1920. After graduation he moved to New York City to study for his master's degree in chemistry, and instead became a pianist who demonstrated songs for Pace and Handy Music Company. When Harry Pace left the company to form Black Swan Records, Henderson joined him. Blues became popular, and Henderson found himself accompanying Ethel Waters in 1921 on road tours. During one of the tours with Waters the group made the first known jazz radio broadcast in New Orleans, in 1922. In 1923 Henderson's reputation as a gifted accompanist for blues singers soared, as he played with the likes of Ma Rainey, Bessie Smith, and many more.

By 1924 Henderson had formed his own group, which performed at the Club Alabam in New York. After this brief engagement he landed the job at Roseland Ballroom, where his band was the house band from 1924 to 1930. Henderson had become a remarkable bandleader, composer, arranger, and pianist in New York City. His style might be characterized as *pre-swing* because over the years he added increasingly more players, creating sections, and he used instrumental arrangements to organize the music. These arrangements were evident even in his early associations with blues singers. Henderson was not a forceful bandleader, but did manage to hire some of the better musicians of the period. He represented the African roots of hot jazz in his transitional big band style that was exciting in a rough manner.

"Smack," as he was nicknamed, had some outstanding soloists such as Coleman Hawkins on tenor saxophone and Don Redman on alto saxophone. Redman, like Henderson, was a gifted composer and arranger who helped create the *swing* style that was to be launched by Benny Goodman. Louis Armstrong joined Henderson for a year, beginning in 1924. Although poorly presented to the American public, Henderson's band became one of the most important developmental jazz links between the dixieland and swing styles. Fletcher Henderson died in New York City in 1952.

Study Guide: Fletcher Henderson

Recordings

"The Stampede"—Fletcher Henderson and His Orchestra.
SCCJ (record side 3, cassette side B, CD II). Recorded in 1926.

Personnel
Fletcher Henderson—piano, Russell Smith—trumpet,
Joe Smith—cornet, Rex Stewart—cornet,
Benny Morton—trombone, Buster Bailey—clarinet/alto sax,
Coleman Hawkins—clarinet/tenor sax, Charlie Dixon—banjo,
Ralph Escudero—tuba, Kaiser Marshall—drums,
Don Redman—arranger
Soloists: Stewart, Hawkins, Joe Smith, Henderson, Stewart

Musical Characteristics
"The Stampede" is musically important because it shows the masterful arranging style of Don Redman. Here, the instruments are assembled into sections that feature call and response, with room for improvisation. Also, the transition from dixieland to swing is evident with the increasing number of sidemen.

Musical Form
AABC

1. Introduction—Stewart cornet solo in a two-beat style.
2. A section—repeated.
3. Hawkins tenor sax solo, followed by an interlude.
4. B section—Joe Smith cornet solo and interlude.
5. C section—features a clarinet trio.
6. Stewart's second cornet solo and interlude.
7. Full band and out.

"Wrappin' It Up"—Fletcher Henderson and His Orchestra.
SCCJ (record side 3, cassette side B, CD II). Recorded in 1934.

Personnel
Henry "Red" Allen—trumpet, Irving Randolph—trumpet,
Russell Smith—trumpet, Keg Johnson—trombone,
Claude Jones—trombone, Buster Bailey—clarinet/alto sax,
Hilton Jefferson—clarinet/alto sax, Russell Procope—clarinet/alto sax,
Ben Webster—tenor sax, Lawrence Lucie—guitar,
Elmer James—bass, Walter Johnson—drums,
Soloists: Jefferson, Allen, Bailey
Arranger: Fletcher Henderson.

Musical Characteristics
Here we can hear the refinement of Henderson's style with a slightly
larger band. It is one of the pieces that was later provided for Benny
Goodman, who recorded it in 1938. "Wrappin' It Up," written in 1934,
might have launched the swing era if it had been properly introduced to
the American public. Recording exposure was one of the unfortunate
problems that plagued Henderson.

Musical Form
1. Introduction—call and response patterns between the brass and saxes.
2. First chorus—saxes play the main theme with brass responses. ABAC.
3. Second chorus—solo by alto sax with muted brass background.
4. Third chorus—solo by trumpet accompanied by saxes and muted brass.
5. Final chorus—A section is brass lead with clarinet ensemble, B section features a clarinet solo, A section is repeated with saxes and the C section ends with the full band.

Developing an American Orchestra, 1923–1937—Fletcher Henderson. **Smithsonian P2-13710 (2 LPs).**
A collection of thirty-two selections, including "Christopher Columbus," "Somebody Loves Me," and "Sugar Foot Stomp." These recordings are of high quality, and the program notes offer extensive study and evaluation of Henderson's formative years. Includes an extensive discography with essays and pictures tracing the history of Henderson's band. Highly recommended.

Paul Whiteman

One of the big orchestras that provides an interesting contrast to Henderson's was that of the very popular Paul Whiteman. While Henderson reflected strong African roots, Whiteman reflected European traditions in his approach. Whiteman was born in Denver, Colorado, in 1890. He moved to the West Coast, then left San Francisco in 1919 for Atlantic City. The following year he came to New York City and made his first recordings, "Whispering" and "The Japanese Sandman," which gained him great fame and popularity in this country. He was one of the most successful bandleaders, with considerable commercial backing by publishers and agents with clever marketing skills. He had great soloists, including the forlorn Bix Beiderbecke.

Whiteman was crowned "King of Jazz" by his publicity agents, rather than by his musical peers. To drive his grandeur home to the American public, Whiteman was shown in a newsreel movie clip conducting his orchestra on a white Arabian stallion borrowed from the Ringling Brothers Circus. The original plan was to mount Whiteman atop an elephant while conducting, but the plan had to be abandoned when the elephant could not fit through the doors of the theater. His music publishers staged a lavish and bizarre homecoming for him in New York Harbor when he returned from his European tour aboard the S.S. Leviathan on August 13, 1923. The *New York Tribune* featured pictures of floating musicians who nearly drowned, and others in biplanes welcoming their hero.

Whiteman's famous concert in Aeolian Hall on February 12, 1924, introduced George Gershwin at the piano playing his *Rhapsody in Blue,* and brought jazz-influenced music to the American public with respectability. This concert was a rather long musical affair, with eleven separate sections featuring the developments of popular music from early dixieland styles to light classics. Some of the other composers featured were Jerome Kern ("Raggedy Ann"), Zez Confrey ("Kitten on the Keys" and "Nickel in the Slot"), Irving Berlin ("Alexander's Ragtime Band"); other works at the concern included "A Pretty Girl Is Like a Melody," and "Orange Blossoms in California," Victor Herbert's "A Suite of Serenades," Edward MacDowell's "To a Wild Rose," and Edward Elgar's *Pomp and Circumstance* as the last piece. A large number of music critics and classical composers attended the event, with highly favorable reactions. *Rhapsody in Blue* was presented before the last piece by Elgar, and was the hit of the concert. The concert was a great success and helped Gershwin to a popular musical career. The Whiteman movie "King of Jazz," released in 1930, staged the famous *Rhapsody in Blue* with Gershwin at the piano. Unfortunately, Bix Beiderbecke was gravely ill and did not appear in the movie. Whiteman passed away in 1968.

Study Guide: Paul Whiteman

Recordings

Paul Whiteman, Vol. I.
RCA. Victor LPV-55.

Musical Characteristics
Listen to the first three recordings: "Whispering," "The Japanese Sandman," and "Anytime, Anyday, Anywhere." These were extremely popu-

lar in 1920, and notice that the polished arrangements have little relation to jazz. A most interesting phenomenon is the tonal vibrato that was used by musicians of the day, particularly saxophone players. The tonal ideal was a sweet, syrupy sound. This overly sentimental sound is very difficult for modern musicians to emulate, but represents an example of the creative mind in the '20s.

Next, listen to the 1927 recording of *Rhapsody in Blue,* and compare this style to that of Fletcher Henderson in the same year. Whiteman's orchestra is more of a classical European style with little room for improvisation. Henderson's band reveals much more emotional content and has many more rhythmic elements of jazz, although it is not as well-polished. "Love Nest," recorded by Whiteman in 1928, features a closing solo by Bix Beiderbecke.

The Best of The Big Bands, Vol. 8—Paul Whiteman and His Orchestra Featuring Bix Beiderbecke.
CSP CBS BT 16784.
This recording features brief solos by Beiderbecke in some of the Whiteman hits: "That's My Weakness Now," "Sweet Sue," "Felix the Cat," "My Melancholy Baby," "China Boy," "Tain't So, Honey," "Gypsy," and "Because My Baby Don't Mean Maybe Now."

An Experiment in Modern Music: Paul Whiteman at Aeolian Hall.
Smithsonian 2028 (2 LPs).
This is a recreation of the original concert in 1924, including George Gershwin performing *Rhapsody in Blue.* The historic concert features recordings of Zez Confrey and other composers represented on the program. There are 32 recordings by Whiteman in this collection.

Video

King of Jazz
MCA Home Video; 93 min.
Produced by Universal in 1930, this was the first all-technicolor feature-length musical film, with seven dazzling production numbers. One of the production numbers is *Rhapsody in Blue,* which features George Gershwin at the piano with the Whiteman Orchestra. This film is quite interesting in capturing the entertainment style of the late '20s.

Duke Ellington—Early

Edward Kennedy "Duke" Ellington was born in Washington, D.C. in 1899 and became one of the true geniuses of jazz. Born in relative middle class comfort and given to a life of elegance, Duke played piano and was greatly influenced by the best ragtime and stride piano players of the day. His reputation as America's foremost jazz composer is well supported by his massive legacy of compositions, some 1500 pieces of music. While Ellington played piano, his real talent was the orchestra as an instrument which he used like an artist uses a palette. He wrote compositions with incomparable tonal beauty and harmonic coloring. A unique quality of his writing was the balance between orchestral composition and individual improvisation. His ability to write for individual members of his band was a stroke of genius.

After coming to Harlem in the '20s, he formed his first important band at the downtown Kentucky Club in New York City, then moved in to the big-time Cotton Club in Harlem from 1927 to 1932. Ellington developed his tonal and harmonic language with pieces like "Black and Tan Fantasy," "The Mooche," "East St. Louis Toodle-oo," "Creole Love Call," and "Mood Indigo." Two of his early sidemen, Bubber Miley on trumpet, who had been influenced by King Oliver, and Joe "Tricky Sam" Nanton on trombone, pioneered the "wa-wa" effects and plunger muted styles. Ellington's development as America's most important composer continued throughout most of the history of jazz until his death in 1974.

Ellington's early band, The Washingtonians featured Miley and Nanton in 1926. The Washingtonians was organized to play theaters, and they played New England tours and at Ciro's before coming to the Cotton Club in 1927. In 1928 Arthur Whetsol replaced Miley in this band, and Miley returned four months later in the Cotton Club Orchestra. Freddie Jenkins was featured on trumpet and Barney Bigard on clarinet as soloists in a two-part composition "Tiger Rag," which was recorded by the Jungle Band in 1929. Cootie Williams replaced Miley after these sessions, while Johnny Hodges and Harry Carney began to develop as fine reed players.

Study Guide: Duke Ellington—Early

Recordings

"East St. Louis Toodle-oo"—Duke Ellington and His Kentucky Club Orchestra.
SCCJ (record side 6, cassette side D, CD III). Recorded in 1927.

Personnel
Duke Ellington—piano, Bubber Miley—trumpet,
Louis Metcalf—trumpet, Joe Nanton—trombone,
Otto Hardwicke—saxophones, Harry Carney—reeds,
Rudy Jackson—reeds, Fred Guy—banjo,
Wellman Brand—bass, Sonny Greer—drums,
Ellington–Miley—arrangers

Soloists: Miley, Carney, Nanton, Jackson, and Miley

Musical Characteristics

This early version shows the influence of Bubber Miley's "wa-wa" plunger effects with his trumpet on the orchestra. This collaboration between Ellington and Miley is important because it reveals an influence that Ellington would carry on with his other soloists throughout his career. It is interesting to note that aside from Whiteman's large concert style orchestra, jazz bands were gradually increasing in size, as evidenced through the Ellington recordings.

Musical Form
AABAC

1. A theme—repeated with Miley's plunger effects (growl) on trumpet.
2. B and A themes—Miley's solo continues.
3. C theme—repeated with Carney on baritone sax.
4. C theme—with Nanton on open trombone.
5. A theme—repeated with Jackson on clarinet.
6. C theme—full band in a dixieland style.
7. A theme—Miley's solo returns.

"The New East St. Louis Toodle-oo"—Duke Ellington and His Famous Orchestra.
SCCJ (record side 6, cassette side D, CD III). Recorded in 1937.

Personnel
Duke Ellington—piano/arranger, Wallace Jones—trumpet,
Cootie Williams—trumpet, Freddy Jenkins—trumpet/drums,
Rex Stewart—cornet, Joe Nanton—trombone,
Lawrence Brown—trombone, Juan Tizol—valve trombone,
Barney Bigard—clarinet/tenor sax,
Johnny Hodges—clarinet/alto and soprano saxes,
Harry Carney—clarinet/baritone sax,
Otto Hardwicke—alto sax, Fred Guy—guitar,
Hayes Alvis or Billy Taylor—bass, Sonny Greer—drums

Soloists: Williams, Bigard, Williams.

Musical Characteristics
This 1937 version of "East St. Louis Toodle-oo" shows the remarkable development of Ellington through ten years. The development of a smoother, polished style is evident as the band is expanded from ten players to fifteen. Also note that the C theme has been dropped. The traditional plunger style of Miley has been preserved by Cootie Williams in a much slower tempo.

Musical Form
AABA

1. Introduction—with chimes, slower tempo.
2. A theme—repeated with Williams' plunger solo, trombones, and trumpets in response.
3. B theme—features sax section with brass response.
4. A theme—repeated with Williams' solo.
5. A theme: Second Chorus—full band, A theme repeated with Bigard clarinet solo.
6. B theme: Second Chorus—clarinet solo continues.
7. A theme: Second Chorus—trumpet solo returns with temple blocks (hoof-beats) and full band to the end.

The Brunswick Era, Vol. 1: 1926–1929—Duke Ellington and His Orchestra. **MCA 42325.**
Although the quality of these recordings has suffered from reissue, there are several early Duke classics that are most worthwhile. In addition to the 1927 "East St. Louis Toodle-oo" recording, listen to "Black and Tan Fantasy" and "The Mooche," 1928. Both pieces are packed with the stylings of early Ellingtonia. You will hear the famous "wa-wa" plunger and "growl" technique of Bubber Miley and the soulful clarinet sounds in both upper and lower registers. The muted brass and doubled woodwinds give the music exotic colors with lush harmonic textures. The early section work clearly defines the emerging direction of the Swing Era.

Video

Duke Ellington and His Orchestra, 1929–1941
Amvest Video, Jazz Classics, 33 min.
This is a wonderful collection of three early short classic films in black and white. It features Duke's band, and reveals the band's musical evolution every six years beginning with the Cotton Club Band in 1929, his 1935 band, and finally the great band of 1941. The program is:

1. *Black and Tan Fantasy,* 1929—The first film features Duke and his Cotton Club Orchestra and is his initial appearance on film. The opening scene shows Duke at the piano with lead trumpet man Arthur Whetsol rehearsing "Black and Tan." Other early pieces are "Black Beauty" and "The Duke Steps Out," which features a five-man dance routine. "Cotton Club Stomp" features female dancer Fredi Washington, and the band closes with "Hot Feet" and a host of chorus girls. The last scene features the full orchestra in a deathbed scene playing

"Black and Tan." These performances were probably part of the regular 1929 Cotton Club show.

Personnel
Arthur Whetsol, Freddie Jenkins, and Cootie Williams—trumpets,
Joe "Tricky Sam" Nanton—trombone,
Barney Bigard, Johnny Hodges, and Harry Carney—reeds,
Duke Ellington—piano, Fred Guy—guitar,
Wellman Braud—bass, Sonny Greer—drums

2. *Symphony in Black*, 1935—Duke and his orchestra are featured in this Paramount short film. *Symphony in Black* is a four-part symphony. Part 1, "The Laborers," opens with Johnny Hodges on sax and Lawrence Brown on trombone. Part 2, "A Triangle," is made up of three sections with a muted Cootie Williams solo in the first section; and nineteen-year-old Billie Holiday sings a mournful blues in the last section, with a Bigard clarinet solo and Nanton playing a trombone plunger solo. Part 3 is "Hymn of Sorrow," with a scene of a silent preacher followed by "Harlem Rhythm," with Snakehips Tucker in a dance routine and some wonderful vintage Ellington.

Personnel
Same as "Black and Tan"—add Otto Hardwicke—reeds, and Lawrence Brown—trombone.

3. *Hot Chocolate*, 1941—with Duke and his orchestra near its peak of fame and achievement. This piece is also known as "Cottontail," featuring tenor sax great Ben Webster. Whitey's Lindy Hoppers also appear.

Personnel
Wardell Jones, Ray Nance, Rex Stewart—trumpets,
Joe Nanton, Juan Tizol—trombones,
Barney Bigard, Johnny Hodges, Otto Hardwicke,
Ben Webster, and Harry Carney—reeds,
Duke Ellington—piano, Fred Guy—guitar,
Jimmy Blanton—bass, Sonny Greer—drums

Reading

Duke Ellington, *Music Is My Mistress*
DaCapo Press, Inc. 1973.
This autobiography by the Duke reveals his love of music and humanity. Great in-depth discussions of his many famous sidemen and musical associates. There is also a discography and an extensive chronological listing of his compositions. Over 100 photographs.

PART III

The Swing Era, 1935–1945

CHAPTER SEVEN

THE BIG BANDS

With the invention of the phonograph and operation of radio stations, the American public became exposed to jazz during the 1920s. During the last half of that decade, talking movies became the vogue. Prior to this time black music was available on *race records* that were sold in African-American neighborhoods; the white public was completely unaware of great black musicians. Jazz had become a household word because of radio and recordings; however, with the crash of the Wall Street stock market in 1929, the country plunged into a deep depression which temporarily stunted this growth until 1935–36.

In the early '30s, great black bands like those led by Fletcher Henderson, Duke Ellington, Bennie Moten, and Count Basie had helped define basic arranging and improvisational concepts for the big band. It wasn't until 1935 that a young white musician named Benny Goodman gave birth to the "Swing Era" on his radio program "Let's Dance." The country began to recover from its economic reeling, and the seeds for a new musical era were firmly planted.

Bennie Moten, a Kansas City band leader from 1922 to 1935, with his arranger-trombonist Eddie Durham, developed a big band style that was heavily influenced by the blues and featured *riffs*. A riff is simply a repeated musical idea, or motive, by the brass and/or woodwind sections. His sidemen, including the famous Count Basie on piano, had helped him create a swing style in Kansas City despite the Depression. Thomas Joseph Prendergast, a political boss, had kept this Southwestern city wide open, and musicians were still able to find work. He was later convicted of evading paying half a million dollars in income tax and sent to Leavenworth Prison. Listen to "Moten Swing," 1932, on SCCJ (record side 4, cassette side C). The predominant style of four strong beats provided by bassist Walter Page became one of the trademarks of the Count Basie Band. "Moten Swing" also features the early stride style of Basie that he would later refine into the right hand alone. The piece ends with the use of riffs and revealed the ability to swing with call and response between sections.

Study Guide: Bennie Moten

Recordings

"Moten Swing"—Bennie Moten's Kansas City Orchestra.
SCCJ (record side 4, cassette side C, CD II). Recorded in 1932.

Personnel
Bennie Moten—director,
Oran "Hot Lips" Page, Dee Stewart—trumpets,
Dan Minor—trombone, Eddie Durham—trombone/guitar,
Eddie Barefield—alto sax, Jack Washington—alto/baritone sax,
Ben Webster—tenor sax, Count Basie—piano,
Leroy Berry—guitar, Walter Page—bass,
Willie McWashington—drums

Soloists: Basie, Durham, Barefield, Page, Webster, Page

Musical Characteristics
The tightly knit rhythm section playing fours in a swing style was demonstrated here very successfully well before the swing era began. The importance of such steady driving pulsations in the rhythm section was an indelible musical characteristic of Basie's later bands.

Musical Form
AABA, fast swing fours

1. First chorus
   A Section—piano solo with bass as intro, 8 bars.
   A Section—piano continues, driving 4s on bass, 8 bars.
   B Section—brass and saxes in call and response, 8 bars.
   A Section—piano continues with bass, 8 bars.
2. Second chorus
   AA Sections—saxes play 4-bar theme with brass response.
   B Section—guitar solo with piano.
   A Section—saxes play the theme.
3. Third chorus
   AA Sections—brass play a riff theme with alto sax solo.
   B Section—sax solo with piano and walking bass.
   A section—brass play the theme.
4. Fourth chorus
   AA Sections—trumpet solo to swing 4s.
   B Section—tenor solo with stride piano style.
   A Section—trumpet solo continues.

5. Final chorus
   AA Sections—full band plays the main theme.
   BA Sections—full band continues.
6. Tag: riff-style with piano, 4 bars.

Characteristics: Swing

Never before or since in the history of jazz has one style of jazz music captivated the popular tastes of the American public as in the swing era. Swing music was fervently listened to by young and old alike in this country as well as by both the Allied Forces and the Axis powers during World War II. The word "swing," like the term "blues," has had some popular misconceptions when used to describe music. Duke Ellington's 1932 hit "It Don't Mean a Thing if It Ain't Got That Swing" was one of the first big band compositions to use the word in its title, as was "Moten Swing." Ever since, modern musicians often use the term "swing" to describe mainstream stylings that reveal true jazz characteristics of rhythm. When used in this context, the word "swing" has nothing to do with the swing era. The use of riffs and *shout choruses*, which pitted the brass against the saxes in call-and-response patterns, provided the musical vehicle for swing.

In the swing era big band music dominated the country and provided work for more musicians than ever before. Swing bandleaders and soloists such as trumpeter Harry James became Hollywood matinee idols, enjoying the same status as the screen stars. James married Betty Grable, who was a popular Hollywood actress and pin-up girl for American G.I.s in World War II.

The characteristics of the swing era big bands were:

1. Expanded instrumentation to a standard big band of five brass, four reeds, and four rhythm.
2. Stress on reading music with precision, and less emphasis on improvisation.
3. Swing music was used primarily for dancing.
4. Heavy use of the riff and shout chorus devices.
5. Swing became popular music.

Riffs were used by Bennie Moten and Count Basie in their early arrangements. The *shout chorus* was the last section of a swing arrangement that featured an exchange of riffs between the brass and woodwinds in a highly punctuated manner. The shout chorus was the musical climax of the piece, adding great excitement to the music and producing a swinging quality. Swing was now more desirable than hot as a musical style.

The height of the swing era in 1937 gave rise to extremely popular figures such as Benny Goodman, Count Basie, and Duke Ellington. Goodman recorded historical performances at Carnegie Hall in 1938. Basie, after leaving Moten's band, recorded "Doggin' Around," "Taxi War Dance" and "Lester Leaps In," and later joined the Goodman Sextet recordings with Charlie Christian. In the '40s, the famous Earl Hines Band began with Charlie Parker and Dizzy Gillespie. Ellington produced a series of great recordings with "Ko Ko," "Concerto for Cootie," "Cottontail," and "In a Mellotone."

Benny Goodman

Goodman, who was born in 1909 in Chicago, was a young clarinet virtuoso and was one of the first artists able to perform classical music as well as jazz with great proficiency. In his early years Goodman became a member of the Ben Pollack band in California and Chicago. He moved to New York City in 1929 and began playing many studio sessions before forming his own band, using Fletcher Henderson's arrangements, in 1934. He had his first big break with his appearances on the "Let's Dance" radio broadcasts from New York City; his overwhelming success at the Palomar Ballroom in Los Angeles in 1935 was a landmark in the beginning of the swing era. He featured some great sidemen, including trumpeters Bunny Berigan and Harry James, vibraphonist Lionel Hampton, and drummer Gene Krupa, who all went on to form their own bands.

Benny Goodman was dubbed The King of Swing by the public and musicians alike. One of his most notable achievements was breaking the color barrier between black and white musicians. The earliest example of this was Goodman's inclusion of Teddy Wilson at the piano; other black musicians followed including Lionel Hampton, Charlie Christian, and Cootie Williams. Goodman excelled in the big band style because he demanded precision and perfection from his sidemen. The Goodman band owed much in their development to black bands like Henderson's, Basie's, and Ellington's. He paid great homage to Fletcher Henderson for his influence.

Along with a big band style filled with riffs and incomparable execution, Goodman featured small groups that began as a trio and later developed into a septet. It must be emphasized that Goodman was actively promoted by impresario John Hammond, who also influenced the careers of Fletcher Henderson, Count Basie, Teddy Wilson, Charlie Christian, Billie Holiday, and Meade Lux Lewis. Hammond's personal effect on the development of jazz was widespread. He became Goodman's brother-in-law in 1942 when Goodman married his sister.

Benny died in 1986, but his legacy as the King of Swing will never diminish.

Study Guide: Benny Goodman

Recordings

"Sing, Sing, Sing"—Benny Goodman.
The Carnegie Hall Concert Jazz Concert.
(Columbia 40244). Recorded in 1938.

Personnel
Benny Goodman—clarinet, Hymie Shertzer—alto sax,
George Koenig, Babe Russin, Art Rollini—tenor saxes,
Harry James, Ziggy Elman, Chris Griffin—trumpets,
Vernon Brown, Red Ballard—trombones,
Gene Krupa—drums, Allan Reuss—guitar,
Jess Stacey—piano, Harry Goodman—bass
Arranger: Louis Prima

Musical Characteristics
This selection shows the great Goodman band at its peak and swinging
best. "Sing, Sing, Sing" in this version is an extended concert piece that
allows time for solo work with the likes of Harry James on trumpet, Goodman on clarinet, and the dominating drummer Gene Krupa with his
"floor-tom" style. There is great emotion and enthusiasm in this live performance as it showcases the riffs and shout choruses with call-and-
response patterns that were to characterize the swing band style.

Musical Form
AABA

1. Introduction is a drum solo (floor-toms), trumpets growl.
2. A Theme repeated—saxes and trumpets.
3. B Theme and A Theme as above.
4. Clarinet solo—trumpets in response.
5. Drum solo.
6. Interlude with trombones and trumpets riff.
7. Drum solo continues.
8. Riff Theme begun by the trumpets.
9. Drum solo continues.
10. Second riff introduced by the trumpets.
11. Drum solo continues.
12. Second riff played by the entire band.
13. Abrupt halt!
14. Drum solo begins softer with tenor solo and brass riffs.
15. Interlude on a riff theme.
16. Drum solo.

17. Trumpet solo by James, begins a dazzling display of execution and technique; trumpet section plays a riff.
18. Clarinet solo enters with hard floor-tom-tom and bass drum.
19. Solo fades to piano accompaniment, ends on high A to C.
20. Piano solo (Stacey) with drums in fours.
21. Abrupt end! (applause)
22. Drum solo begins with a cowbell.
23. Shout chorus played by the entire band in an exhilarating climax.

"I Found a New Baby"—Benny Goodman Sextet.
***SCCJ* (record side 6, cassette side D, CD II). Recorded in 1941.**

Personnel
Benny Goodman—clarinet,
Cootie Williams—trumpet, George Auld—tenor sax,
Count Basie—piano, Charlie Christian—guitar,
Artie Bernstein—bass, Jo Jones—drums

Musical Characteristics
The Goodman Sextet is a superb example of the rare combo style of the swing era. Using sidemen of the Basie Band provides a curious mixture of two approaches to jazz. Charlie Christian's great solo work on guitar is much more advanced and modern in the jazz language than those of Goodman, Basie, Williams, or Auld. Although dead at the age of 25, Christian's work on electric guitar was of great influence to all guitar players. Listen to "Breakfast Feud," *SCCJ*, following this cut, for further evidence of Christian's blues work. "Breakfast Feud" and other pieces like "Flying Home," "Memories of You," "AC/DC Current," "These Foolish Things," and "The Shiek of Araby" are available on digital remasters by Columbia: *The Benny Goodman Sextet Featuring Charlie Christian (1939–1941)* (CK 45144).

Musical Form
AABA (Basie-style 4/4 rhythm)

1. Introduction—begins with a cymbal figure.
2. A Theme—clarinet plays the melody in paraphrased improvisation. B and A themes are the same.
3. Second Chorus—guitar solo by Christian, very original.
4. Third Chorus—piano solo by Basie, guitar and clarinet background.
5. Fourth Chorus—trumpet solo muted on AA sections, tenor sax plays BA sections.
6. Fifth Chorus—abbreviated with a trumpet lead into a dixieland-style ending.

Reading

James L. Collier, *Benny Goodman and the Swing Era*
Oxford University Press, 1989.
This recent biography portrays both the legendary Benny Goodman and
the fabulous era over which he was to reign. In center stage throughout
this period stood Benny Goodman—a virtuoso player adored by millions
of fans but disliked by most musicians. Collier offers both the man and
the era in great detail, along with an examination of his major recordings.

Benny Goodman and Irving Kolodin, *The Kingdom of Swing*
Stackpole, 1939.
This is Benny Goodman's autobiography.

White Big Bands

Many other white big bands enjoyed great success and popularity during
the swing era. Harry James and Gene Krupa left Goodman to form their
own bands, while the Dorsey Brothers and Glenn Miller became household favorites. Glenn Miller, one of the most popular bandleaders of the
period, used a clarinet lead in his sax section, which produced a melancholy sound and achieved great notoriety in 1939 with hits like "Moonlight Serenade" and "Sunrise Serenade." Other hits like "Little Brown
Jug" and "In the Mood" were fine examples of the faster swing style.
Glenn Miller entered the American Air Force in 1942, during World War
II, and disappeared in a flight over the English Channel in 1944. When
Miller was lost the American newspapers announced it with more cover-
age than one of the most significant American victories in the European
theater, the Battle of the Bulge.

Tommy Dorsey, who began as a youthful musician with Bix Beiderbecke in the Midwest was very influential in the early days of swing, along
with the Casa Loma Orchestra. He was a bandleader and trombone solo-
ist, with his trademark solo on "I'm Getting Sentimental Over You."
Tommy had formed a band with his brother Jimmy early in 1933 to 1935.
Jimmy was a fine clarinet and alto saxophone soloist whose recording "So
Rare" became very popular. A fine technician on the alto sax, he was not
highly rated as a jazz musician, but was admired by other players like
Charlie Parker. Many fine sidemen passed through the ranks of the
Tommy Dorsey Orchestra, including Bunny Berigan, Pee Wee Erwin,
Charlie Shavers, Ziggy Elman on trumpet; and reedmen Buddy De-
Franco and Bud Freeman. Featured also were drummers Dave Tough,
Buddy Rich, and the great Louis Bellson. Tommy Dorsey introduced
singer Frank Sinatra in one of his hit records, "I'll Never Smile Again."
Another famous bandleader and a clarinet soloist who rivaled Goodman

Bunny Berigan (*Photo courtesy of RCA/Bluebird*)

was Artie Shaw, with his famous recording of "Begin the Beguine" in 1938. Like Harry James, he married Hollywood actresses; his most famous wives were Lana Turner and Ava Gardner among others. Shaw's recordings in the 1950s revealed a surprising tendency toward modern jazz.

Black Big Bands

Many black big bands sprung up during the swing era and followed on the heels of Ellington and Basie. They played a less commercial style than their white counterparts, with more true jazz elements, and their bands did not receive nearly the publicity. Jimmie Lunceford led an orchestra with arrangements by Sy Oliver, and his was one of the finest disciplined black bands. Although lacking in famous sidemen, the Lunceford band played with a tight, well-rehearsed swing style. Listen to his "Organ Grinder's Swing," 1936, on *SCCJ* (record 5, cassette side C), arranged by

Sy Oliver. His Ellington-influenced music is characterized by a disciplined sound full of precision and incomparable swing.

Fletcher Henderson's band continued into the swing era with "Wrappin' It Up" in late 1934. Andy Kirk led a band that featured composer-pianist Mary Lou Williams and easy-swinging arrangements. Chick Webb's band featured the compositions of Edgar Sampson, whose "Stompin' at the Savoy" and "Don't Be That Way" would be used later by Goodman. Webb also introduced the great vocalist Ella Fitzgerald. Cab Calloway's band was an exotic presentation much in the mold of the earlier Duke Ellington. Unlike the white bands, the black bands evolved more musically in modern jazz styles, particularly with arrangers and soloists. The era of bebop was more clearly forecast by the black bands, while the white bands tended to imitate each other. The die was cast when Duke Ellington claimed that the riff was overused and no longer useful as an expressive jazz element.

Artie Shaw (*Photo courtesy of RCA Archives*)

Study Guide: Black Big Bands—Lionel Hampton

Recordings

"When Lights Are Low"—Lionel Hampton and His Orchestra.
SCCJ (record side 5, cassette side D, CD II). Recorded in 1939.

Personnel
Dizzy Gillespie—trumpet, Benny Carter—alto sax,
Coleman Hawkins, Ben Webster, Chu Berry—tenor saxes,
Clyde Hart—piano, Charlie Christian—guitar,
Milt Hinton—bass, Cozy Cole—drums,
Lionel Hampton—vibraphone

Soloists: Hampton, Carter, Hampton, Hawkins, Hart
Arranger: Benny Carter

Musical Characteristics
Lionel Hampton was one of the first musicians to use the vibraphone
(vibes) in jazz. He, like Gene Krupa and Harry James, formed their own
bands after leaving Goodman. This smaller version of the swing band features some of the finest musicians of the swing era.

Musical Form
AABA, medium swing fours

1. First chorus
   A Theme—muted brass, repeated, 16 bars.
   B Theme—vibes improvise with straight fours in rhythm.
   A Theme—alto sax solo is improvised.
2. Second chorus
   A Theme—vibes improvise, repeated, 16 bars.
   B Theme—vibes solo continues.
   A Theme—vibes plays a blues style.
3. Third chorus
   A Theme—tenor sax solo, repeated, 16 bars.
   B Theme—piano solo.
   A Theme—trumpet lead with full band and vibes in the background.
4. Tag: ends with the vibes.

Duke Ellington—Later

By 1940 Duke Ellington had met a young composer-arranger, Billy Strayhorn, who exerted a tremendous influence on him. Ellington and Strayhorn
held great respect for each other, and developed a very close personal and

Duke Ellington with guitarist Fred Guy (*Photo courtesy of Duncan P. Schiedt*)

professional relationship. Strayhorn contributed a great number of tunes for the Ellington Band during this period, including "Lush Life," "Take the A Train," and collaborated with Duke on "Satin Doll." Ellington increased the size of his orchestra to fifteen, as shown in chapter 6, on "New East St. Louis Toodle-oo" in 1937. The orchestra went through a number of personnel changes, including trumpeter Cootie Williams who replaced Bubber Miley in 1929. Valve trombonist Juan Tizol also came in 1929 and wrote the Latin-tinged "Caravan" and other works before leaving in 1944.

When Cootie Williams left Ellington for Goodman in 1940, he was replaced by Ray Nance. Others who came into the band were Ben Webster on tenor sax, Rex Stewart on cornet, and Jimmy Blanton on bass. By the '50s modern replacements like Clark Terry and William "Cat" Anderson were added on trumpet with Paul Gonsalves on tenor sax and Russell Procope on alto sax. Johnny Hodges, a mainstay on alto sax since 1928, left the band in 1951, and returned in 1955. Ellington had developed a great sense of empathy with all of his musicians, and wrote biographical sketches with amazing recollections of most of his sidemen in *Music Is My Mistress,* his autobiography. Duke unfurled a musical legacy that was filled with elegance and sensitivity for his musicians. Being highly unselfish, he wrote pieces featuring his sidemen rather than himself. Furthermore, he encouraged Miley and Strayhorn, among others, to compose and arrange for his band, even though he was obviously the greatest jazz composer in history.

In 1989 Duke's lifetime output was donated to the Smithsonian Institution in his home town, Washington, D.C. His music, correspondence, and memorabilia are currently being catalogued at the Duke Ellington Archives at the Smithsonian. The exact number of his compositions will be known when this monumental task is completed. The Ellington Collection numbers 200,000 pages of documents. Included are 2,000 photographs, five hundred recordings, as well as scripts, clippings, work notes, financial records, and several hundred trophies, medals, and plaques. Address: The Duke Ellington Collection, Archives Center, National Museum of Natural History, Room C340, Smithsonian Institution, Washington, D.C. 20560; telephone (202) 357-3270.

The Eighteenth Annual International Association of Jazz Educators Conference held in Washington D.C. on January 10-13, 1991 was presented as "Celebrating Duke Ellington." Over one hundred jazz artists and groups gathered to honor this great composer with concerts and symposiums, with a keynote address by Wynton Marsalis and a retrospective of his music presented by Gunther Schuller and Orrin Keepnews.

Study Guide: Duke Ellington—Later, and Big Band Jazz

Recordings

"Concerto for Cootie"—Duke Ellington and His Famous Orchestra. *SCCJ* (record side 7, cassette side E, CD III). Recorded in 1940.

Personnel
Duke Ellington—piano/composer,
Wallace Jones, Cootie Williams—trumpets,
Rex Stewart—cornet, Joe Nanton—trombone,
Juan Tizol—valve trombone, Barney Bigard—woodwinds
Otto Hardwicke, Johnny Hodges—alto saxes,
Ben Webster—tenor sax, Harry Carney—baritone sax,
Fred Guy—guitar, Jimmy Blanton—bass,
Sonny Greer—drums

Soloist: Williams

Musical Characteristics
Duke's preoccupation with innovative forms and color is set to the stylings of Cootie Williams. On this recording Cootie plays both plunger-muted and open-horn styles for a variety of tonal colors. The piece is cast in a form that extends the A sections and coda to ten bars each.

Musical Form
AABACA, slow fours

1. Intoduction—muted solo trumpet, 8 bars.
2. A section—muted solo 6 bars, full band 4 bars.
   A section—repeated
   B section—trumpet plunger growls, 8 bars.
   A section—same as before.
3. Interlude—change of key, 4 bars.
4. C section—open trumpet solo, repeated, 16 bars.
5. Bridge—full band, 2 bars.
6. A section—muted solo trumpet, 6 bars.
7. Coda—solo joined by full band, 10 bars.

"In a Mellotone"—Duke Ellington and His Famous Orchestra.
SCCJ (record side 7, cassette side E, CD III). Recorded in 1940.

Personnel
Same as in "Concerto for Cootie."

Musical Characteristics
This is one example of the classic Ellington during the '40s. His compositional skills and ability to write space for his soloists are an important feature as they are refined. Notice that the trombone section becomes more prominent throughout the piece.

Listen also to "Cottontail" (record side 7, cassette side E), with soloists Williams, Webster, Carney, and Ellington; and "Ko Ko" (record side 6, cassette side D), which features Tizol, Nanton, Ellington, and Blanton. Both compositions, like "Mellotone," were recorded in 1940 and give rich examples of Ellington's famous soloists and his own compositional development.

Highly recommended is the later Ellington album of July 7, 1956, *Ellington at Newport*, CBS 40587, which features the famous 28-chorus solo by Paul Gonsalves on "Diminuendo and Crescendo in Blue." Many believe that this was the last great performance of Duke.

Musical Form
ABAB

1. Introduction—piano with bass fills, 8 bars.
2. A Theme—saxes play melody with trombone fills, 8 bars.
3. BAB Themes—same
4. Interlude—piano
5. Trumpet Solo—Williams uses a plunger, saxes fill and trumpet growls.
6. Alto Sax Solo—Hodges uses double-time with piano accompaniment.
7. Solo plays double-time with the rhythm in regular fours.
8. Entire band plays the melody to the end with sax fills.

Big Band Jazz: From the Beginnings to the Fifties
Smithsonian (4 CDs—2202, 6 LPs—2200, 3 CA—2201).
This double Grammy-winning album features the distinctive sounds of America's big bands. There are eighty classic performances by the bands of Louis Armstrong, Fletcher Henderson, Earl Hines, Chick Webb, Benny Goodman, Tommy Dorsey, Count Basie, Charlie Barnet, Artie Shaw, Glenn Miller, Harry James, Woody Herman, Dizzy Gillespie, Stan Kenton, and others. The collection includes a fifty-two-page listening guide written by Gunther Schuller and Martin Williams.

Videos

The Best of the Big Bands, Vols. I-IV.
MCA; 50 min. each.
These four volumes are an interesting collection of swing era bands, vocalists, and soloists compiled through the archives of Universal Studios.

Vol. I. Tommy Dorsey plays "Opus One" and "Boogie Woogie"; Hi-Los; Benny Carter with Nat King Cole; Rosemary Clooney and Louis Prima; Harry James performs "Charmaine" and "Trumpet Blues"; Billie Holiday sings "God Bless the Child" and "Now Baby or Never"; Charlie Barnet; Duke Ellington plays "On a Turquoise Cloud," sung by Kay Davis, and "Frankie and Johnnie," featuring the plunger-mute style of Joe Nanton on trombone; The Blackburn Twins; Gene Krupa with "Lover" and "Lover's Leap."

Vol. II. Charlie Barnet; Lionel Hampton; Ralph Marterie; Gene Krupa; The Dorsey Brothers; Tex Beneke; Nat King Cole; Stan Kenton performs "Eager Beaver" and "Reed Rapture"; Sarah Vaughan sings "Don't Blame Me" and "I Cried For You"; Woody Herman offers "Caldonia" and "Northwest Passage," with Stan Getz on tenor sax and Shorty Rogers on trumpet.

Vol. III. Jimmy Dorsey; Billy Daniels; Les Brown; Freddie Martin; Duke Ellington performs "History of Jazz" and "Violet Blue" with Kay Davis on vocals and Johnny Hodges on alto sax; Harry James; Count Basie plays "Red Bank Boogie"; Teresa Brewer; Gene Krupa; The Ink Spots; Charlie Barnet.

Vol. IV. Count Basie with "One O'Clock Jump" and "Swingin' the Blues"; Jimmy Dorsey; Tex Beneke; The Mills Brothers; Ray Anthony; The Skylarks; Stan Kenton plays "Artistry in Rhythm"; Louis Prima; Buddy Rich plays a great solo.

Jazz Legends 1, '30s and '40s
The Music Hall of Fame Collection; 39 min.
Features Fats Waller, Albert Ammons and Pete Johnson, Lena Horne and Teddy Wilson, Cab Calloway, Benny Goodman, and Peggy Lee, Nat King Cole, Louis Jordan, Art Tatum, Louis Armstrong, Duke Ellington, Jimmy Rushing, and Joe Williams.

Count Basie

William "Count" Basie was born in Red Bank, New Jersey, in 1904. He played piano in early childhood and was influenced by the early Harlem pianists. While traveling with a vaudeville show he was stranded in Kansas City and soon joined Walter Page's Blue Devils, featuring singer Jimmy Rushing, during 1928–29. He then became a member of the Bennie Moten Band until Moten's death in 1935. Basie formed his own band with many of the Moten sidemen and was brought to New York City by John Hammond in 1936; with an enlarged personnel, the band made its first recording in 1937. Basie's band, with the rich blues tradition of the Southwest, developed a precision rhythm section with Jo Jones' sock cymbal style, Freddie Green on guitar, Walter Page on bass, and Basie himself.

The band also featured great soloists like Jimmy Rushing and Joe Williams singing the blues, trumpeters Buck Clayton, Joe Newman, and in later years, Thad Jones. Tenor saxophone player Lester Young, who was nicknaned *Pres* (for president), was one of the most famous Basie sidemen. Young's style revolutionalized sax soloing with his laid-back, cool approach.

Basie soon abandoned the early stride piano style he used with the Moten Band, refining it into a simple right hand technique which became highly influential to other pianists. Jo Jones' syncopated hi-hat style on floor cymbals was an innovative approach in drumming while swinging the band to the steady fours supplied by guitarist Freddie Green and bassist Walter Page. Basie had helped set the swing era in motion with his characteristic use of riffs behind his fine soloists. His bands were noted for fine precision in later years, with their adherence to the early rhythmic princi-

Count Basie (*Photo courtesy of RCA Archives*)

ples. He was known as The Kid from Red Bank. Many of his arrangements in the '50s were by Ernie Wilkins and Neal Hefti. Basie remained one of the key figures in jazz, with his bands playing a consistently high caliber of jazz. He died of cancer at the age of seventy-nine in 1984.

Study Guide: Count Basie

Recordings

"Doggin' Around"—Count Basie and His Orchestra.
SCCJ **(record side 5, cassette side D, CD II). Recorded in 1938.**

Personnel
Count Basie—piano,
Buck Clayton, Ed Lewis, Harry Edison—trumpets,
Eddie Durham—trombone/guitar,
Benny Morton, Dan Minor—trombones,

Earl Warren—alto sax, Jack Washington—saxophones,
Hershel Evans—tenor sax/arranger,
Lester Young—tenor sax, Freddie Green—guitar,
Walter Page—bass, Jo Jones—drums

Musical Characteristics
The first selection of Basie is a furious up-tempo beat that shows off the skill of his band wound together by a very tight rhythm section. Lester Young's fresh style of improvisation could be described as understated, laid back, and relaxed, with a very cool tone that lacked vibrato. His style was very fresh and different, at a time when most players were adopting a hot approach with wider vibratos in their tonal concepts.

Musical Form
AABA form.

1. Introduction—piano in a fast tempo, stride style.
2. A theme—saxes play the lead with trumpets growling in response.
   B theme—alto sax solo in acrobatic style (Warren).
   A theme—same as before
3. Second chorus—tenor sax solo (Evans) with muted trumpets playing riffs.
4. Third chorus—trumpet solo (Edison) plays AA theme, baritone sax (Washington) plays B and A themes with solid 4s in the bass.
5. Fourth chorus—piano solo (Basie) displays the refined right hand style.
6. Fifth chorus—tenor solo (Young) with brass riffs.
7. Bridge—transitional drum solo, 4 bars. Trombone gliss into full band shout chorus and out.

"Taxi War Dance"—Count Basie and His Orchestra.
SCCJ (record side 6, cassette side D, CD II). Recorded in 1939.

Personnel
Same as "Doggin' Around," except Buddy Tate, tenor sax, replaced Evans; Dicky Wells, trombone, replaces Durham; add Shad Collins, trumpet.

Musical Characteristics
Again this is a showcase for the talent of Lester Young, although he is a little more relaxed this time, and appears to play slightly behind the chords and beat. Young's approach to improvisation could be compared to Beiderbecke's earlier, cool, liquid sound on the cornet. Pres was the first to use this style on tenor sax and many West Coast sax men copied

this approach in the early '50s. "Taxi War Dance" is different than "Doggin' Around" not only because it is a slower medium tempo, but also in the treatment of the arrangement. More space is given to the soloists, with the band playing 4-bar shout choruses in between. This is called *trading fours*.

Musical Form
1. Introduction with piano (Basie) beginning boogie style in medium tempo.
2. Tenor sax solo (Young) plays very laid back in 4/4.
3. Bridge and boogie-woogie rhythm.
4. Trombone solo (Wells).
5. Full band shout, 4 bars; tenor solo (Tate), 4 bars.
6. Full band shout, 4 bars; Tate solo, 4 bars.
7. Piano solo by Basie; right hand dominates; band shout.
8. Piano plays boogie-woogie pattern again with full band.
9. Tenor solo (Young) with full band.
10. Piano solo on bridge, 8 bars.
11. Full band shout 4 bars, tenor solo (Young) 4 bars.
12. Piano solo 2 bars, tenor solo (Tate) 2 bars, bass solo (Page) 2 bars, drum solo (Jones) 2 bars.
13. Band shout and out.

Video

The Last of the Blue Devils
Rhapsody Films; 90 min.
This movie about Kansas City jazz and blues features Big Joe Turner, Jay McShann, and Count Basie and His Orchestra. The early days of the jazz tradition are seen in a series of informal sessions featuring the deep-rooted blues and rock and roll. Like the early New Orleans background provided by Punch Miller in "Til the Butcher Cuts Him Down," the early Kansas City days of the territory bands are vividly depicted by the men who shaped its future.

Count Basie and Friends, 1943–1945
Jazz Classics; 60 min.
Features the early Basie Band with the Delta Rhythm Boys, Bobby Brooks Quartet, Jimmy Rushing, and Louis Jordan and His Tympany Five. Tunes include "Band Parade," "Take Me Back Baby," "Just a Sittin' and a Rockin'," and "Caldonia."

CHAPTER EIGHT

SWING ERA ARTISTS

Many great soloists and vocalists became famous during the swing era besides former sidemen like Harry James, Gene Krupa. Bunny Berigan, and Lionel Hampton, all of whom went on to front their own bands. Lester Young had made his reputation as a highly innovative tenor sax soloist in the cool style. Coleman Hawkins, nicknamed *Bean* and *Hawk*, also came into great prominence during the swing era as a daring tenor sax improviser. His style was very different from Lester Young primarily because of his wider tonal vibrato and very active improvised lines around a melody in a hotter style. Roy Eldridge was the successor to Louis Armstrong as a great trumpet soloist and would later influence Dizzy Gillespie, among others. Nicknamed *Little Jazz*, Eldridge played in a number of bands, becoming a featured soloist with Gene Krupa and Artie Shaw. In addition to playing some very powerful lines in all registers of the trumpet with great emotion, he was, like Armstrong, a master at accompanying a vocalist.

Coleman Hawkins

The great tenor sax player Coleman Hawkins was born in St. Joseph, Missouri, in 1904. He played several instruments before beginning tenor sax at the age of nine, and toured with Mamie Smith's Jazz Hounds as a teenager before coming to New York. His first important appearance was with Fletcher Henderson in New York City in 1923, with whom he was a featured soloist until 1933. He performed abroad after the Henderson years and returned to the U.S. in 1939, when he recorded "Body and Soul," which became his biggest hit. He also appeared in the Sound of Jazz television show for CBS in 1957, with a host of other great musicians of the swing era. Hawkins developed a broad improvisational style on the tenor with a hot, full-bodied vibrato and superb feel for rhythmic nuances. He established a new standard on the instrument until the bebop era, when

Coleman Hawkins (*Photo courtesy of RCA/Bluebird*)

the cool style became popular. Hawkins had been one of the first soloists on tenor sax in jazz history; he died in 1969.

Study Guide: Coleman Hawkins

Recordings

"Body and Soul"—Coleman Hawkins and His Orchestra.
SCCJ (record side 4, cassette side C, CD II). Recorded in 1939.

Personnel
Coleman Hawkins—tenor sax, Earl Hardy—trombone,
Joe Guy, Tommy Lindsay—trumpets,
Jackie Fields, Eustis Moore—alto saxes,
Gene Rodgers—piano, William Oscar—bass,
Arthur Herbert—drums

Musical Characteristics

Hawkins' approach on tenor sax is stylistically opposite from that of Lester Young. With a richer tone and full vibrato, he is more of a vertical player, exploring ascending and descending chords, while Young's style is more laid back, with long, flowing lines in a horizontal approach. Bean uses a more technical musical format to his solos. Compare this recording of Hawkins with the solos of Young.

Musical Form

AABA, slow 2/4 rhythm

1. Introduction—piano in slow tempo, 4 bars.
2. First Chorus
   A theme—tenor solo (Hawkins) paraphrases melody.
   A theme—repeated, Hawkins plays more of a chordal style in double-time, straying from the melody.
   B theme—change of key; Hawkins plays double-time runs.
   A theme—continues in this style.
3. Second chorus
   AA themes—Hawkins builds intensity with vertical leaps, brass hold chords in background.
   B theme—solo now explores new changes in chordal style without the background.
   A theme—solo continues in a leaping style with background.
4. Tag—with short solo cadenza, band returns for the last chord.

Lester Young

Born some five years later than Hawkins, Young also became one of the leading jazz soloists on the tenor sax. Nicknamed "Pres" by Billie Holiday, Young was born in 1909 in Woodville, Mississippi, to a family of trained musicians. He began playing drums at an early age, as did Roy Eldridge, and was trained on the clarinet, alto sax, and violin. Young's early inspiration came from C-melody saxophonist Frankie Trumbauer. He began his career in the Southwest, coming into his own with the Blue Devils and Bennie Moten in the early '30s. His influence was widely felt with Count Basie. Young was also one of the featured soloists on the "Sound of Jazz" CBS telecast. He eventually died in poor health, a victim of alcohol abuse, in New York City in 1959. Pres is to be remembered as the first tenor player to play in a *cool style* that was laid-back, in contrast to the more fashionable, hot-blooded styles of the swing era. His tone was subtle, as were his musical ideas in solo.

Study Guide: Lester Young

Recordings

"Lester Leaps In"—Count Basie's Kansas City Seven.
SCCJ (record side 6, cassette side D, CD II). Recorded in 1939.

Personnel
Lester Young—tenor sax,
Buck Clayton—trumpet, Dickie Wells—trombone,
Count Basie—piano, Freddy Green—guitar,
Walter Page—bass, Jo Jones—drums

Musical Characteristics
This recording of Young with Basie's rhythm section features two of the modern innovators of jazz during the swing era. Young's cool approach style in this fast-paced tune reveals a very light sound without much vibrato, laced in romanticism. Basie streamlined a new approach to the keyboard by simplifying the heavy-handed stride style with a simple right hand. Both Young and Basie had tremendous impact on musicians of the bebop era.

Musical Form
AABA, up-tempo fours

1. Introduction—piano solo
2. First chorus
    AA themes—ensemble plays a repeated riff, 16 bars.
    B theme—piano solo with walking bass, 8 bars.
    A theme—ensemble repeats the riff, 8 bars.
3. Second chorus—tenor solo improvises riff theme.
4. Third chorus—tenor solo continues with rhythm breaks.
5. Fourth chorus—piano and tenor trade fours.
6. Fifth chorus
    AA themes—ensemble trades fours with tenor and piano.
    B theme—piano solo.
    A theme—ensemble trades with the tenor.
7. Final chorus
    AA themes—ensemble trades with the piano.
    B theme—piano solo.
    A theme—ensemble plays the 4 bar riff and final 4-bar tag in collective improvisation.

Roy Eldridge

David "Roy" Eldridge, nicknamed "Little Jazz," was born in 1911 in Pittsburgh. After playing several instruments as a youngster, Eldridge came to New York City as a young singing and trumpet-playing talent in 1930. He played with Teddy Hill's band and the Fletcher Henderson Band in the late '30s. Little Jazz became famous as a soloist with the Gene Krupa Band in the '40s and joined the JATP (Jazz At The Philharmonic) tours abroad in the '50s. Eldridge is considered the most important trumpet player of the '30s as a successor to Louis Armstrong and the leading influence on Dizzy Gillespie, who dominated '40s trumpeters. He was not only a gifted soloist with sheer power and melodic invention, he was a back-up and accompanist for prominent singers such as Billie Holiday's "Fine and Mellow," which is included on the video "The Ladies Sing the Blues." He was also featured in a famous duet with Anita O'Day in the Gene Krupa Band's "Let Me Off Uptown" in 1941, and he appeared with Ella Fitzgerald and her combo in 1964 in "You'd Be So Nice to Come Home To" in the SCCJ set.

Study Guide: Roy Eldridge

Recordings

"Rockin' Chair"—Gene Krupa and His Orchestra.
SCCJ (record side 5, cassette side D, CD II). Recorded in 1941.

Personnel
Roy Eldridge, Graham Young—trumpets,
Torg Halten, Norman Murphy—trumpets,
Babe Wagner, Jay Kelliher, John Grassi—trombones,
Mascagni Ruffo, Sam Listengart—alto saxes,
Sam Musiker, Walter Bates—tenor saxes,
Milton Raskin—piano, Ray Biondi—guitar,
Gene Krupa—leader/drums

Soloist: Eldridge

Musical Characteristics
"Rockin' Chair" is a showcase for the extraordinary talents of trumpeter Roy Eldridge. His ability to front the band with his soaring trumpet lines placed him between Armstrong and Gillespie as one of the most original trumpet soloists in jazz history.

Musical Form
slow ballad in fours

1. Introduction—solo trumpet against sustained chords of the band, 8 bars.
2. A theme—trumpet solo of 8 bars with walking bass and brushes on snare.
3. A theme—trumpet solo continues with more daring improvisations, sax section sustains chords, 8 bars.
4. B theme—trumpet solo with sax section, 8 bars.
5. A theme—repeated with continued improvisation.
6. C section—trumpet solo in soaring lines played over the band, 8 bars.
7. A section—solo builds continual excitement over the band.
8. Coda—features a trumpet cadenza with breaks and response from clarinet, ends on a high sustained note like Bunny Berigan's "I Can't Get Started."

Billie Holiday

Billie Holiday was born in Baltimore, Maryland, in 1915 and became one of the greatest vocal stylists since Bessie Smith. She was discovered by John Hammond and made her first recording with Benny Goodman in 1933. She later joined Teddy Wilson in 1935, Count Basie in 1937, and Artie Shaw in 1938. Her increasing fame brought on a destructive drug addiction that plagued her through three marriages. Her tragic life, which ended in 1959, was laced with child abuse, prostitution, and drug abuse.

Unlike Bessie Smith, *Lady Day*, as she was called, possessed a small voice filled with great intimacy. She sang a highly personal style that was laid back and influenced by the blues. Holiday learned a great deal about phrasing from Louis Armstrong and her good friend Lester Young. Some of her greatest recordings are "Strange Fruit" and "Fine and Mellow" in 1939, and "Lover Man" in 1944. Another great jazz vocalist became important during the swing era, Ella Fitzgerald. This great singer, like Holiday, fashioned a musical bridge between her early swing years and the modern stylings of bebop.

Study Guide: Billie Holiday

Recording

"He's Funny That Way"—Billie Holiday and Her Orchestra.
SCCJ (record side 4, cassette side C, CD II). Recorded in 1937.

Personnel
Billie Holiday—vocals, Buck Clayton—trumpet,
Buster Bailey—clarinet, Lester Young—tenor sax,
Claude Thornhill—piano, Freddy Green—guitar,
Walter Page—bass, Jo Jones—drums

Musical Characteristics
This is from a series of recordings that Billie organized with her own recording bands in 1937. Her laid-back style with a small intimate voice is a
trademark of Billie's emotional and romantic approach. On this cut, Lester Young's similarly styled tenor sax forms a perfect dialogue with Holiday's voice. As you listen to the famous Holiday style, compare once
again Young to fellow tenorman Coleman Hawkins.

Musical Form
AABAC

1. Introduction—tenor solo, 4 bars.
2. First chorus
   A theme—vocal begins with dialogue from the tenor and continues
   throughout repeated A theme with voice inflections.
   B theme—vocal continues with piano fills.
   A theme—vocals are accompanied by the return of tenor.
3. Second chorus
   A theme—muted trumpet paraphrases the melody.
   A theme—solo trumpet strays more from the melody.
   B theme—vocal solo returns.
   C theme—vocal solo continues with heightened emotion, band en-
   ters, and out.

For an example of Holiday's later stylistic development, listen to
"These Foolish Things," 1952, on *SCCJ* (record side 4, cassette side C
CD II), immediately following "He's Funny That Way." Although the recording technology is somewhat improved on "These Foolish Things,"
one can notice a decline in Billie's voice due to her heavy substance
abuse. Although her voice is in a state of decline, she reveals a great deal
of musical maturity with her treatment of the melody and her thorough
command of the underlying harmonic structure. The great musicians
who are the sidemen contribute very effectively to this famous jazz standard. Also, the musical illustration of the A section melody in the *SCCJ*
booklet guide on page 54 is a fine musical example and stylistic guide to
Holiday's inventive melodic approach. Notice how laid-back her technique is to each phrase, as the musical illustration reveals rests in each of
the first four bars of her interpretation.

Video

The Ladies Sing the Blues
V.I.E.W. Video; 60 min.
Here is a fine compilation of some of the greatest singers in the history of jazz. This video features Billie singing "Fine and Mellow," which must not be missed! With the exception of Bessie Smith, most are captured in their early years, with a brief biographical narrative of their careers. There are some errors, such as identifying Bessie Smith as a country blues singer; however, the biographical data is fairly accurate with some interesting performances. Highly recommended!

The program is:

1. "St. Louis Blues"—Bessie Smith in one of the earliest performances of a blues singer on film in a Hollywood set.
2. "Darkies Never Dream"—Sung by Ethel Waters, capturing her clear and eloquent diction in her early years.
3. "Quicksand"—A staged presentation with Ethel Waters and the Count Basie Band.
4. "Fine and Mellow"—Billie Holiday is featured in the 1957 CBS telecast "The Sound of Jazz" as she sings, surrounded by some of the greatest jazz artists. Solos are by Ben Webster and Lester Young on tenor saxes, Gerry Mulligan on baritone sax, Coleman Hawkins on tenor sax, and Roy Eldridge, trumpet.
5. "When You Lose Your Money Blues"—Sung by Ida Cox with husband Jesse Crump on piano.
6. "The Lonesome Road"—A revive clip with Sister Rosetta Tharp and dancers.
7. "Nobody's Sweetheart Now"—Sung by Connie Boswell.
8. "Lean Baby"—Sung by Dinah Washington.
9. "Only a Moment Ago"—A slower ballad with Dinah Washington at the Apollo Theatre.
10. "Have a Good Time"—Sung by Ruth Brown, also at the Apollo Theatre.
11. "The Man I Love"—Sung by lovely Lena Horne, showing the early influences of Ethel Waters on her style.
12. "Unlucky Woman"—Sung by Lena Horne with the Teddy Wilson Orchestra, in an early experimental film clip.
13. "You're Mine You"—Sung by Sarah Vaughan.
14. "I Cried for You"—Sung by Helen Humes with the Count Basie Orchestra.
15. "Why Don't You Do Right"—Peggy Lee scintillates in her early years with the Benny Goodman Orchestra, from 1941. Fine solos by Benny.
16. "I Cover the Waterfront"—This jazz standard is sung by Peggy Lee with Dave Barbour on guitar.

Ella Fitzgerald

Ella Fitzgerald was born in Newport News, Virginia, in 1918, and was discovered in 1934 in an amateur show in Harlem. She began her career with Chick Webb in 1935 as a vocalist, and continued her brilliant development from the early swing years to the modern period. Fitzgerald's singing style is best characterized as one of remarkable control and command of vocal technique. She is possibly one of the best pure singers in the field of jazz. Her ability to sing consistently with perfect intonation is one of her enduring qualities. Ella worked with both Count Basie and Duke Ellington before appearing in combo formats with the great pianists Oscar Peterson and Tommy Flanagan. Fitzgerald's flexible register and uncanny ability to *scat* (sing without lyrics) were showcased in "How High the Moon," which became a model for all jazz singers. She became an international sensation when she began the JATP tours with famous jazz stars, produced by Norman Granz, beginning in 1946. Ever since the mid-'50s, she has been a favorite in this country with her many concerts.

Study Guide: Ella Fitzgerald

Recordings

"You'd Be So Nice to Come Home To"—Ella Fitzgerald.
SCCJ (record side 5, cassette side C, CD II). Recorded in 1964.

Personnel
Ella Fitzgerald—vocalist,
Roy Eldridge—trumpet, Tommy Flanagan—piano,
Bill Yancey—bass, Gus Johnson—drums

Musical Characteristics
This is an example of the modern style of Ella, accompanied by a combo, unlike her early swing style with Chick Webb's big band, when she sang tunes like "A Tisket A Tasket." Here Ella displays her great vocal facility and ability to create exciting melodic improvisations that have an extremely swinging sensation with an outstanding sense of rhythm.

Musical Form
ABAB, 32 bars

A theme: "You'd be so nice to come home to,
        you'd be so nice by the fire.
B theme: While the breeze on high, sang a lullaby,
        you'd be all that I could desire.

A theme: Under stars chilled by the winter,
            under August moon, burning above.
B theme: You'd be so nice, you'd be paradise,
            to come home to, and love."*

1. Introduction—piano and muted trumpet play descending figures.
2. First chorus—straight vocals with muted trumpet.
3. Second chorus—vocal improvisations begin with muted trumpet.
4. Third chorus—vocal improvisations with trumpet lead.
5. Fourth chorus—vocals with continuing descending trumpet figures to end.

Sarah Vaughan

Sarah Vaughan, nicknamed *Sassy* and *The Divine One*, was born in Newark, New Jersey, in 1924. She took piano lessons and studied organ, and sang at the Mt. Zion Baptist Church. She, like Ella, won an amateur contest at the Apollo Theatre in New York City; Vaughan began her career with the bands of Earl Hines and vocalist Billy Eckstine toward the end of the swing era in 1943. Vaughan became a favorite in the vocal bop style of Charlie Parker and Dizzy Gillespie. Her style was different from the style of Fitzgerald, in that she was more emotional and sophisticated as a vocalist, with great control and a variety of mood swings. Her first hit was "It's Magic" in 1947. She died of cancer in 1990, and was buried at her birthplace in Newark.

Listen to her later recordings "All Alone" (1967) and "My Funny Valentine" (1973) on *SCCJ* (record side 9, cassette side F, CD IV). Although, like Fitzgerald's "You'd Be So Nice," these represent the modern period, the dramatic qualities of her voice are richly exemplified and rewarding. The video "The Ladies Sing the Blues" features Sarah's "You're Mine You" early in her career. For a full-blown example of her modern style, try the video "Sass and Brass" (HBO 1502, 1987) with Sarah singing "I Can't Give You Anything but Love," "Just Friends," and her famous dramatic rendition of "Send in the Clowns."

Boogie Woogie

Another popular piano style to emerge after ragtime and stride piano was boogie woogie, which gained great popularity in the '30s.

This style was basically blues with a syncopated bass in a continuous pattern: By repeating each of the four accents in each bar, a recognizable pattern of eight notes were played by a strong left hand. One of the earliest pioneers of the boogie-woogie style before its craze in the 30s was Clarence "Pine Top" Smith, who recorded "Pine Top's Boogie Woogie" in 1928. The boogie-woogie style is rooted in the early black *functions,* or social gatherings. One of the most exciting boogie pianists during the swing era was Meade "Lux" Lewis, whose recording of "Honky Tonk Train Blues" (1937) (*SCCJ* record side 4, cassette side C, CD II) is a fine example of this style. The left hand hammers out an eight-beat *ostinato* pattern that is a repeated rhythmic pattern also played in right-hand figures. The heavy left hand plays dotted eighth note and sixteenth note figures that were repeated in ascending and descending motion.

The boogie-woogie craze continued into the early '40s and many big bands like Benny Goodman featured pieces like "Boogie Woogie Bugle Boy," which was also sung by the Andrews Sisters. Jimmy Yancey was another famous boogie pianist. Boogie woogie later formed much of the early musical inspiration of early rock and roll in the '50s.

Dixieland Revival

During the late '30s, another movement was popularized by critics of traditional jazz like Frederick Ramsey, Jr., who reintroduced many New Orleans dixieland jazzmen who never left the South after the closing of Storyville. A new dixieland movement was set in motion. Trumpet player Bunk Johnson, Edward "Kid" Ory, the trombonist, and Sidney Bechet, who played both clarinet and soprano saxophone, became prominent during this revival. Some of the others who had been coaxed out of retirement or had been re-discovered were Alphonse Picou on clarinet and trumpeter Thomas "Papa Mutt" Carey.

This revival of the golden days of early New Orleans dixieland was one of the earliest traditionalist movements in jazz, although the history of jazz was barely twenty years old. Listen to "Blue Horizon," by Sidney Bechet and His Blue Note Jazz Men (1944) for a fine example of this revived music. Today a second revival is being seen with the Marsalis retrospect of the seminal figures of the hard bop movement.

Study Guide: Sidney Bechet

Recordings

"Blue Horizon"—Sidney Bechet and His Blue Note Jazz Men. *SCCJ* (record side 2, cassette side A, CD I). Recorded in 1944.

Sidney Bechet (*Photo courtesy of RCA/Bluebird*)

Personnel
Sidney Bechet—clarinet,
Sidney DeParis—trumpet, Vic Dickenson—trombone,
Art Hodes—piano, George "Pops" Foster—bass,
Manzie Johnson—drums

Musical Characteristics
Although Bechet made his reputation on the soprano saxophone, this recording reveals much of the early New Orleans approach to improvisation. Bechet and Armstrong represent two of the most innovative soloists of the early New Orleans period. Notice that he uses a very wide vibrato, which was common with the early New Orleans players. The entire piece is a six-chorus solo by Bechet.

Musical Form
Slow blues, six choruses

1. First chorus—Bechet begins the clarinet solo in the low register.
2. Second chorus—solo continues, exploring the middle register.
3. Third chorus—solo continues with a very wide vibrato.

4. Fourth chorus—solo begins with blues lines in the upper register.
5. Fifth chorus—solo continues with high sustained blues, finishing in the low register.
6. Sixth chorus—solo builds excitement with flat-fours in rhythm and horn accompaniment.
7. Ending—sustained notes.

Earl Hines

Another musician who was a prominent figure throughout the late 1920's until his death, in 1983, was pianist Earl Kenneth "Fatha" Hines. Hardly a revivalist, Hines had been active continuously after his work in the Hot Five recordings with Louis Armstrong in 1927. He formed a big band in 1928, and performed on tour with several editions of it until 1948. His early '40s band included bebop players such as Charlie Parker and Dizzy Gillespie. He began working with small groups in 1951 until his New York concerts thrust him back into public recognition.

For a fine example of his early collaboration with Louis Armstrong, listen to "Weather Bird," (1928) (*SCCJ* record side 3, cassette side B, CD I).

Study Guide: Earl Hines

Video

Earl Hines and Coleman Hawkins
Jazzland; 28 min.
This is a 1965 session in which these two great jazz figures head a quartet late in their careers. Most of the musical focus is on Hines, with his superb finger technique; Hawkins is featured on two tunes.

PART IV

The Bebop Era, 1945–1955

CHAPTER NINE

BEBOP MUSIC

World War II had depleted most big bands through the mandatory military draft during the early '40s, and most musicians, including Duke Ellington, agreed that the riff as a musical device had effectively sanitized swing music. By 1945 the big band boom had ended, and a recording ban by the musicians union, when musicians requested trust funds from record companies, from 1942 to 1944, further exacerbated the situation. A second ban took place in 1948.

A musical revolution had begun by black musicians to reclaim the music that was so successfully commercialized and marketed by the white bands. The new music was formulated at Minton's Playhouse in Harlem on 118th Street between St. Nicholas and Seventh Avenues. The club was owned by Henry Minton, and jazz activity flourished there from 1939 to 1942. Three musicians who were largely responsible for this revolution were trumpeter Dizzy Gillespie, pianist Thelonious Monk, and Charlie Parker, an alto saxophone player. Monk and drummer Kenny Clarke were members of the house band; however, Minton's became a haven for musicians like pianist Bud Powell to sit in during after-hours *jam sessions* (see glossary). The musical experiments in harmony were led by Gillespie and Monk, with Parker coming on the scene in 1942. Dizzy reports in his memoirs *To Be or Not to Bop:*

> What we were doing at Minton's was playing, seriously, creating a new dialogue among ourselves, blending our ideas into a new style of music. You only have so many notes, and what makes a style is how you get from one note to the other. We had some fundamental background training in European harmony and music theory superimposed on our own knowledge from Afro American musical tradition. We invented our own way of getting from one place to the next. I taught myself chords on the piano beginning at Laurinburg because I could hear chords in European music without anybody telling me what they were. Our phrases were different. We phrased differently from the older guys. Perhaps the only real difference in our music was that we phrased differently. Musically, we were

changing the way that we spoke, to reflect the way that we felt. New phrasing came in with the new accent. Our music had a new accent.*

Because of the recording ban few examples of this music were available until 1945. Although Monk, Dizzy, and Parker were at the forefront of this new musical development, many other musicians like guitarist Charlie Christian, drummer Kenny Clarke, bassists Milt Hinton and Nick Fenton, and tenor players Don Byas, Lucky Thompson, Horace "Hoss" Collar and Rudy Williams were regular performers at the jam sessions. The new bop music germinated at Minton's, often referred to as the University of Minton or Minton's Conservatory, before moving downtown in 1945 to 52nd Street, where a series of clubs like the Spotlite, Three Deuces, Kelly's Stable, and the Onyx featured this music primarily for white patrons. This series of clubs was known as *the street*. It was here that bebop was nurtured and matured.

Characteristics: Bebop

The unusual label *bebop* was applied to the music by the musicians themselves. Monk had referred to it earlier as "bip bop," and many other labels like "rebop" followed. These two-syllable words described the characteristic rhythmic endings of phrases, and "bebop" finally caught on as the accepted term. The social and musical characteristics of bebop were not an evolution of swing music, in the way swing was an evolution of dixieland, but rather a complete revision in just about every way.

A Bohemian lifestyle modeled after that of European painters characterized this new social setting. Musicians kept the music mostly for themselves, with little regard for public taste, in contrast to the swing years. Bebop was a triumph of the highest artistic achievement over commercialization. A picture of Dizzy Gillespie wearing a fez and facing the East toward Mecca in a popular magazine conveyed a new image that was somewhat overdone. Bebop was largely an esoteric art that was known by and for a few chosen musicians.

The new music was intended for listening rather than dancing, and was performed by small groups or combos rather than big bands. The classic bebop group usually included a rhythm section of bass, drums, and piano, with a front line of, usually two horns, a saxophone and trumpet. The music was intended for musical intellectuals rather than the masses, and came under sharp criticism from many other musicians like Louis Armstrong in a famous tirade.

---

*Dizzy Gillespie, *To Be or Not to Bop*. Doubleday, a division of Bantam Doubleday Dell Publishing Group, Inc. Used by permission.

Bebop music stressed improvisation with players *stretching out* in longer extended solos. Music of the swing era was mostly read and highly organized, but bebop used *head* tunes or arrangements that were memorized. Along with the rhythmic figures and new phrasing that gave the music its name, a new harmonic language was created that greatly affected the *tonal colors* and *texture* of the music. Around 1939, Dizzy, Monk, and later, Parker began using *alterations* and *extensions* to chords such as ♭5th, ♭9th, and ♯9th to dominant chords and 7th, 9th, and ♯11th to major chords. They also used *chord substitutions*. The harmony became very complex, making great theoretical demands on musicians who attempted to play the music. In bebop music *the soloist became a virtuoso*, showing off his improvisational skills with furiously fast lines and acrobatic figures. This was very much unlike the swing bands, where the band was in the spotlight with little attention paid to the limited space for the soloists. The great demands made on musicians, which humbled quite a few of them, were learned in informal jam sessions in which soloists could learn the tunes and embroider them with skillful improvisations. One of the impacts of bebop on jazz was that it elevated jazz theory—in phrasing, harmony, and rhythm—in no uncertain terms.

The characteristics of bebop are:

1. Decreased size of the bands from a big band to a combo. Usually a rhythm section with a front line of two horns.
2. Stress on improvisation with memorized head charts, less on reading.
3. Music was primarily intended for listening rather than dancing.
4. Heavy use of chord and melodic extensions with substitute chords in new phrasing.
5. It became much less commercialized.
6. Melodies or themes became intricate and highly ornamented.

An association with hard drugs and an underground lifestyle produced a negative effect on the new music. Another phenomenon that rose from bebop was a new language or slang used by musicians called "bop talk." Musicians communicated with each other with words like "hip," "cool," "man," "cat," or "dig" to form their own lexicon, which became part of the jazz musician's heritage. Boppers became so aloof that many of their social and musical antics were largely exaggerated, finding much disfavor elsewhere in musical circles. However, a spawning of great musicians emerged from the ashes of bebop to produce some of the greatest musicians in the history of jazz. Others like tenor saxophonist Lester Young were key figures in developing the new modern jazz style, although they were not involved with the sessions at Minton's. Soloists from the Basie and Ellington bands also bridged the stylistic changes from swing to bop.

Bebop was the beginning of the modern age in jazz, and left an indelible mark on the evolution of its musical style. Since 1917, this movement represented the first complete revision socially and musically. Until the bebop era, jazz had gone through gradual changes, as shown by New Orleans and Chicago dixieland, pre–swing, and swing. The modern movement was now in full bloom and its evolutionary path would be realized and imitated with the coming years. The "Bebop Era" lasted about ten years, until the death of Charlie Parker in 1955.

Charlie Parker

Charlie Parker was one of the key figures associated with bebop, and his legend as one of the greatest alto saxophone soloists in the history of jazz is still with us. Born in 1920 in Kansas City, Charles Parker, Jr. began playing baritone horn in the school band and alto sax in 1931. His early influences were the recordings of Lester Young and Charlie Christian. He worked with Jay McShann from 1937–39 and developed a narcotics habit as a teenager. Parker's second visit to New York City resulted in a strong association with Dizzy Gillespie in 1942, and together they formed a partnership that led to the bebop movement. He joined the Earl Hines Band in 1943 as a tenor sax player, along with Dizzy Gillespie on trumpet, and later in 1944 went on to play alto sax in vocalist Billy Eckstine's Band. In 1945 Parker made his first combo recordings with Dizzy Gillespie, and both men became seminal figures of the bebop movement.

In 1945 Parker left for the West Coast, where he worked unsuccessfully with Gillespie until 1946, and became deeply involved with his drug habit. He later returned to New York and played in festivals in Paris and Scandinavia. Parker's last five years were marked by repeated illness and addiction that caused many inconsistencies in his appearances. One of his remarkable achievements was the album he made in 1950 featuring a string section. He was the first jazz musician to do so, leading other artists to follow this kind of showcase. His last appearance was in Birdland in New York City, a club that was named for him, and he died of a heart seizure on March 4, 1955 a week later.

Nicknamed *"Bird"* or *"Yardbird,"* Parker is one of the most important musicians of modern jazz. He was truly a genius, with his variations on blues styles and incomparable technique on the alto saxophone. One of his musical legacies was to create new melodies based on the chords of standards, or older tunes. Some examples of Parker originals based on standards are "Anthropology," "Confirmation," "Moose the Mooche," based on "I Got Rhythm"; "Ko Ko" on "Cherokee"; "Donna Lee" on "Indiana"; "Ornithology" on "How High the Moon."

All of Parker's music has been published by Atlantic Music Corp. in the *Charlie Parker Omnibook*. This is virtually a bible for all young saxo-

phonists and professional musicians alike. The examples in figure 9.1
show how Parker used the chords of "How High the Moon"* for his melody "Ornithology."† Notice how the melody is much more active and ornamented in "Ornithology" compared with "How High The Moon,"
which uses basically the same chords.

Figure 9.1: "How High the Moon" and " Ornithology"

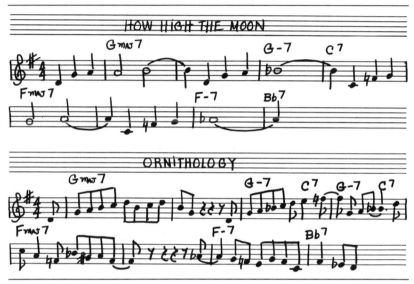

Study Guide: Charlie Parker

Recordings

"Ko Ko"—Charlie Parker's Re-Boppers.
SCCJ (record side 7, cassette side E, CD III). Recorded in 1945.

Personnel
Charlie Parker—alto saxophone/composer,
Dizzy Gillespie—trumpet/piano,
Curly Russell—bass, Max Roach—drums.

Musical Characteristics
As illustrated, Parker often used the chordal structures from standard tunes to create new melodies in order to avoid copyright infringements. In this case "Ko Ko" used the basic chords from "Cherokee"; he transformed the tempo into a furious double time with a variety of accents, particularly in the "bombs" played on the bass drum. Notice that the signature ending has a two-note bebop rhythmic sound. The drumming of Max Roach was a clear innovation in this early modern style. Parker's "Ko Ko" is a different composition than Ellington's "Ko Ko."

Musical Form
AABA, up-tempo

1. Introduction—begins with a unison melody in double time by alto and muted trumpet; alto and trumpet solo, with brushes on drums; ends with a duet.
2. First chorus—alto sax solo with swing 4s by rhythm; Gillespie comps on piano.
3. Second chorus—alto solo continues, building melodic extensions and dazzling chordal improvisations in descending patterns on B section.
4. Break—drum solo by Roach, with a variety of accents.
5. Ending—unison melody returns with solo breaks by trumpet and alto with the ride cymbal, before returning to the duet and out.

"Parker's Mood"—Charlie Parker All Stars.
SCCJ (record side 8, cassette side F, CD III). Recorded in 1948.

Personnel
Charlie Parker—alto sax/composer,
John Lewis—piano, Curly Russell—bass,
Max Roach—drums.

Musical Characteristics
Parker's many variations on the blues was another outstanding feature of his contributions to jazz. This recording reveals a slower paced style of bebop that was an exception rather than a rule. His complete mastery of improvising *inside the changes* in a blues style is quite evident. The pianist John Lewis was another early modern soloist who became an important figure with his stylistic innovations. "Parker's Mood" gives the listener a chance to hear bebop in slow motion.

Musical Form
Slow blues

1. Introduction—opens with alto sax *cadenza* followed by a piano solo with slow 4/4 rhythm.
2. First chorus—alto solo continues with highly inflected blues melody.
3. Second chorus—solo continues with relaxed laid-back style.
4. Third chorus—piano solo with the simple right hand style made famous by Basie.
5. Fourth chorus—alto solo enters with a variety of double-time rhythms.
6. Coda—closing statement by the alto, as in the introduction.

For further study of Parker listen to some of the cuts on *Bird: The Savoy Original Master Takes* (Savoy ZDS 8801), Vols. 1 and 2. These recordings are examples of Bird's finest playing from 1944 to 1948. Included are "Ko Ko" and "Parker's Mood." Listen to Parker on some of his other famous pieces in this collection for an overview of his magnificent improvisational skills. Charlie Parker has remained a legend in jazz, and his music forms the basis for all students of modern jazz music.

Video

Celebrating Bird: The Triumph of Charlie Parker
Sony; 58 min.
This documentary about Charlie Parker includes interviews with Rebecca Parker Davis, Jay McShann, Dizzy Gillespie, Leonard Feather, Roy Porter, Chan Parker, Roy Haynes, and Ted Ross. Among the musicians appearing in film clips are Parker, Dizzy Gillespie, Louis Armstrong, Count Basie, Jimmy Dorsey, Charlie Barnet, Billy Eckstine, Coleman Hawkins, Ben Webster, Lester Young, Thelonious Monk, Kenny Clarke, and Lucky Thompson.
The program includes "Ko Ko," "Confirmation," "Ballade," "Night in Tunisia," "Yardbird Suite," "Ornithology," "Kim," "Lover Man," "Just Friends," "Lady Be Good," and "Funky Blues." Parker's music and personal life are closely examined in great detail. The film also offers a first hand look at the bebop era. *Highly recommended!*

Reading

Gary Giddins, *Celebrating Bird: The Triumph of Charlie Parker*
Beech Tree Books/William Morrow, N.Y. 1987.
The book by author and director Gary Giddins illustrates the video, with interviews that were adapted for the documentary. It is a clear, unsenti-

mental portrait of one of the world's great artists tracing the evolution of jazz from the Armstrong era in the '20s to bebop in the '40s and '50s.

Dizzy Gillespie

John Birks "Dizzy" Gillespie was born in 1917 in Cheraw, South Carolina. His father played several instruments; Dizzy began playing trombone at age 14, and later trumpet. Dizzy studied harmony and theory at Laurinburg Institute in North Carolina. His first professional work was at age 18, with the Frank Fairfax band, in 1935. His first inspiration on trumpet was Roy Eldridge, whom he replaced in the Teddy Hill band, in 1937, with which he toured abroad. He came to New York City in 1939 and joined Cab Calloway as a featured soloist for two years. Dizzy began his after-work jam sessions at Minton's and began to develop the style that became known as bebop. For the next few years he played with several groups before joining Billy Eckstine in 1944. Dizzy gained great musical stature during 1944–45 and then formed his first big band.

Dizzy toured Scandinavia in 1946 with the big band, then returned to Europe with a quintet in 1952–53. He continued touring with the JATP All Stars and then went to the Middle East in 1956 on a U.S. State Department tour organized by Quincy Jones. He continued this new federal jazz program later in Latin America on a second goodwill tour. He and other jazz artists were honored by an invitation to the White House in 1978 by President Jimmy Carter. As a musical joke alluding to Carter's former occupation as a peanut farmer, Dizzy offered "Salt Peanuts" as a musical parody. Since then he has appeared with numerous small groups. His 1987 big band tour featured his student trumpet player, Jon Faddis, and visited Europe, the Far East, and the United States.

Gillespie's contribution to modern jazz with the advent of bebop was tremendous. He certainly must be given credit for developing much of the harmonic and theoretical basis of the new music, even before Parker arrived on the scene to galvanize it in 1942. Dizzy remained the archetype of the hipster or bopper with his goatee, beret, sun glasses, and manner of dressing in his early years. His trumpet, which has the bell upturned because of an accident in his early years, and his puffed-out cheeks are symbols of his unorthodox stylistic approach. He was always extremely outgoing, with his onstage singing and dancing. His style on trumpet was virtuosic with powerful *chops* (see glossary); he was able to play rapid figures, often descending from very high pitches, with great technique. Dizzy's solos stand with those of Bird in representing the best of the bebop tradition. One of his most important innovations in jazz was to combine African-American music with Cuban music. He was one of the geniuses and legends of modern jazz spanning its entire development through fifty years. He passed away in 1993 in Englewood Cliffs, New Jersey.

Dizzy Gillespie (*Photo courtesy of David Gahr*)

Study Guide: Dizzy Gillespie

Recordings

"I Can't Get Started"—Dizzy Gillespie Sextet.
SCCJ (record side 7, cassette side E, CD III). Recorded in 1945.

Personnel
Dizzy Gillespie—trumpet soloist,
Trummy Young—trombone, Don Byas—tenor sax,
Clyde Hart—piano, Oscar Pettiford—bass,
Shelley Manne—drums.

Musical Characteristics
Vernon Duke's "I Can't Get Started" has become a signature ballad for
Dizzy, with other modern trumpet players like Maynard Ferguson emu-
lating the earlier singing and playing style of Bunny Berigan, who had
played it originally with great success. Gillespie had many versions of this
famous theme and was able to develop several improvisational approaches. Here, he added a number of ornamental lines to the melody,

completely transforming it into his own personal vehicle. His improvised lines, which are very active and rhythmic, characterize the bop style and give evidence of the shift to bebop from swing.

Musical Form
AABA, ballad in 4/4

1. Introduction—trumpet solo begins as a cadenza on the chords from the A theme. Horns sustain chords while rhythm plays a slow 4/4.
2. A theme—solo begins by paraphrasing the melody with slight melodic extensions.
3. A theme—repeated in a transformed style with new material.
4. B theme—melody is briefly stated before continuing elaborate ascending and descending chordal lines.
5. A theme—solo continues through the chord changes with ornamentations.
6. Coda—ends with the introduction and a short solo break before the final chords.

"Shaw 'Nuff"—Dizzy Gillespie All-Star Quintette.
SCCJ (record side 7, cassette side E, CD III). Recorded in 1945.

Personnel
Dizzy Gillespie—trumpet/arranger,
Charlie Parker—alto sax, Al Haig—piano,
Curly Russell—bass, Sid Catlett—drums.

Musical Characteristics
The performances of Parker and Gillespie together became notable events in the jazz world. "Shaw 'Nuff" was a prime example of bebop, with its virtuoso demands and furious pace. Note that the melody lines are very difficult to remember, compared with swing style-themes. The fast pace of the tune became another important characteristic of the bebop tradition. "Shaw 'Nuff" is also programmed in the video "Jivin' in Bebop"

Musical Form
AABA, up-tempo swing 4s

1. Introduction—begins with a heavy rhythmic vamp before the alto and trumpet join with a theme in an American Indian mode. Piano leads to the first chorus.

2. First chorus—alto and trumpet play the head theme with breakneck speed, using extended melodic lines crossing the phrases. The rhythm stays in fast swing four.
3. Second chorus—Bird plays the first solo, actively exploring the chordal structure with extended lines. The bridge is treated with running chords.
4. Third chorus—Dizzy's trumpet solo opens with a trademark high burst before settling into continuous phrase patterns of eighth notes in ascending and descending lines. The bridge is played in a lead trumpet riff style.
5. Fourth chorus—piano solo with walking bass and swing fours by drums.
6. Fifth chorus—the first chorus restated.
7. Coda—ends with the Indian-style treatment of the introduction, with the same bebop signature accents.

For examples of Dizzy's Afro-Cuban style, with his great conga player Chano Pozo and big band from 1947 to 1949, listen to "Manteca," "Cubana Be," and "Cubana Bop" on *Dizziest* (RCA 5785-4-RB). Also included in the album are many of the band's early arrangements such as "Two Bass Hit," "Ol' Man Rebop," "Minor Walk," "Good Bait," "Swedish Suite," and "Dizzier and Dizzier." Earlier, Gil Fuller had composed such Gillespie landmarks as "Things to Come" and "One Bass Hit."

Video

"Jivin' in Be-Bop"—Dizzy Gillespie
Amvest Jazz Clasics; 60 min.
This full-length feature film from 1947 has nineteen music and dance routines with interludes of bop talk between the master of ceremonies and Dizzy.

1. "Salt Peanuts"—opens the program in a fast bop pace with solos by Dizzy and his drummer.
2. "Be Bop a Lu La"—features vocalist Helen Humes and a Dizzy solo.
3. "Oop Bop Sh' Bam"—the band opens with vocals and a Dizzy solo begins in double time, also some of the famous Dizzy antics.
4. "Dance Duo"—with orchestra accompaniment, vibes solo by Milt Jackson.
5. "Shaw 'Nuff"—Charlie Parker tune with an exotic female dancer, very fast solo by Dizzy to the up-tempo tune, and another vibes solo.
6. "I Waited for You"—vocal ballad sung by Billy Eckstine with a Dizzy solo.
7. Piano and organ duet

8. "Night in Tunisia"—opens with two dancers and Afro-Cuban drums. Jackson plays a vibes solo in the Latin section and Dizzy solos on the swing-style bridge.
9. "Crazy about a Man"—a slow classic blues sung by Helen Humes and the orchestra.
10. "Two Bass Hit"—features Ray Brown on bass with a solo by Dizzy. Call and response between the band and bass.
11. "Boogie in C"—features an exotic dancer with piano and organ.
12. "Jitterbug Dance"—with four dancers to a bop tune by the orchestra; solo by Dizzy.
13. "Ornithology"—features a tap dancer in top hat with the orchestra.
14. "Beep Instead of Bop"—vocal with Dizzy and the orchestra; Dizzy solo.
15. Female Dance Feature
16. "Be Bop"—a furious up-tempo tune in bop style with the orchestra, with a virtuoso solo by Gillespie and a Jackson solo on vibes.
17. Dance feature—Ron Brown in a tap dance with orchestra.
18. Dance feature—boogie woogie with John Lewis on piano and Milt Jackson on vibes.
19. Dance feature—female dancer to a boogie woogie with piano and organ.

Reading

**Dizzy Gillespie with Al Fraser, *To Be or Not to Bop: Memoirs*
Doubleday and Co., Inc.; 1979.**
A very interesting autobiography of one of America's greatest modern jazz figures. Sometimes very humorous, with Dizzy recalling his early years. Based on interviews with many musicians, and great storytelling by Dizzy. Good fun!

Thelonious Monk

Another of the important musicians during the bebop era was pianist-composer Thelonious Sphere Monk. Monk was a musical eccentric who kept to himself rather than exhibiting the extroverted trappings of Dizzy. He was born in 1917 in Rocky Mount, North Carolina, and moved to New York City with his mother at an early age. He began piano lessons at age eleven and was highly influenced by the stride style preferred by the Harlem masters such as Fats Waller and James P. Johnson. His most significant work began at Minton's Playhouse in 1939, when he and drummer Kenny Clarke played in a house band that featured many after-hour jam sessions with other greats like Dizzy Gillespie, Don Byas, Charlie Christian, and Charlie Parker. It was at Minton's that Monk began to formulate bebop's new harmonic language with Dizzy.

Monk remained mostly on his own after playing as a sideman with Lucky Millender, Dizzy Gillespie, and Coleman Hawkins in the mid-'40s. Most of his efforts were ignored by musicians and fans alike until the late '50s when he was featured with a quartet at the Five Spot Cafe in New York City with John Coltrane as a sideman. Monk encountered some personal difficulties when he lost his cabaret card in 1951 due to a narcotics-related arrest; a wealthy jazz patroness, Baroness Pannoica "Nica" de Koenigswarter, helped in renewing his card in 1957. His bizarre behavior led to another loss of his card for two more years and he turned to a Town Hall concert appearance in 1959 with a ten-piece orchestra.

Monk enjoyed great success in the '60s with numerous club dates and appearances in a quartet format. In the 70s he toured with Dizzy Gillespie in a group called The Giants of Jazz. While in declining health, Monk appeared successfully at the Newport Jazz Festival in 1975 and passed away in 1982. Monk's major contribution to bebop was as a composer with elaborate harmonic schemes that featured dissonant compositions that were characterized as "angular." Although Monk was a product of the bebop movement his style could be more properly called "modern," since he did not reflect the styles of either Bird or Dizzy. Many of his compositions like "'Round Midnight," "Straight No Chaser," "Ruby My Dear," "Off Minor," "Well You Needn't," and "Blue Monk" have become jazz standards, and his reputation as one of the first great composers of modern jazz continues to grow. His compositions are rich examples of extensions, dissonance, and angular or vertical contrasts in a modern jazz style.

Study Guide: Thelonious Monk

Recordings

"Misterioso"—Thelonious Monk Quartet.
SCCJ (record side 10, cassette side G, CD IV). Recorded in 1948.

Personnel
Thelonious Monk—piano, Milt Jackson—vibes,
John Simmons—bass, Shadow Wilson—drums.

Musical Characteristics
Monk's interpretation of the blues is unveiled in a modern bop form. While remaining in the blues form of chord progressions the melodic material presents an angular approach with dissonances and whole tone scale extensions. The opening and closing themes are in double time while the solos by Jackson and Monk are in a slow blues groove. This is a

good example of his harmonic approach and subsequent contributions to modern jazz.

Musical Form
Slow blues

1. Introduction—first 4 bars of the theme are repeated by solo piano featuring "walking sixths."
2. First, second choruses—theme is joined by vibes and bass in leaping 6ths and 9ths.
3. Third chorus—half-tempo solo by vibes, with piano comping in accented 7ths.
4. Fourth, fifth choruses—piano solo uses whole tone scale extensions and accented minor-second dissonances. Monk's second chorus features large leaps of accented 7ths with descending whole tone *licks*.
5. Sixth chorus—opening theme returns in double time with vibes and bass; piano begins with accompaniment, then joins the melody, slowing to the ending which features a descending whole tone scale.

"I Should Care"—Thelonious Monk, piano solo.
SCCJ (record side 10, cassette side G, CD IV). Recorded in 1957.

Musical Characteristics
This beautiful jazz standard undergoes a complete musical metamorphosis in Monk's treatment, with surprising nuances and an array of melodic, harmonic, and rhythmic devices. Without a rhythm section, Monk demonstrates a free use of time, lingering over the bar lines with fresh ideas that include an innovative technique of striking four chords and using the piano's damper and sustaining pedals to release all but one, for an eerie effect in the middle of the last strain. His musical innovations are completely unpredictable, and compel careful listening. This is a wonderful example of fully realized Monk, in a spellbinding performance. If possible, the tune should be played from a *fake book* before listening to Monk's version.

Musical Form
ABAB, rhythmically free style

A section—begins with a sustained chordal outline of the melody before proceeding with the theme.
B section—a slow melodic treatment with innovative use of substitute chords and extensions.
A section—the melodic material is framed in quickly moving, ascending figures and chordal extensions.

B section—the rhythmic delay in tempo is more pronounced with trilled notes and a bop lick in double time throughout, which he "hums." The four sustained chords with single release follow with a modulation (key change) to a new chord before the sustained final chord.

Video

Thelonious Monk, Straight No Chaser
Warner Bros., 89 min.
A full-length feature film about this great personality. Includes interviews with Monk's friends and colleagues plus footage shot backstage, on the road, and in the studio in 1967–68. The program includes twenty-five tunes, including Monk's "'Round Midnight," "Ask Me Now," and "Ruby My Dear."

CHAPTER TEN

BIG BANDS

Stan Kenton

One of the earliest big band leaders to make a decided musical break from the cloned swing era bands was Stan Kenton. Stanley Newcomb Kenton was a leader, composer, and pianist born in Wichita, Kansas, in 1912. He moved to Southern California at an early age, and became infatuated with the piano while still a teenager. Kenton wrote his first arrangement in 1928 and was hired in his first big job as pianist and arranger with the Everett Hoagland band in 1934. Beginning in 1936, he played with Gus Arnheim and several other groups, before forming his own band in 1941.

His first band was a hit; it recorded "Artistry in Rhythm," which became his theme song. Kenton featured his own arrangements in these early years, for a seventeen-piece band that included outstanding bop soloists like trumpeter Buddy Childers and saxophonist Art Pepper. In the middle '40s Kenton began to feature vocalists such as Anita O'Day and June Christy. Pete Rugolo joined the band as an arranger in 1946, and produced such hits as "Interlude" and "Unison Riff" in 1947. Rugolo's music, along with Kenton's arrangements of his earlier compositions "Artistry in Rhythm" and "Eager Beaver," shaped the lush modernistic palette of the large band. It expanded into a twenty-piece orchestra in 1947, and its music became known as *progressive jazz*, which was a modern compositional style featuring bop-style solos. After exhaustive tours and concert dates, Kenton retired briefly in 1949. He had been a victim of much public criticism: His music was deemed undanceable and harsh to the ears of those who clung nostalgically to the sounds of the swing bands.

A year later, Kenton reorganized again with a forty-piece concert orchestra that included strings. This orchestra featured a modern classical format and bore the slogan Innovations in Modern Music. This large ensemble included great soloists like the *scream trumpet* player Maynard Ferguson, who like Cat Anderson specialized in extreme high notes, and played works by a host of composers and arrangers. The orchestra survived for two years, but had to be abandoned due to its large financial overhead. The failure of this orchestra and more deep personal problems pushed Kenton into psychological counseling.

From 1952 to 1955 Kenton introduced new soloists, including alto saxophonist Lee Konitz, trombonist Frank Rosolino, and trumpeter Conte Candoli, in his nineteen-piece band called New Concepts in Rhythm. Kenton's contribution to big band jazz in the '40s are:

1. Expanded big band instrumentation
2. Introduced modern composers and arrangers
3. Began using Afro-Cuban rhythms
4. Music became concert-oriented progressive jazz.

Kenton's bands created a strong following by the late '50s, marked by many *Down Beat* awards.

Study Guide: Stan Kenton

Recordings

Stan Kenton's Greatest Hits.
Capitol 48437, 16182. Recorded 1943–51.

Musical Characteristics
This album certainly does not present an overview of Kenton's achievements; however, it does present his early band of the '40s. The early characteristics that were true Kenton innovations are apparent in many of the compositions. A sampling of arrangements by Kenton and Rugolo with modernistic big band tendencies is heard. Most of these innovations in concert style music produced thick textures through an expanded instrumentation. Listen to:

1. "Artistry in Rhythm," 1943—written by Kenton; features abrupt tempo changes and modern harmonic material.
2. "Eager Beaver," 1943—another Kenton tune; shows his transition from swing to a more progressive style, with abrupt rhythm breaks and exciting climactic modulations.
3. "Interlude," 1947—composed and arranged by Pete Rugolo; begins with a haunting piano solo (Kenton) followed by lush writing featuring the trombone section. The piece settles into slow walking 4s shifting back and forth from a two beat, solo features chordal extensions.
4. "The Peanut Vendor," 1947—features the Afro-Cuban sounds that would characterize much of Kenton's later music. Also notable is the

bold use of dissonance, with the trumpet section producing minor seconds in the last section of the composition. Kenton would frequently have his brass section play various Latin percussion implements.

Video

The Best of the Big Bands, Vols. II and IV
MCA; 50 min. each.
Vol. II. Stan Kenton's early band performs "Eager Beaver" and "Reed Rapture"
Vol. IV. Stan Kenton's early band performs "Artistry in Rhythm"

Woody Herman

Another big band leader who emerged during the '40s was clarinetist-saxophonist and leader Woodrow Charles Herman. Woody was born in Milwaukee, Wisconsin, in 1913; there he began singing and dancing in local theatres at age six and began playing saxophone by the time he was nine. After playing locally he left his hometown in 1930 with the Tom Gerun band, then was featured on clarinet and vocals with Isham Jones from 1934 to 1936. When Jones' band disbanded, Woody took over the remnants and produced its biggest hit in the 1939 "Woodchoppers Ball." His early bands had garnered their reputation from playing blues and in a dixieland style. In the '40s, however, Herman changed his style to an updated, swinging ensemble in the best of modern jazz taste.

In 1944 he organized a band that became known as the *First Herd*. This band featured a rhythm section of pianist Ralph Burns, bassist Chubby Jackson, guitarist Billy Bauer, and drummer Dave Tough. Trumpeter Neal Hefti and Burns contributed swinging arrangements that brought the band a special distinction. The powerful brass section was led by trumpeters Pete Candoli and Sonny Berman, with exciting solos by Flip Phillips on tenor sax and Bill Harris on trombone. Herman's First Herd became one of America's favorite bands. Igor Stravinsky was commissioned by Herman to write *Ebony Concerto*, which the Herd performed at Carnegie Hall in 1946.

Herman retired for a year, then organized the *Second Herd* in 1947. This was a bop band expanded to a large ensemble and featured the composition "Four Brothers" voiced for three tenor saxes and a baritone sax. The Four Brothers were tenor saxophonists Stan Getz, Zoot Sims, Herbie Steward, and baritonist Serge Chaloff. The Second Herd gave way to the *Third Herd* in 1950; Herman's subsequent bands continued their excellence, drawing on many college and conservatory musicians.

Woody's much-publicized problems with the Internal Revenue Service grew out of crooked management that began in the '60s and surfaced in 1987. The jazz community was shocked by his one-and-a-half-million dollar penalty, and staged a massive campaign of concerts and benefits to aid him. Woody died in 1987, not forgotten by the musicians and public.

Herman's band was different from Kenton's in that he featured soloists and arrangements that reflected a swinging bop style. While Kenton's focus was on the ensemble, through the efforts of his many writers, Herman was mostly concerned with the quality of his soloists. Woody had often said that the two main ingredients for a hard-swinging band were a powerful lead trumpet player and a swinging, steady drummer. It must be remembered that the Dizzy Gillespie big band during the period of the late '40s was quite a formidable swinging bop-styled band, too.

Study Guide: Woody Herman

Recordings

The Thundering Herds—Woody Herman.
Columbia 44108. Recorded 1945–47.

Musical Characteristics
This collection of the First and Second Herds showcases some of the most popular pieces by Herman in the mid-'40s. The selections from this period give evidence to Herman's commitment to a hard-swinging modern style full of muscle and excitement. After hearing the following selections, compare Herman's big band style to that of Kenton during the '40s.

1. "Woodchopper's Ball," 1946—from the First Herd's final recording session; this was written by Joe Bishop and is a variation on "Tiger Rag." Solos are Herman on clarinet, Bill Harris on trombone, and Flip Phillips on tenor sax.
2. "Apple Honey," 1945—this is a head arrangement built on the changes of "I Got Rhythm." Noteworthy is the cheering behind the Harris solo. Also features Herman on clarinet and Pete Candoli on trumpet.
3. "Northwest Passage," 1945—this is a classic swinger featuring solos by Ralph Burns on piano and Herman, which lead to a brass-driven solo by Phillips and a climactic riff for a Harris solo.
4. "Four Brothers," 1947—one of the popular showcase pieces of the Second Herd, written by Jimmy Giuffre. The solos are by Zoot Sims on tenor, Serge Chaloff on baritone, and Herbie Steward and Stan Getz on tenors.

Video

The Best of the Big Bands, Vol. II.
MCA; 50 min. each.
Woody Herman's early band plays "Caldonia" and "Northwest Passage,"
featuring Stan Getz on tenor sax and Shorty Rogers on trumpet.

Bebop Artists

Many fine musicians thoroughly absorbed the new harmonic, rhythmic,
and melodic language forged by Charlie Parker, Dizzy Gillespie, and
Thelonious Monk, and expanded it with several approaches during the
late '40s. Some players began to refine bebop, while others turned to a
cool style. Pianists Bud Powell, Tadd Dameron, and Lennie Tristano varied between these concepts, while tenor saxophonists Don Byas and
Dexter Gordon blended new elements with their playing as they worked
the 52nd Street clubs. Among rhythm section players, Oscar Pettiford redefined the work of Ellington's Jimmy Blanton on bass and 'cello, while
Max Roach and Kenny Clarke reshaped the role of a drummer as something other than a pure time-keeper. Charlie Christian anticipated this
new modern style and was simply much further advanced as a soloist on
guitar, as was Louis Armstrong on the trumpet earlier in the mid-'20s.

Young trumpet players like Red Rodney and Miles Davis had mastered the bebop technique by the late '40s, and a new trumpeter, Fats
Navarro, modeled his bebop style on Dizzy Gillespie's. Many bebop soloists had served their apprenticeships in the jam sessions at Minton's or as
sidemen with the big bands of Earl Hines and Billy Eckstine. By 1949 the
bebop movement was being modified into a *cool* concept by Miles Davis,
Gerry Mulligan, Stan Getz, and Lennie Tristano. The cool movement
eventually produced the West Coast School, led by Gerry Mulligan's
pianoless quartet with trumpeter Chet Baker in the early '50s.

Bud Powell

Born in 1924, pianist Earl "Bud" Powell grew up in New York City and
left school as a young teenager to play with local groups. He was introduced to the sessions at Minton's by Monk, and became a disciple of the
bop movement. Powell moved downtown to the 52nd street clubs and
played in recordings with Parker and others for the Savoy label. Unfortunately, in 1945, he began to suffer severe mental breakdowns during the
time he became a prominent jazz figure. Powell played with many of the
bop greats in New York during the late '40s, with continued lapses in
mental hospitals. In 1959 he moved to France, where his health became
much improved and he received many accolades. After contracting tu-

berculosis in 1962 he returned to the United States having never fully recovered and died in 1966.

Powell was one of the foremost bebop piano players; he was often considered the piano counterpart to saxophonist Charlie Parker.

Study Guide: Bud Powell

Recordings

"Night in Tunisia"—Bud Powell Trio.
SCCJ (record side 8, cassette side F, CD III). Recorded in 1951.

Personnel
Bud Powell—piano, Curly Russell—bass, Max Roach—drums

Musical Characteristics
Compare Powell's piano style to those of Dizzy Gillespie on trumpet and Charlie Parker on alto saxophone. This Dizzy Gillespie piece is the perfect vehicle for Powell, as it shifts back and forth between Afro-Cuban and straight swing rhythms. He begins his solo in double-time, with the right hand outlining the scales of the chords in swing fours. His ornamentations in the bridge of the first solo are reminiscent of Bird. In the second chorus the bridge receives an extended melodic treatment in double-time.

Lennie Tristano

Leonard Joseph Tristano was born in Chicago in 1919. By the time he was nine years old he was totally blind from a birth defect. He played reed instruments in local clubs, but gradually settled on piano. Lennie moved to New York, with the encouragement of bass player Chubby Jackson, in 1946. His early influence was Earl Hines, but during the late '40s he had formed his own combo and began to experiment with bebop theory and harmony. Tristano's new cool style led to recordings for Capitol in 1949 featuring saxophonists Lee Konitz and Warne Marsh and guitarist Billy Bauer. During his second session with Capitol he began a free style concept without a drummer in the group. A highly influential teacher, he opened his own school in 1951. His innovations were felt deeply by tenor saxophonist Warne Marsh. Tristano passed away in 1978.

Study Guide: Lennie Tristano

Recordings

"Subconscious Lee"—Lennie Tristano Quintet.
SCCJ (record side 9, cassette side F, CD IV). Recorded in 1949.

Personnel
Lennie Tristano—piano/composer,
Lee Konitz—alto sax, Billy Bauer—guitar,
Arnold Fishkin—bass, Shelley Manne—drums

Musical Characteristics
The cool interpretation of the bop style is evident here in the solos of
Tristano and Konitz with their laid-back treatment of these changes to
"What Is This Thing Called Love?" Manne's use of brushes keeps the
emotions on a low level, and notice how Tristano's first solo is mostly *outside the changes* (see glossary). The trading of solos on the last chorus is
clearly not intended as a carving contest, but the solos were a cohesive
forerunner of West Coast jazz style. Compare Tristano's approach to Powell's.

Tadd Dameron

Tadley Ewing Dameron was born in 1917, two years earlier than Tristano, in Cleveland. He learned musical elements early from his brother
Caesar, an alto sax player. Tadd began his professional career with trumpeter Freddie Webster, playing piano, then in 1940 he played with the
Zack Whyte and Blanche Calloway bands. He had become an arranger in
Chicago during this time, then worked in New York City with saxophonist Vido Musso and in Kansas City with the Harlan Leonard band. Dameron wrote for many artists in New York during the '40s including Jimmie Lunceford, Georgie Auld, Sarah Vaughan, and Dizzy Gillespie.
Beginning in 1947 he led his own small groups featuring the outstanding
young bop trumpeter Fats Navarro. In 1949 he played with Miles Davis in
Paris, and then worked in England as an arranger for Ted Heath's big
band.

Dameron returned to the United States in 1951 and formed another
band in 1953, which introduced trumpeter Clifford Brown. Afterwards
he was incarcerated for a long period in the late '50s due to drug abuse.
He returned to writing and arranging in 1961 and died of cancer in 1965.
Dameron's style falls between the driving bop style of Powell and the laid-
back, cool approach of Tristano.

Fats Navarro

Trumpet player Theodore Navarro was born in 1923 and died relatively
young, at the age of 27. He first played piano and tenor sax before turning
to trumpet. In 1941–42 he played with Snookum Russell, and joined
Andy Kirk's band in 1943–44. Navarro emerged as a notable bop soloist,
taking Gillespie's place in the Billy Eckstine band. In 1947–48 Navarro

appeared with Illinois Jacquet, Lionel Hampton, and Coleman Hawkins, before his brilliant work with Tadd Dameron. He became inactive for a year with drug problems and tuberculosis that eventually claimed his life in 1950. Fats Navarro was deeply influenced by Dizzy Gillespie, developing an excitingly clean bebop trumpet style that was taken up by Clifford Brown after Navarro's passing. His solo on the second chorus of "Lady Bird" is a testimony to his glorious bebop trumpet.

Study Guide: Tadd Dameron and Fats Navarro

Recordings

"Lady Bird"—Tadd Dameron Sextet with Fats Navarro.
SCCJ (record side 9, cassette side F, CD III). Recorded in 1948.

Personnel
Tadd Dameron—piano/arranger,
Fats Navarro—trumpet,
Wardell Gray, Allen Eager—tenor saxes,
Curly Russell—bass, Kenny Clarke—drums

Musical Characteristics
This neatly arranged version of "Lady Bird" features a consummate swinging feel in bop style. The wonderful solo by Navarro shows an ebullient refinement of Gillespie's style, overflowing with a golden tone. The tenor players solo in a laid-back style reflecting Lester Young, rather than the hard-boiled sound of Coleman Hawkins. The arrangement is as important as the solos in providing balance for the composition.

Don Byas

Born Carlos Wesley Byas in Muskogee, Oklahoma, in 1912 he came from a musical family. As a tenor saxophonist Don had his own college group in 1930 before working in Los Angeles with Eddie Barefield in 1935. He later worked with Don Redman, Lucky Millander, Eddie Mallory, and Andy Kirk. Byas joined Count Basie in 1941, then played with Coleman Hawkins on 52nd street at the Yacht Club in 1943 and Dizzy Gillespie at the Onyx in 1944. He toured Europe with Don Redman's band in 1946, and remained there, settling in France and Holland. His chief influence was Coleman Hawkins on the tenor. Byas had been active on continental tours and recordings with Quincy Jones and Art Blakey before succumbing to cancer in Holland in 1972. He was one of the figures at Minton's Playhouse active with Gillespie in the early years of bebop.

Study Guide: Don Byas

Recordings

"I Got Rhythm"—Don Byas and Slam Stewart.
SCCJ (record side 7, cassette side E, CD III). Recorded in 1945.

Personnel
Don Byas—tenor sax, Slam Stewart—bass

Musical Characteristics
Here is an unlikely version of "I Got Rhythm," when these two men
played duets at Town Hall in New York City. Byas shows off his Hawkins
influence with great creativity very early in the bop movement (1945).
Stewart provides a perfect foil with a slapping and fast walking bass, providing percussion effects along the way. His unison humming while bow-
ing the bass provide great interest and excitement in the performance.
Byas runs the chords with great vigor and command of his instrument. A
truly amazing performance!

Dexter Gordon

Dexter was born in 1923 in Los Angeles to a father who was a physician.
He studied harmony, theory, and clarinet as a teenager, and left school at
age seventeen to play tenor sax with a local band, the Harlem Collegians.
In 1940 he joined Lionel Hampton's band for several years. His next big
band engagement was with Louis Armstrong in 1944, and he gained recognition playing and recording with Billy Eckstine. He appeared at the
52nd street clubs with Charlie Parker, Miles Davis, Bud Powell, Max
Roach, and his own group, before returning to the West Coast in 1946. In
the '50s he served two years in prison in California on drug charges. Gordon was strongly influenced by Lester Young and Herschel Evans, and in
turn he influenced bop-style tenormen John Coltrane and Sonny Rollins.
He toured Europe and the Far East after moving to Denmark in 1962. His
career was reinvigorated with the Oscar nomination for his role in the
1986 film " 'Round Midnight," which was based on expatriate Bud Powell's life in Paris. Gordon died in 1990 in Philadelphia of cancer.

Study Guide: Dexter Gordon

Recordings

"Bikini"—Dexter Gordon Quartet.
SCCJ (record side 9, cassette side F, CD III). Recorded in 1947.

Personnel
Dexter Gordon—tenor sax, Jimmy Bunn—piano,
Red Callender—bass, Chuck Thompson—drums

Musical Characteristics
The minor blues form here is an AABA form with a B section of eight bars
instead of the customary twelve. After a short introduction by the piano,
Gordon plays straight-ahead swinging 4s with a well-gleaned tenor solo.
His *laid-back* style resembles Young, but with the tonal excitement of
Hawkins, although Gordon's vibrato is not quite as wide. His sound was
definitely a very modern concept on tenor sax at this early date.

Miles Davis—Early

Miles Dewey Davis, Jr. was born in Alton, Illinois in 1926 before moving
to East St. Louis in 1927. He came from a prominent background, as his
father was a dentist. Davis received a trumpet for his thirteenth birthday, and played in the local high school band and with Eddie Randall in
St. Louis in 1941-43. Miles had been influenced early by trumpeter
Clark Terry, a St. Louis native. Miles was sent to the Julliard School of
Music in New York City in 1945, and eventually left school in pursuit of
Charlie Parker and Dizzy Gillespie. He met both musicians and began
to play on 52nd street and record with Parker (on the Savoy label) in
1945. Miles had mastered the bebop style early in his career, and began
a nine-piece group that recorded the album *Birth of The Cool* in
1949-50 for Capitol. These sessions shifted much of the jazz world from
bebop to the new cool style.

Davis has gone through three basic periods of jazz development leading each transition. After his early bebop work, he began to emphasize
the new style of *cool jazz* in 1949. In 1959 he began to simplify harmonic
construction with a style known as *modal jazz*. His last style, *electric jazz*
or *jazz-fusion*, began in 1969. Miles' impact on the evolution of jazz, particularly from 1949 to 1969, has placed him as one of our true geniuses.
No other living figure has had more effect or influence on the stylistic
development of jazz than Miles Davis. In this section of the book we are
directed to the early cool jazz movement that he influenced in 1949.

Study Guide: Miles Davis—Early

Recordings

"Boplicity"—Miles Davis and His Orchestra.
SCCJ (record side 9, cassette side F, CD IV). Recorded in 1949.

Personnel
Miles Davis—trumpet, J.J. Johnson—trombone,
Sandy Siegelstein—French horn, Bill Barber—tuba,
Lee Konitz—alto sax, Gerry Mulligan—baritone sax,
John Lewis—piano, Nelson Boyd—bass,
Kenny Clarke—drums

Arranger—Gil Evans

Musical Characteristics
Miles' work in this selection from *Complete Birth of the Cool* exhibits a
new cool approach that had far-reaching influences in the '50s and the
West Coast School, with its *laid-back* style. Players like Lennie Tristano,
Lee Konitz, and Gerry Mulligan began to re-translate bop into a more
understated style. One of the most significant features in these recordings was the arrangements of Gil Evans, who struck a perfect balance between the ensemble and the new solo style of Davis. This was Miles' first
great impact on the history of jazz in collaboration with Evans. Also available: The album *Complete Birth of the Cool*, on Capitol Jazz CDP7
92862-2.
    Notice that the emotional level is toned down considerably from bop,
into a very gentle swing style. The use of French horn and tuba were unusual in a jazz group, providing an orchestral setting which produced a
laid-back unemotional sound. Gerry Mulligan, the baritone sax player,
had contributed some of this band's other arrangements, like "Jeru" and
"Venus De Milo" in the 1949 sessions and "Rocker" in 1950. Mulligan
went on to lead the West Coast School based on the cool style heard in
these recordings.

Musical Form
AABA

1. A theme—tightly arranged ensemble writing with trumpet lead, gentle swing fours; 8 bars.
2. A theme—repeated as above, 8 bars.
3. B theme—alto sax takes the lead with trumpet, 8 bars.
4. A theme—repeated with trumpet lead, 8 bars.
5. Solos—baritone sax plays laid back in the AA sections; sax section
   plays in the B section; brief trumpet solo with alto lead in final A section.
6. Last chorus—AA sections feature trumpet solo with alternate chords
   in bop style; B section is a piano solo with walking bass.
7. Ending—brief, one measure.

PART V

Jazz in the '50s

CHAPTER ELEVEN

COOL JAZZ

The reaction to the more explosive style of bebop was led by Miles Davis and his first collaboration with Gil Evans in the *Birth of the Cool* 1949–50 sessions. Other musicians such as saxophonists Gerry Mulligan, Lee Konitz, and Stan Getz had begun to exhibit the cool tendencies. The new cool style was more highly organized with sophisticated arrangements in a classical approach. More attention was given to each performance structure as a whole with a balance of solos that were noticeably shorter in length. Cool jazz was laid-back, unemotional, and musically subdued, inspired by classical music, particularly the Baroque style. Gerry Mulligan had launched the West Coast School in California in the early '50s with trumpeter Chet Baker and arrangements that featured themes in *counterpoint* (idea against idea), much as J. S. Bach had done in his early 18th century clavier works.

This basically white movement of West Coast jazz included Shorty Rogers who was a transplanted trumpet-flugelhorn player and arranger from the Northeast. He was one of the first jazzmen to solo exclusively on the flugelhorn. His group Shorty Rogers and the Giants were featured in jazz sequences arranged by Rogers in the Otto Preminger film "The Man With the Golden Arm." This grim movie was about a dope addict drummer named Frankie Machine (Frank Sinatra), with drum solos by Shelley Manne and a musical score by Elmer Bernstein. The soundtrack was released by Decca (DL 8257) in the late '50s. Other musicians strongly associated with the cool jazz style were alto saxophonist Art Pepper and pianist Dave Brubeck. Brubeck and his fine quartet featured the gifted alto sax player Paul Desmond in popular jazz hits like "Take Five" and "Blue Rondo a la Turk" on the *Time Out* album in the late '50s (CBS 40585). The West Coast movement has remained one of the most controversial periods of cool jazz.

John Lewis, the pianist and composer-arranger on *Birth of the Cool*, formed the Modern Jazz Quartet, with vibraphonist Milt Jackson, in

1952. The MJQ featured a cool style in the blues idiom and classical arrangements that set unprecedented standards. Miles Davis, in 1959, refined cool jazz with a modal style, which gave more emphasis to soloists in
a revolt against bop's numerous chord changes. Davis again became a major influence in the jazz world with his 1959 album *Kind of Blue* (CBS CK
40579). This has become one of the all-time best selling albums in the history of jazz.

The recordings Miles had done in Paris earlier in 1957 with original
music to the movie "Elevator to the Scaffold" ("L'Ascenseur pour l'echafaud") by Louis Malle (on Phillips 822566-2) is perhaps an example of his
finest playing in the cool style.

Writer Jack Kerouac produced a novel in 1955, *On the Road* (Pen-
guin Books), that became a classic of the *Beat Generation.* Kerouac had
strong associations with many of the cool musicians, and reflected the
new social values of a group of free spirits, artists, writers, and musicians
of the '50s. These creative people were called *beats* or *beatniks.* This

Shorty Rogers (*Photo courtesy of RCA/Bluebird*)

Dave Brubeck Quartet (*Photo courtesy of Dave Brubeck*)

post–World War II novel paved the way as a bible of nonconformity for a new lifestyle and philosophy that made strong social departures from prevailing attitudes. A recent video release *"What Happened to Kerouac?"* features a score by Thelonious Monk to the story of Kerouac, the heart and mind of the beat generation. Also featured in the film is a clip of Charlie Parker.

West Coast Jazz—Gerry Mulligan

Baritone saxophonist and arranger Gerry Mulligan was born in New York City in 1927. He produced a remarkable series of recordings for Fantasy in 1952. His quartet, which featured his own compositions and arrangements of standard tunes, created considerable excitement on the jazz scene, causing a shift of interest from East to West. Mulligan's pianoless quartet featured a great young trumpet player, Chet Baker, with Carson Smith on bass and Chico Hamilton on drums. Mulligan had been a graduate of the Gene Krupa and Charlie Barnet bands, and established a reputation with his writing for the Miles Davis Capitol recordings. His arrangements with the Stan Kenton Orchestra and his

Figure 11.1: Comparison Chart
Cool Jazz vs. Hard Bop

Cool Jazz	Hard Bop
1. Smooth, light sound	1. Hard-driving sound
2. Little emotion	2. Much emotion
3. Use of classical elements	3. Use of bebop elements and funk-based blues
4. Balance between writing and improvisation	4. Emphasis on improvisation, with memorized head tunes
5. Small groups emphasized, mixed instrumentation	5. Small groups emphasized; usual front line of two horns and three rhythm
6. Tempos varied from slow to fast	6. Tempos were usually fast
7. Melodies were often simple, based on standards, with skillful arranging	7. Melodies were usually irregular and angular, with substitute harmonies
8. Featured the composer as well as soloist	8. Featured the soloist as a virtuoso

own quartet broadened public knowledge of his work. He was also featured in a '50s movie "The Subteranneans" based on a Kerouac novel and appeared as a soloist with Billie Holiday in *The Sound of Jazz* television show in 1957.

Study Guide: Gerry Mulligan

Recordings

"Line for Lyons"—Gerry Mulligan.
Gerry Mulligan and Chet Baker.
(Prestige 24106 (2)). Recorded in 1952.

Personnel
Gerry Mulligan—baritone sax/composer,
Chet Baker—trumpet,
Carson Smith—bass, Chico Hamilton—drums

Musical Characteristics
All of the essential West Coast style musical elements are apparent in this prototypical Mulligan composition. Cast in gentle swing fours with brushes on drums and walking bass, the horn duet is very subdued and laid-back in the ultimate cool approach. Notice how the solos are restrained and unemotional, with hardly a trace of vibrato. Mulligan gives the composition a classical Baroque treatment in the third chorus, when he weaves a countermelody to Baker's melody, creating counterpoint. The absence of a piano is not felt because the bass provides

steady, moving chordal roots and the horns' countermelodies outline the harmonic feel.

Musical Form

AABA, easy swing fours

1. First chorus:
   AA sections—trumpet lead with baritone sax duet.
   B section—baritone sax plays countermelodies off the trumpet lead.
   A section—same as before.
2. Second chorus:
   AA sections—baritone sax solo.
   BA sections—trumpet solo

Gerry Mulligan, Chet Baker, and Lee Konitz (1952) (*Photo courtesy of William Claxton*)

Gerry Mulligan with Chet Baker (*Photo courtesy of William Claxton*)

3. Third chorus:
   AA sections—contrapuntal treatment between trumpet and sax.
   B section—trumpet lead as before.
   A section—same as beginning.
4. Tag—4-bar repeated phrase with final hold.

West Coast Jazz—Chet Baker

Trumpet player Chet Baker was born in 1929 in Yale, Oklahoma, and then moved with his family to Glendale, California where he attended high school and then moved to Hermosa Beach. He was drafted in 1946 and in an Army band he learned marches by ear, because of his inability to read music. Baker returned to civilian life two years later, then re-enlisted with the Sixth Army Band in San Francisco, where he played in the after-hours club Bop City. After going AWOL from his post, he was found unadaptable to Army life and discharged. Chet played in Los Angeles with Vido Musso, Stan Getz and Charlie Parker. Gerry Mulligan came to the city, and one night in 1952 when his piano player didn't come to work, the pianoless quartet was formed with the formidable front line of Mulligan and Baker. Baker's rendition of

Chet Baker (*Photo courtesy of William Claxton*)

"My Funny Valentine" became a jazz favorite, and he quickly became a young cult figure. With his good looks and nonconformist views, he was cast in the same mold as the Hollywood screen actor James Dean.

Baker's reputation in the early '50s grew not only in the United States, but also abroad. When Mulligan served a six-month prison term for narcotics charges, beginning in June, 1953, Baker continued on with the regular band members at the time and hired Russ Freeman as a pianist and writer for the group. Freeman was a fine complement for Baker producing arrangements such as "All the Things You Are," "Moon Love," and "Imagination" and compositions such as "Bea's Flat," "No Ties," and "Russ Job" in 1953–54. These recordings reveal the best of Chet Baker's playing, with his detached, subdued tone and highly romantic flavor. They are available on *The Complete Pacific Jazz Live Recordings of the Chet Baker Quartet with Russ Freeman* (Mosaic MR4-113) and *The Complete Pacific Jazz Studio Recordings of the Chet Baker Quartet with Russ Freeman* (Mosaic MR4-122).

Chet's fame as a trumpet player and singer found him much in demand, and after returning to the United States from a 1955–1956 European tour he started using drugs at the age of twenty-seven. His life became a roller-coaster nightmare with a series of drug-related incidents, including one in which he had his teeth knocked out by five men who were after his narcotics money. Chet's life came to a tragic end on Friday, May 13, 1988, when he fell from his hotel window in Amsterdam at the age of fifty-nine. This accident was under criminal investigation with charges to several men by local authorities. Bruce Weber released a documentary film in 1990, "Let's Get Lost," which details Baker's real life, which was much like the horrors of Otto Preminger's fictional film "The Man with the Golden Arm."

Study Guide: Chet Baker

Recordings

"My Funny Valentine"—Gerry Mulligan.
Gerry Mulligan and Chet Baker.
(Prestige 24106 (2)). Recorded in 1952.

Personnel
Chet Baker—trumpet, Gerry Mulligan—baritone sax,
Carson Smith—bass, Chico Hamilton—drums

Musical Characteristics
This hauntingly beautiful rendition of "My Funny Valentine" is one of Baker's most famous ballads. His restrained tonal approach results in a "breathy cracked note" (E) in the bridge. The early years of Baker's style not only typified the West Coast sound, but also featured some of his fin-

est playing. After listening to "My Funny Valentine" try some of his other early ballads like "Moon Love," "Moonlight Becomes You," "Imagination," "Little Man You've Had a Busy Day," or "Good-bye." For his approach to up-tempo and medium swing pieces listen to "All the Things You Are," "No Ties," "Happy Little Sunbeam," "Bea's Flat," or "Russ Job." These compositions are all included in the Pacific Jazz reissues, and include some of Baker's all-time best performances on trumpet.

Musical Forms
slow ballad, AABA

1. A theme—Baker plays the opening 8 bars with a walking bass: Mulligan joins with sustained notes, over light brushes on drums.
2. B theme—Baker's laid-back style continues when he "cracks" a note, as he gently paraphrases the melody.
3. A theme—trumpet solo continues with a highly romantic ascending embellishment on the melody.
4. A theme—last A theme is repeated with Mulligan for 8 bars; Baker joins, playing the melody with interweaving counterpoint.
5. Tag—ends with a West Coast subdued style.

Video

Let's Get Lost—**Chet Baker**
(Film by Bruce Weber)
BMG (RCA); 118 min.
This stark black and white documentary opens with the late stages of Chet Baker's life. An early '50s pictorial follows, with some of the famous photographs of a young Baker by photographer William Claxton, whose photographs are featured in this chapter. Baker's performances include footage of the 1956 San Remo Festival, a vocal rendition of "Imagination," the "Funny Valentine" track, "My Old Flame," and an appearance on the Steve Allen television show. There are interviews with Dick Bock, director of Pacific Jazz Records, trumpet player/actor Jack Sheldon, and Baker's former wives. The film is a graphic testament to the horrors of drugs. His appearance is shocking in the last years, with his tortured career revealed on his face. *Very highly recommended!*

Modal Jazz—Miles Davis

Miles Davis fashioned the cool style into a fine art with solos that rivaled the impressionistic strokes of the French painters and classical impressionistic music of French composers. This musical style was reflected with compelling solos in his *Elevator to the Scaffold* sound track in 1957.

Chet Baker (*Photo courtesy of RCA/Novus*)

His compositions with the quintet and Harmon-muted trumpet solos minus the stem revealed a haunting modal approach over sustained (pedal point) chords. The opening theme from "Generique," which he plays on the open horn, is a cool blues in the best manner of this period.

The first great group of Davis included Julian "Cannonball" Adderley on alto sax, John Coltrane on tenor sax, and Bill Evans on piano. This remarkable group recorded "On Green Dolphin Street," "Put Your Little Foot Right Out," and "Stella by Starlight" on *Jazz Track* for Columbia on May 26, 1958. The album revealed the differences of solo styles between Miles' cooler, laid-back style, accompanied by drums on brushes, and the brash hard bop stylings of Coltrane and Adderley with the explosive bomb style in the drums. A second collaboration with Gil Evans, later in 1958, was George Gershwin's *Porgy and Bess*. Using a large orchestra, Evans was able to again effectively showcase Miles' cool style with elaborate arranging in a classical style.

Cool jazz continued with a new refinement, *modal jazz*, in 1959. Miles became disenchanted with the many different and complicated chords used in the bop style, and began to streamline his music, limiting it to a few chords. Instead of improvising in a chordal, or vertical manner, as in bop, Miles began to use a linear, or horizontal technique which stressed variations on the few scales or modes which he assigned to his soloists.

Modal jazz reflected these cool tendencies in 1959, with Davis' *Kind of Blue* album, in which five compositions followed a simple formula in their harmonic schemes. The modal style permitted the soloist to play notes based on scales such as the Dorian mode. In order to avoid repetition in their solos, performers were forced to play *extensions* on the existing chords and create melodies *outside* the harmonic structures. Since modal compositions used only a few chords, the possibilities for the soloist included new-found freedom to stretch out beyond the chords once he or she had established the mode through scales.

Miles had established himself as a star in the galaxy of cool jazz. His manner of dressing in the best of fashion lured many female fans and admirers during the '50s. He had provided yet another direction in modern jazz, with an ardent following of musicians. His collaborations with Gil Evans during this period cannot be overemphasized, because of the mutual respect each had for the other and the musical success which resulted. Evans named his son Miles in honor of Davis. Despite cooling out from a four-year heroin addiction, Miles became the consummate hipster of the '50s.

Study Guide: Modal Jazz—Miles Davis

Recordings

**"Summertime"—Miles Davis with the Gil Evans Orchestra.
SCCJ (record side 11, cassette side G, CD IV). Recorded in 1958.**

Personnel
Gil Evans—arranger, Miles Davis—solo trumpet (muted),
John Coles, Bernie Glow, Ernie Royal, Louis Mucci—trumpets,
Joe Bennett, Fran Rehak, Jimmy Cleveland—trombones,
Dick Hixon—bass trombone,

Miles Davis (*Photo by Jim Marshall/Courtesy of Fantasy, Inc.*)

Bill Barber—tuba,
Willie Ruff, Julius Watkins, Gunther Schuller—French horns,
Julian "Cannonball" Adderley, Daniel Banks—saxophones,
Phil Bodner, Romeo Penque—flutes,
Danny Bank—bass clarinet,
Paul Chambers—bass, Philly Joe Jones—drums.

Musical Characteristics

The rich scoring of Gil Evans with a large orchestra included French horns and tuba, as used in *Birth of the Cool*, in addition to flutes and bass clarinet, for a more pronounced classical sound. This treatment of instrumentation provided a very richly sedated orchestral texture showcasing Miles' cool approach on the muted trumpet. Miles was one of the first trumpet players of repute to remove the stem from a stock Harmon mute, producing highly impressionistic colors that were important to his style. His improvisations, with linear movements above the chords, were as important as his limited but *well-placed choices of notes.* This was Davis and Evans' third collaboration in developing an orchestral texture in the cool style.

Musical Form
medium ballad, 16 bars of 4/4meter

1. First chorus—solo muted trumpet begins paraphrases of the melody, with horns playing a repeated riff.
2. Second chorus—Miles begins to use melodic extensions; flutes join the horns' figure.
3. Third chorus—solo extensions continue, with the flutes playing the riff one octave higher.
4. Fourth chorus—pattern and texture continues under the solo with tuba fills.
5. Fifth chorus—solo paraphrases final chorus before moving to extensions with a slight ritard; tuba fills between riffs and hold at the end.

"So What"—Miles Davis Sextet.
***SCCJ* (record side 12, cassette side H, CD V). Recorded in 1959.**

Personnel
Miles Davis—trumpet/composer,
Julian "Cannonball" Adderley—alto sax,
John Coltrane—tenor sax, Bill Evans—piano,
James Cobb—drums, Paul Chambers—bass.

Musical Characteristics
The front line of Davis, Adderley, and Coltrane formed one of the most creative groups in early modern jazz. Young Bill Evans had begun to emerge as an innovative keyboard player, with great imagination in chord voicing. "So What" is an ideal classic modal piece that uses only two chords in a minor key (the Dorian mode), D minor and E♭ minor. Davis and Evans solo in a cool, laid-back style while Coltrane and Adderley play a more emotional hard bop style in their solos.

Musical Form
AABA, modal swing fours

1. Introduction—free style with bass and piano
2. First chorus:
   A section—bass solo begins the theme, with piano response of two chords. (8 bars in D minor)

A section—bass continues as horns join the two chord response. (8 bars in D minor)

B section—change of key with the same pattern. (8 bars in E♭ minor)

A section—same as second A strain (8 bars in D minor)

3. Second chorus—Rhythm shifts to swing 4s with trumpet solo in a cool style, piano plays extensions.

4. Third chorus—Trumpet solo continues with some *Porgy and Bess* licks, bass plays off-beats or weak beats on 2 and 4 before returning to walking style of swing 4s.

5. Fourth, fifth choruses—Tenor solo begins with swing rhythm, plays double-time figures, strays outside the changes in a hard bop style, exploring the entire register of the horn.

6. Sixth, seventh choruses—Alto solo plays with a more melodic approach in bop style, builds short melodic sequences before returning to double-time licks.

7. Eighth chorus—Piano solo begins in a light cool style with horns accompanying with the two chord pattern. Solo continues with extensions that are laid back, leads to the original bass theme.

8. Final chorus—Bass plays the original theme with horns' response, leading to fadeout after the final B section.

Cool Jazz—Modern Jazz Quartet

The MJQ has been a model of sustained durability throughout the history of modern jazz. The quartet was formed of former musicians from Dizzy Gillespie's big band in late 1952. John Lewis, the brilliant composer and pianist, became the creative force behind the quartet, with Milt "Bags" Jackson on vibes. Kenny Clarke, who was replaced by Connie Kay in 1955, was the original drummer and Percy Heath was the bassist. The group became very influential in the cool jazz style, with concert tours abroad. It ultimately disbanded between 1974 and 1984, re-formed in the early '80s, and has become a staple in modern jazz ever since. Lewis' style on piano is conservative, well thought-out, and essentially classical in nature, with a dominant right hand.

John Lewis

John Lewis, born in 1920 of musical parents, began piano and violin lessons at age seven. He settled on piano, and studied at the University of New Mexico; drafted into the Army, in 1942, he played in Special Services bands for three years. After leaving the Army he went to New York City and joined Dizzy Gillespie's band. He was well educated at the Manhattan School of Music, and strongly influenced by classical masters such as J. S. Bach. After touring with Gillespie he returned to New York in

1948, recording with Charlie Parker and Lester Young. In 1949 he played piano and wrote some of the arrangements on the famous *Birth of the Cool* recordings. Rejoining Gillespie, he played with Milt Jackson, Percy Heath, and Kenny Clarke in the rhythm section which ultimately led to the MJQ.

Milt Jackson

Milt "Bags" Jackson was born in Detroit in 1923 and studied music at Michigan State University. He had first played piano and guitar, and became the first bop musician to solo on the vibraphone. Jackson was heard by Gillespie, who brought him to New York City in 1945. He free-lanced with some of the great musicians of the bebop era, including Tadd Dameron and Thelonious Monk, and joined the Woody Herman band in 1949. Jackson rejoined Gillespie in 1950, until his association with the MJQ began in 1952. His style is a very distinctive approach, with colorful blues licks and a slow, wide vibrato, producing an unmistakable cool sound that is the characteristic principal voice of the MJQ.

Study Guide: Modern Jazz Quartet

Recordings

"Django"—Modern Jazz Quartet.
SCCJ (record side 11, cassette side H, CD IV). Recorded in 1960.

Personnel
John Lewis—piano/composer, Milt Jackson—vibraphone,
Percy Heath—bass, Connie Kay—drums

Musical Characteristics
"Django" is considered one of Lewis' finest compositions. It is a mixture of the blues and classical elements that provided the cool color for the MJQ. This piece was dedicated to the late guitarist, Django Reinhardt, who was a Belgian-born gypsy. The themes alternate between a slow dirge treatment and a joyous swing section that recalls the early New Orleans funerals. There is a masterful mix of arranging and improvising which gives the composition great unity. Also, the continued use of classical elements in Lewis' music points the way to *third stream music*, which became prevalent in the '60s.

Musical Form
  1. Slow dirge-like theme played by the vibes, supported by the bass and piano.

2. Medium swing tempo with brushes on the drums; vibes solo in a bluesy bop style.
3. Pedal point in the bass, repeats the same note—8 bars.
4. Vibes solo continues; drummer plays brushes and then ride cymbal to push the tempo.
5. Vibes plays a bop and blues style with double-time figures, accompanied by snare accents.
6. Composed interlude in double time.
7. Piano solo begins with simple right hand in classical Baroque style, continues in swing feel with walking bass and back beats from the snare.
8. Piano and bass gradually slow the pace, leading to the opening slow dirge theme.
9. Ending with the vibes and piano improvising arpeggios and a cymbal roll for the final held tones.

CHAPTER TWELVE

HARD BOP

With the passing of Charlie Parker in 1955, bebop in its earliest form passed on to many of his followers who chose to embellish the hard-driving style and maintain its high emotional content. This was distinctly a different approach from the cool style led by Davis on the East Coast and the cool style led by Mulligan on the West Coast. In 1954 pianist Horace Silver and drummer Art Blakey organized the Jazz Messengers, which added new elements to bop. This new style called *hard bop*, was characterized by funk and soul, which were derived from gospel music and down-home blues.

In early jazz's New Orleans days *funk* and *funky* had connotations of highly repugnant smells or distasteful situations. "Funk" as used in hard bop, however, referred to the music's bluesy, down-home, gospel feel derived from the music of "sanctified" churches. Trumpeters Kenny Dorham and Clifford Brown led the way in developing the new, hard-driving bop style, with numerous ornamentations and inflections in their playing. Tenor saxophonists Sonny Rollins and John Coltrane redefined their playing with these same tendencies, as did drummers Art Blakey and Max Roach. In 1955 the Jazz Messengers recorded "The Preacher" with Hank Mobley on tenor sax, Dorham on trumpet, Silver on piano, Doug Watkins on bass, and Blakey on drums. This music represented hard bop, which was somewhat of a reaction to the less emotional strains of West Coast jazz. The blues in a gospel or soul style was brought into focus with great vocalists like Ray Charles.

The Clifford Brown–Max Roach Quintet produced electrifying results in 1955 with *Study in Brown* (Emarcy 814 646-2). This album represented some of the finest playing in the hard bop style by Clifford Brown with the driving force of Max Roach. Sonny Rollins' work with Brown and the same rhythm section offers another glimpse of that style in "Pent-up House," which is included in the Study Guide that follows. John Coltrane had gone through three periods of development; his early style was set during his years with the Miles Davis and Thelonious Monk groups; then, setting out on his own, he produced the ultimate hard bop "burner," "Giant Steps," with his furious chordal improvisations called *sheets of sound*. Like Davis, he also later reacted against abundant chord changes, and came to produce modal tunes such as "Impressions," which was built on the same two minor chords as Miles' "So What." He began to free his sound by adding soprano sax to his performances with a famous rendition of "My Favorite Things." Another of his simplified chordal pieces was "A Love Supreme."

Sonny Rollins has remained an important tenor player throughout the history of modern jazz. His tunes "Oleo," "Airegin," "Doxy," "St. Thomas," and "Pent-up House" are favorites of jazz musicians everywhere. The tunes John Coltrane recorded for Blue Note, such as "Blue Train," "Locomotion," "Moment's Notice," and "Lazy Bird," have likewise found their way into the standard modern jazz repertory.

Art Blakey

Art Blakey was born in Pittsburgh, Pennsylvania, in 1919. He was raised by his mother's first cousin, and began as a pianist, leading his own band in 1936. According to Blakey, the Democratic Club, where he was playing piano, was run by gangsters, and when they heard Erroll Garner, Blakey was moved to drums. Blakey played with Fletcher Henderson in 1939 and with Mary Lou Williams in 1940 before working with Billy Eckstine from 1944 to 1947. In 1947 he formed an early edition of the Jazz Messengers with an octet that recorded for Blue Note. With his small groups, especially, after 1954, the Jazz Messengers, he became known as "The Professor," for he taught a host of noteworthy artists, including a famous line of trumpet players: Kenny Dorham, Clifford Brown, Donald Byrd, Bill Hardman, Lee Morgan, Freddie Hubbard, Chuck Mangione, Woody Shaw, Wynton Marsalis, and Terence Blanchard. Blakey died from lung cancer at the age of seventy-one in 1990 at St. Vincent's Hospital in New York City. His drumming was explosive and his groups represented the best of hard bop. Listen to his *One Night in Birdland*, 1954 (Blue Note 81521, 81552).

Study Guide: Art Blakey

Videos

The Jazz Life—Art Blakey and the Jazz Messengers
Sony; 55 min.
Features Branford Marsalis, Donald Brown, Bill Pierce, Charles Fambrough, and Wynton Marsalis. Filmed live at Seventh Avenue South in New York City in 1982. The program includes "Fuller Love," "Little Man," "Ms. B.C.," "My Ship," "Webb City," and "New York."

The Jazz Messengers—Art Blakey
Rhapsody Films; 78 min.
This 1987 film is a celebration of Blakey's past and present commitment
to jazz. Conversations with Dizzy Gillespie, Blakey, Roy Haynes, and
Walter Davis, Jr. reveal the spirit of bop. Includes archival footage of Blakey with the Billy Eckstine Band. The film records Blakey's collaboration
with British musicians and dancers who have created an authentic jazz
revival.

Clifford Brown

Trumpeter Clifford Brown was born in 1930 in Wilmington, Delaware,
and was killed in a car crash on the Pennsylvania Turnpike in 1956. He
began trumpet when he entered high school in Delaware, and studied
with Robert Lowery in Wilmington. Clifford began playing in Philadelphia in 1948 with Miles Davis and Fats Navarro, who encouraged him.
Brown attended Maryland State on a scholarship and was hospitalized
after a car crash in 1950. In 1953 he played with Chris Powell, Tadd Dameron, Lionel Hampton, and Max Roach. He was widely recognized in
the jazz polls as one of the most brilliant young bop trumpet players with
amazing technical qualities in his solos. "Brownie," as he was called, was
on his way to becoming a giant before the fatal accident claimed his life at
the age of 26.

Study Guide: Clifford Brown

Recordings

"Swingin' "—Clifford Brown–Max Roach Quintet.
Study in Brown **(Emarcy 814 646-2). Recorded in 1955.**

Personnel
Clifford Brown—trumpet/composer,
Max Roach—drums, Harold Land—tenor sax,
George Morrow—bass, Richie Powell—piano.

Musical Characteristics
Clifford Brown's "Swingin' " is a quintessential example of hard bop.
This explosive piece is taken at an unbelievable up tempo, with Roach in
control on the drums. The main theme features a blues-based triplet in
funk style that is repeated and played four times. Brown's Herculean solos and Roach's unrelenting driving force propel this piece into a true jazz
adventure; his playing is flawless. The chord changes are based on the
standard tune "I Never Knew." Miles Davis believed that Max Roach

played at his all-time best when he was with Brown. Listen to "Cherokee" also; it is a hard bop classic, and Brown's solos are very exciting.

Musical Form
AABA, up tempo in swing fours (four beats to a measure).

1. Introduction—Trumpet and alto play a descending unison lick with the rhythm in off-beats in twos (two beats to a measure).
2. First chorus:
   AA theme—trumpet and alto play the head in unison while the rhythm shifts into high gear on swing fours. The repeated triplet is a good example of the funk-based style hard bop.
   B theme—piano solo on the bridge with fast moving melody.
   A theme—as in previous A strains
3. Second chorus—Brown's trumpet solo is well-conceived with continuous linear movement and phrase extensions in hard bop style.
4. Third chorus—Land's tenor solo follows the bop style.
5. Fourth chorus—Piano solo by Richie Powell (Bud Powell's brother) begins with descending figures and continues with melodic extensions.
6. Fifth chorus—Horns trade fours with the drums in the A sections, B section is a drum solo, A section continues as before. See glossary, *trading solos.*
7. Tag—As played in the introduction

Sonny Rollins

Tenor sax player Theodore Walter "Sonny" Rollins was born in New York City in 1929. He began piano lessons briefly at age nine, before taking up alto sax in high school in 1944. After finishing high school he began to work some clubs in New York City. Late in 1948 Rollins made his first record date as sideman on Capitol with Babs Gonzales; he then recorded with Bud Powell and J. J. Johnson, who recorded his first composition "Audubon." Sonny continued his work with Art Blakey in 1949, played with Tadd Dameron and Powell in 1950, also making his first trip to Chicago; in 1951 he spent six months with Miles Davis, then freelanced around New York for several years. He went to Chicago for a second time and returned to New York in 1956 with the Brown-Roach Quintet. After leaving Roach in 1957 he worked with his own pianoless trio; that same year he recorded *Way out West* on Contemporary, accompanied only by bassist Ray Brown and drummer Shelley Manne. During this period he began his great ascension as one of the leading hard bop tenor men. At the height of his career, in August, 1959, he abruptly stopped performing in public for some two years, due to personal problems and self-reevaluation on his instrument. His ability to develop a me-

Sonny Rollins (*Photo courtesy of David Gahr*)

lodic theme with brilliant structures and great continuity was noted by writer Martin Williams.

Study Guide: Sonny Rollins

Recordings

"Pent-up House"—Sonny Rollins Plus Four.
SCCJ (record side 11, cassette side H, CD IV). Recorded in 1956.

Personnel
Sonny Rollins—tenor sax/composer,
Clifford Brown—trumpet, Richie Powell—piano,
George Morrow—bass, Max Roach—drums

Musical Characteristics
Here is another superb example of the hard bop style with the celebrated Brown-Roach Quintet. Rollins and Brown are two virtuosi of the style and form an exciting front line, with Rollins' melodic structures providing a springboard for Brown's joyous figures. Roach is also at his best, with innovative soloing on drums.

Musical Form
AABA, medium swing fours

1. First chorus—tenor leads the group into the theme with trumpet unison, rhythm accents in two.
2. Second chorus—trumpet solo with Brown's inventive melodic extensions, rhythm in swing fours.
3. Third chorus—trumpet continues with high shouts on the repeat and double time figures.
4. Fourth chorus—trumpet uses ornamental embellishments and grace notes in bop style.
5. Fifth chorus—tenor solo begins late with sustained tones paraphrasing the melody before moving away in chordal style.
6. Sixth chorus—tenor continues with double-time passages on the repeat.
7. Seventh chorus—tenor uses more melodic material in a highly swinging manner.
8. Eighth chorus—piano begins with simple right hand, left hand blocks the chords.
9. Ninth chorus—tenor and trumpet alternate, trading twos with the drums.
10. Tenth chorus—drum solo by Roach
11. Final chorus—same as beginning with a two-note tag.

Video

Saxophone Colossus—Sonny Rollins
Sony; 101 min.
Part documentary and part performance, this film records Rollins' 1986 concerts in Tokyo and New York and shows the definitive tenor saxophonist at his finest, with an orchestra, fronting his own quintet, and playing a solo. An in-depth musical portrait of this supreme jazz artist. Features Clifton Anderson, Mark Soskin, Bob Cranshaw, Marvin Smith, and the Yomiuri Nippon Symphony Orchestra conducted by Helkid Searmanto. The program includes "G-Man," "The Bridge," *Concerto for Tenor Saxophone and Orchestra,* "Don't Stop the Carnival," and "Tenor Saxophone Solo."

John Coltrane

John William Coltrane was born in 1926 in Hamlet, North Carolina. His father, a tailor, played several instruments, as did John, including the E♭ horn and tenor saxophone in high school. After Coltrane's father died, the family moved to Philadelphia and he studied at the Granoff Studios and the Ornstein School of Music. He began his professional career in 1945, playing in combos, and in 1945–46 toured with a Navy band in Hawaii. After the Navy he worked with the Joe Webb band in 1947, Bud Powell in 1949, and then Dizzy Gillespie and Johnny Hodges in 1953.

Coltrane's style and musical attributes are not easily summarized because of his enigmatic development through several styles and influences. Even though he is indebted to the styles of Dexter Gordon and Sonny Stitt, he has acknowledged the influences of Lester Young, Johnny Hodges, and Charlie Parker on his playing. Coltrane first worked with Miles Davis in 1955, and began his ascent as one of the leading tenormen of the late '50s. After leaving Davis in 1957, he joined Thelonious Monk and began to assimilate theoretical and technical knowledge that brought him to his next level of development. Monk's quartet included drummer Shadow Wilson and was heard at the Five Spot Cafe. Later, Coltrane returned to Davis and the modal style.

He began to influence other players with his *sheets of sound*, playing entire scales on a single chord, with long, rapid lines. His style was marked by long solos with fierce slashing lines. As a leader Coltrane recorded for Prestige, and then Atlantic, with his own compositions on *Giant Steps*. In the opening of his song "Giant Steps" he used a series of substitutions for the standard ii-V-I chord progression, producing key areas a major third apart. With Rollins' two-year hiatus, Coltrane became the dominating tenorman by 1959. In 1960 he left Davis for yet another group and began to play soprano saxophone, which gained him even greater popularity.

Trane had become deeply involved with the music of India and was impressed by the great Indian sitarist Ravi Shankar, who played *ragas*, which were patterns that musically reflected certain daily religious prayers or utilitarian functions. Ragas were made of quarter-tone scales with free improvisations that became quite popular in this country during the '60s. Coltrane also became influenced by Ornette Coleman during this period, and produced a fifteen-minute blues with bass and drums accompaniment on "Chasin' the Trane." His constant chordal and theoretical experimentations and unrelenting improvisational intensity have given him a lofty place in the history of jazz as one of the greatest modern tenor players. Coltrane was a deeply religious man whose beliefs were embodied in his music; he died in 1967.

Study Guide: John Coltrane

Recordings

"Giant Steps"—John Coltrane Quartet.
Giant Steps (Atlantic 1311). Recorded in 1959.

Personnel
John Coltrane—tenor sax/composer,
Tommy Flanagan—piano, Paul Chambers—bass,
Art Taylor—drums.

Musical Characteristics
"Giant Steps" is another hard bop "burner" classic. It is well known for its very fast tempo and its series of quickly changing chordal patterns, called *Coltrane substitutions*. The term "giant step" is derived from the harmonic movement and leap from the beginning B to E♭, with thirds in both the melody and harmony. Coltrane's solo is remarkable because he outlines the very rapid chordal substitutions in his improvisations and strings out long, virtuoso phrases. This is another truly exciting piece. For an example of his meditative side, listen to "Alabama" (on *SCCJ*, record side 1, cassette side J, CD V), recorded in 1963. The composition begins and ends in a slow solemn theme, with a medium-tempo swinging section. The slow sections use an Indian drone in the piano which shows Coltrane's style during this period of ballad playing in a deeply seated religious mode.

Musical Form
Up-tempo swing fours, 16 bars repeated (32)

1. Opening theme—group begins on the chordal theme with changes in twos accented by the rhythm before swinging into fours; 32 bars.
2. Six choruses—tenor solo runs the chords in a furious manner, with long, fast-moving phrases; this is Coltrane at his best in this style.
3. Piano solo—plays two choruses; begins right-hand melody with left-hand comping the chords, then moves to a sustained block style with both hands playing together.
4. Tenor solo—returns for one chorus, as in the *head*.
5. Last chorus—as in the opening theme, ends with held notes and descending flurry by the tenor.

Video

The Coltrane Legacy—John Coltrane
VAI; 61 min.
Coltrane is highlighted in this compilation of rare footage taken from international television specials. Interviews with Reggie Workman, Elvin Jones, and Jimmy Cobb describe the unique spirit, virtuosity, and mystique of Coltrane. The program includes "So What," from 1959, with the Miles Davis Quintet and Coltrane on tenor sax; "Every Time We Say Goodbye," "Impressions," and "My Favorite Things," from 1961, with

Coltrane on soprano and tenor saxes, Eric Dolphy on alto sax/flute, Mc-
Coy Tyner on piano, Reggie Workman on bass, and Elvin Jones on
drums: "Afro Blue," "Impressions," and "Alabama," from 1964, with
Coltrane on soprano and tenor saxes, Tyner on piano, Jimmy Garrison on
bass, and Jones on drums. These selections cover most of Coltrane's musical development. *Very Strongly Recommended!*

Big Bands in the '50s

The big band format had begun to decline from the end of World War II,
with just a handful of bands managing to survive. Small groups in the
hard bop and West Coast styles that featured a front line generally of two
horns and rhythm became the musical mainstay during the '50s. Stan
Kenton had recorded *City of Glass/This Modern World* (Creative World
1006E) in the early '50s, with compositions by Robert Graettinger. *City of
Glass* represented an avant garde approach to music in a neo-classical
style with a large orchestra. This innovations orchestra of Kenton's featured some forty players. Woody Herman had continued his swinging
herds and maintained a strong following with such hits as the follow-up to
"Four Brothers," "Four Others" (Columbia JCL-592), composed by
Jimmy Guiffre in 1953, which maintained the balance between bop and
swing.

Maynard Ferguson led his own band in his native Canada before
joining the bands of Boyd Raeburn, Jimmy Dorsey, and Charlie Barnet.
He finally made his reputation as a prodigious technician and strato-
spheric trumpet player for Stan Kenton from 1950 to 1953. From 1954 to
1956 he settled in California, working with small groups and as the top
brass man in the Paramount film studio orchestra. Afterwards he returned to the big band scene with a group of excellent musicians and writers, to form a high-powered, swinging band with hard bop soloists in 1956.
The combination of three trumpets, two trombones, four reeds, and
three rhythm, with Ferguson playing trumpet or valve trombone, proved
to be an exciting band in the tradition of modern swing. His 1958 album *A
Message From Newport* (Roulette R-52012) featured "The Fugue," "The
Waltz," "Slide's Derangement," and "Three Foxes," arranged by south-
paw trombonist Slide Hampton. Hampton's trombone partner, Don Sebesky, began to emerge as an important writer with "Fan It, Janet" and
"Humbug" on the same album. Tenorman Willie Maiden wrote "Tag
Team" and alto man Bob Freedman wrote "And We Listened." Although this album is presently out of print, it presents some of the best
big band jazz of Maynard Ferguson in the '50s.

Certainly one of the most notable big band events was the Duke Ellington performance at the Newport Jazz Festival in 1956, which featured his 1937 compositions "Diminuendo in Blue" and "Crescendo in

Blue" combined together, featuring a twenty-seven chorus solo by Paul
Gonsalves on tenor sax. This inspired a remarkable return of interest in
Duke's band; the album *Ellington at Newport* (Columbia 40587) became
one of his all-time best sellers.

After touring with a septet in 1950–51, Count Basie reformed his big
band in 1954, and in 1955 he introduced many new stars, including Thad
Jones and Joe Wilder on trumpets, Benny Powell and Henry Coker on
trombones, and Frank Wess and Frank Foster on tenors. This band featured arrangements by Ernie Wilkins, Neal Hefti, and Johnny Mandel.
The band toured Europe extensively and Great Britain during 1956–57.
Basie returned with his band to New York City in 1957 with a thirteen-
week engagement at the Waldorf-Astoria Hotel. The Basie band won numerous jazz polls during the late '50s. The current Basie aggregation is
led by Frank Foster.

Other bands recorded and toured, including Les Brown's Band of
Renown, which promoted musical excellence in a popular entertainment
style, and Billy May, a composer-leader-trumpet player who recorded on
Capitol in 1951 with his big band featuring a unison glissando style in the
sax section. West Coast flugelhorn player and writer Shorty Rogers also
led a recording big band Shorty Rogers and His Giants on the Capitol and
RCA labels. One of the most experimental bands of the period was led by
writers Eddie Sauter and Bill Finegan. The Sauter-Finegan Orchestra
was an early attempt to bridge the gap between jazz and classical music,
particularly the French impressionist masters. Earlier, Sauter had arranged for Benny Goodman and Finegan had been an arranger for Glenn
Miller.

Experimentalists, Modernists

George Russell has been one of the highly influential figures in the evolution of modern jazz. Russell, who was a former big band drummer and
small group pianist, contributed more as a theorist and composer than as
a performer. This musical visionary introduced *Bitonality* (two tonal centers) and advanced *Polyrhythms* with model techniques to Dizzy Gillespie's big band, with its Afro-Cuban styling, in 1947. In 1959 he published
The Lydian Chromatic Concept of Tonal Organization, which was a
highly advanced harmonic treatise. Two of his massive undertakings was
the albums *New York, N.Y.* and *Jazz in the Space Age* (both in MCA 2-
4017), which he composed from 1958 to 1960. The title and music of *Jazz
in the Space Age* were inspired by Sputnik I's first circling of the earth in
October, 1957. The large orchestras of Russell's included some of the biggest names in jazz at the time.

Ornette Coleman turned the jazz world upside-down in 1959 with
his debut at the Five Spot Cafe in New York City. The young alto sax

player from Texas had begun to free jazz from its traditional melodic, harmonic, and rhythmic underpinnings. His radical and controversial approach in the late '50s spilled over into the '60s, causing a major revolution in jazz. With Don Cherry on trumpet, Charlie Haden on bass, and Billy Higgins on drums, Coleman explored and developed pre-set motives or themes without strict adherence to chord progressions. The Coleman group's improvisational style was the *outide the changes* approach that has become a major influence with so many young players in the '80s and '90s. Listen to "Lonely Woman" (*SCCJ*, record side 13, cassette side I, CD V), 1959, which has a dirge-like theme. It uses a basic, rhythmically repetitive motive played by trumpet and alto, driven by a fast counter-rhythm by the drums. Without a keyboard the group is free to explore and develop around this motive. The quicker-paced "Congeniality" (*SCCJ* record side 14, cassette side J, CD V), from the same date, reveals much the same free-wheeling technique of developing a motive and turning it in many directions.

Pianist Cecil Taylor, with his musical complexity, became one of the most controversial keyboard figures since Monk. Taylor was at first largely ignored because his music was considered too demanding. Taylor's intensely thick textures and percussive playing were highly influenced by neoclassical masters such as Igor Stravinsky and Bela Bartok. His assimilation of modern classical music with jazz had made him one of the avant garde jazz pianists. Ellington's compositional influence was strong on Taylor, who attempted to fuse it with European precepts. Listen to "Enter Evening" (*SCCJ*, record side 13, cassette side I, CD V) for an example of his style. This music has irregular and jagged edges much like the music of Stravinsky and Monk.

Charles Mingus was a bassist and composer who was born in 1922 and grew up in Los Angeles. He began as a trombone and 'cello player, and began studying bass at age 16. His early jobs were with Buddy Collette, Louis Armstrong, and Barney Bigard in California. In 1947–48 he played with Lionel Hampton and gained recognition with the Red Norvo Trio when he moved to New York in 1951. There, too, Mingus played with Billy Taylor, Charlie Parker, Stan Getz, Bud Powell, and Art Tatum. He and Max Roach began their own record company, Debut, and joined the Jazz Workshop of composer/players. Mingus was influenced by Ellington, Parker, African-American church music, and modern classical music. In 1971 he published his autobiography *Beneath the Underdog*.

Mingus was one of the greatest bass players ever in the history of jazz. A highly controversial figure, his compositions have had far-reaching effects on modern musicians. During the period between 1966 and 1970 Mingus temporarily retired, suffering from periods of severe depression, and eventually committed himself to the psychiatric ward of Bellevue Hospital in New York. His life was a neurotic behavioral pattern of both extroverted and introverted tendencies. He was known to frequently stop his band in the middle of a piece and begin over during performances. His autobiography reveals much about the complexity of his lifestyle. Mingus had contracted a form of sclerosis which affected his nervous system and ultimately lead to his death in 1979.

A recently discovered Mingus work, *Epitaph,* was written for a thirty-piece orchestra and premiered ten years after his death under the direction of Gunther Schuller on June 3, 1989, at Lincoln Center in New York City. The two-hour work was an attempt by Mingus to integrate composition and improvisation in orchestral forms in very general terms. A recent

George Adams (*Photo courtesy of Shigeru Uchiyama*)

group, Mingus Dynasty, which took its name from one of Mingus's albums, was formed to help perpetuate his great musical legacy. The Dynasty's changing membership has included George Adams, Victor Lewis, John Hicks, Jack Walrath, Ray Drummond, John Handy, Alex Foster, Craig Handy, Lew Soloff, Sam Burtis, and Roland Hanna.

Study Guide: Charles Mingus

Recordings

"Haitian Fight Song"—Charles Mingus Quintet.
SCCJ (record side 11, cassette side G, CD IV). Recorded in 1957.

Personnel
Charles Mingus—bass/composer,
Jimmy Knepper—trombone, Curtis Porter—alto sax,
Wade Legge—piano, Danny Richmond—drums.

Musical Characteristics
The various styles of Mingus can not be showcased in one piece; however, this composition does reveal the gifts of Mingus as a composer and bassist. It must be remembered that he was one of the first modern bass players to use the instrument as a solo voice and in conjunction with horn lines. This piece demonstrates his turbulent, fiery leadership. After listening to "Haitian Fight Song," listen to *Mingus Ah Um* (on CBS CJT 40648), from 1959. "Better Git It In Your Soul" is a fine example of the church-oriented blues that inspired Mingus. "Fables of Faubus" was an expression of Mingus's feelings about the attitude of segregationist governor Orville Faubus of Arkansas during the Civil Rights Movement. This work uses a boisterous first theme with a raucous second strain and a third which is highly funky.

Musical Form
Swing fours, hard bop

1. Bass solo—begins unaccompanied with free extended blues, developing a thematic motive, joined by a tambourine shake and ride cymbal in fours.
2. Ensemble—trombone plays lead in the blues theme with full band, plunger muted trombone.
3. Trombone solo—begins in swing fours, switches to double time and back to swing fours; briefly, the band plays a straight march-like rhythm, then the solo continues in hard bop style with swing fours and walking bass.

4. Piano solo—tones down the intensity before going to the march rhythm and returning to hard bop.
5. Alto solo—picks up on the hard bop sound with blues, switches to double time with running melodic figures before returning to hard swinging 4s.
6. Bass solo—extended, begins with a ride cymbal and piano fills; Mingus explores both registers of the instrument before settling into swing fours. Solo ends unaccompanied with blues influence.
7. Original blues riff—bass begins with the tambourine shake, other instruments join as the intensity builds.
8. Ensemble—plays the theme, with trombone lead in a loud raucous style before slowing down to the bowed bass and final cymbal click.

Video

Mingus—Charlie Mingus.
Rhapsody Films; 58 min.
Shows Mingus in action at a club near Boston, with performances of "All the Things You Are," "Secret Love," and "Take The A Train." Members of the group are Dannie Richmond, Walter Bishop, John Gilmore, and Charles McPherson. The film shows Mingus conducting his own band, composing, singing, and reciting his own poetry. Most of the film was shot in his New York City loft while he was awaiting eviction in 1968.

Reading

Joe Goldberg, *Jazz Masters of the '50s*
DeCapo Press, 1965
In this series of jazz profiles, Goldberg examines the lives and the conflicting aesthetics of musicians during the '50s. Gerry Mulligan, Thelonious Monk, Art Blakey, Miles Davis, Sonny Rollins, MJQ, Charles Mingus, Paul Desmond, Cecil Taylor, and Ornette Coleman are the artists Goldberg presents.

PART VI

Jazz in the '60s

CHAPTER THIRTEEN

ECLECTIC JAZZ

The '60s in many ways recalled the social upheaval and nonconformity of the '20s. Flower children and drugs replaced flappers and bootleg gin. Modern space technology was developed, and the first series of manned orbital space flights began in 1961, by Yuri A. Gagarin of the U.S.S.R. and Alan B. Shepard, Jr. of the U.S. John Glenn, Jr. became the first American in orbit in 1962. The daring space program climaxed with the Apollo 11 moon landing in 1969, with Neil A. Armstrong, Edwin E. Aldrin, Jr., and Michael Collins.

The civil rights movement progressed, with a rally in Washington D.C. of over 200,000 people in 1963. Malcom X, the black nationalist leader, was shot to death at a Harlem rally in New York City in 1965. Martin Luther King, Jr., the civil rights leader, was slain in Memphis, Tennessee, in 1968, and Senator Robert F. Kennedy was shot and mortally wounded in Los Angeles after winning the California presidential primary in the same year.

The impact of modern rock was set in motion by the arrival of a group from Great Britain, the Beatles, and the 1969 Woodstock festival featured one of the largest outdoor concerts in the history of the entertainment world. Jimi Hendrix startled the rock world with his version of the National Anthem with feedback and distortions on electric guitar. The flower children and hippies became part of a popular new drug culture, led by Timothy Leary, which replaced the subterranean foothold of the earlier beatniks with musicians, artists, and writers.

A post–Korean cold war syndrome surfaced in 1962 during the Cuban missile crisis, with President John F. Kennedy's blockade of Cuba and the Russians finally backing down. John F. Kennedy was shot and killed by a sniper in Dallas in 1963, and the Vietnam War began in 1964; public discontent was great during the late '60s, as over a half million American military personnel entered the field of operations.

The '60s represented one of the most diverse periods of jazz history, with several styles carried over from the '50s, those developed during the '60s, and new influences that would become an important part of the '70s. Early European classical music influenced important styles in the '50s that developed into third stream music and free jazz. John Lewis with the MJQ, Gunther Schuller, and Gil Evans were among those who had begun to use classical elements in their compositions and performances. This musical ambivalence resulted in *third stream music,* a combination of jazz and classical music. The musical aberrations produced by such musicians as Ornette Coleman, Charles Mingus, and George Russell were evident in the *free jazz* movement with neo-classical elements. This music provided little harmonic base, in an attempt to free melody and rhythm with improvisational spontaneity.

Many hard bop and post-bop musicians had extended the modal influences in their music, reflecting both the cool view and hard bop stylings in a *mainstream* approach. Musicians such as Bill Evans, Stan Getz, Kenny Burrell, Herbie Mann, Gary Burton, Herbie Hancock, Miles Davis, Wayne Shorter, and McCoy Tyner represented this view until the late '60s. There was a growing tendency to produce showcase albums with jazz stars fronting large orchestral settings. In 1964 Miles Davis began another direction by forming his second great group, with Tony Williams on drums, Ron Carter on bass, Wayne Shorter on tenor sax, and Herbie Hancock on piano. Shorter's imaginative compositions such as those on Davis's *Nefertiti* (Columbia PC9594) and his own group's *Speak No Evil* (Blue Note 84194) were destined to become classics.

Earlier in the '60s Rahsaan Roland Kirk created a new dimension by simultaneously playing several woodwind instruments at the same time in albums such as *Case of the 3-Sided Dream in Color* (on Atlantic 1674) in 1962, and *We Free Kings* (for Mercury 826455) in 1961. Toward the end of the '60s, Miles Davis recorded two albums with new personnel that turned jazz in another direction. Miles' recording of *In a Silent Way* spawned new ideas in electric rock and jazz, which led to one of the most important jazz albums in history, *Bitches Brew* for Columbia Records. His electronic experimentations led to a new kind of music called *fusion music.* Trumpeter Don Ellis also began to experiment with electronic devices within his big band, producing *Electric Bath,* also for Columbia.

The many different styles that occurred during the '60s was the reason the period was called "Eclectic." It also represented one of the golden eras of jazz, with a flurry of recording activities, and many artists who had begun to mature and gain recognition as stars. The important new developments of third stream, free jazz, and electric jazz were balanced by mainstream traditionalists who maintained the hard bop and cool tenets of jazz.

Third Stream Music—Gunther Schuller

The advent of third stream music had a somewhat stultifying effect on the development of jazz in the '60s. Gunther Schuller coined the term "third stream" in a 1957 lecture. Schuller is a French horn player, composer, conductor, and author who was born in 1925 in Jackson Heights, New York. He studied French horn at the Metropolitan Opera and with Robert Schulze of the Manhattan School of Music. Schuller played two years with the Cincinnati Symphony and ten years with the Metropolitan Opera. He was one of the first musicians to exhibit extensive knowledge in both classical and jazz music. In 1950 Schuller played French horn on the third of the Miles Davis *Birth of the Cool* recording sessions. He began to appear in jazz concerts in close association with John Lewis. In 1959 his third stream work, *Conversations*, was performed at Town Hall in New York City by the Modern Jazz Quartet and the Beaux Arts String Quartet.

Schuller was director of the New England Conservatory from 1967 to 1977, leading a revival of ragtime with his recording of Scott Joplin's *Red Back Book* by his New England Conservatory Ragtime Ensemble (Angel Records S-36060). As an author he has written two volumes on the history of jazz that have become critical references in the field: *Early Jazz: Its Roots and Musical Development* (1968) and *The Swing Era: The Development of Jazz* (1930–1945)(1989). Both books are published by Oxford University Press in New York. More recently, he conducted the premiere of the Charles Mingus work *Epitaph* at Lincoln Center in 1989.

Third stream music had some far-reaching effects on jazz. The movie and television industries began to use jazz more often, and new demands were suddenly thrust on the shoulders of musicians. Jazz musicians were now expected to be able to perform in a classical style as well as in the jazz idiom. This meant more early classical training at the conservatories; also, musicians were expected to double on several instruments. Saxophone players in increasing numbers began to double on traditional classical woodwinds such as the oboe and bassoon, in addition to flutes and clarinets. The success of Shorty Rogers, Art Farmer, and Miles Davis on flugelhorn suggested a natural doubling for trumpet players, who began to pack two horns at a *gig*.

John Lewis—MJQ

John Lewis and the MJQ had an early influence on third stream in the late '50s. Gunther Schuller continued his collaboration with the MJQ and John Lewis as the conductor of John Lewis's "England's Carol (God Rest Ye Merry Gentlemen)" with the MJQ and Orchestra, and his own composition *Concertina for Jazz Quartet and Orchestra*. Both of these

The Modern Jazz Quartet (*Photo: Atlantic Records*)

pieces were reissued on *The Art of the Modern Jazz Quartet: The Atlantic Years* (Atlantic SD2-301, CS2-301). This music was largely conceived by John Lewis in the early '60s. He founded Orchestra U.S.A., which was the first large ensemble devoted to third stream music, in 1962. Lewis organized some thirty musicians, conducted by Gunther Schuller in 1963–64, with first appearances at Philharmonic Hall in New York City. Orchestra U.S.A. was an artistic success, and gave many concerts in the New York metropolitan area.

In 1964–65, with Harold Farberman taking over as conductor from Schuller, Orchestra U.S.A. presented several programs at Carnegie Hall.

Most of this music is included in the album *Orchestra U.S.A. Sonorities* (on Columbia 9195). The compositions include *The Spiritual* by John Lewis, based on "Swing Low Sweet Chariot"; *Concerto No. 2 for Orchestra* by Yugoslavian Milijenko Prohaska: *Sonorities for Orchestra* by Hall Overton; *Hex* by Jimmy Giuffre; and *Pressure*, which is an atonal work by Teo Macero. Like George Russell's earlier *Space Age* album, these recordings featured some of New York's finest musicians, including trumpeters Joe Newman and Thad Jones.

Study Guide: John Lewis, MJQ

Recordings

"England's Carol"—Modern Jazz Quartet with Orchestra.
The Art of the Modern Jazz Quartet: The Atlantic Years
(Atlantic 2-301). Recorded in 1960–61

Personnel
John Lewis—piano/composer, Milt Jackson—vibraphone,
Percy Heath—bass, Connie Kay—drums.
Symphony Orchestra conducted by Gunther Schuller.

Musical Characteristics
This is an ideal introduction to third stream music because of the distinct separation of the orchestra and jazz group. The orchestra introduces the classical style playing the theme "God Rest Ye Merry Gentlemen" and the MJQ follows with jazz improvisations by the vibes. The blending of strings with oboe and bassoon counter-themes is skillfully fused with the cool blues of the MJQ, striking an ideal balance between classical music and jazz. Try to identify each style as you hear them.

Musical Form
1. Orchestra begins with an introduction by the strings, then the main theme, with responses from the oboe and bassoon.
2. MJQ begins jazz improvisations on the classical theme with a vibes solo. The strings provide sustained accompaniment on the bridge before shifting back to swinging jazz fours.
3. Orchestra returns to the classical style, with counterpoint from the vibes.
4. Piano solo begins in a jazz style, with accompaniment from sustained strings and oboe/bassoon responses.
5. Strings play the theme in a classical style, with responses in lower strings and oboe.
6. Orchestra plays the final chorus in classical style, as in the beginning.

The Swingle Singers

Ward Swingle studied at the Cincinnati Music Conservatory from 1947 to 1951, during the beginning of the bebop era. It was there that he met his wife, Francoise Demorest, a violin student from Paris. He and his wife-to-be sailed on the *Liberté* to Paris, where they were married, and Ward began serious musical training through a scholarship. In spite of a strict classical education he began to experiment with the music of J.S. Bach, who had been one of the early great improvisers of Baroque clavier (keyboard) works. Swingle's Parisian connections led him in the '60s to found the Swingle Singers, a French group of eight professional musicians, basically instrumentalists except for Christiaine Legrand. Their unique performance style blended elements of Baroque classical music with jazz, using their voices as instruments. The Swingle Singers began to scat the works of J.S. Bach out of boredom during long practice sessions, and found that by adding bass and drums, they could sing Bach's music adhering to the strict contrapuntal rhythms and lines with a natural, swinging jazz feel.

When the group disbanded in 1973, Swingle formed a London-based organization, The New Swingle Singers. The English group of Swingle Singers were all hand-picked voice majors from conservatories. Ward Swingle's imaginative vocal approach to third stream music had much impact on the movie and television industry. Since 1984 Swingle has made his home in New Jersey, where he has established a publishing company Swingle Music. His innovative choral techniques have led him to travel extensively while working with groups in Holland, Australia, Israel, and England.

Study Guide: Swingle Singers (French)

Recordings

"Sinfonia, Partita No. 2—Swingle Singers.
Jazz Sebastian Bach (Phillips 824544).

Musical Characteristics
The most remarkable facet of vocal third stream in this style is that this was done with J.S. Bach's music *as it was written*, with few changes, deletions, or additions except for the addition of bass and drums, and the music's transposition from C minor to G minor in order to accommodate the limits of the human voice. Bach was a great classical improviser, and the addition of solo scat singing in the jazz section seems quite natural. This, like Lewis's "England's Carol," provides an easy example of the third

stream style, with the strict version of the group's classical singing in the beginning of the piece, before giving way to the exciting jazz style, featuring a dazzling female scat solo. Listen to some other cuts, and identify the classical and jazz styles.

Musical Form

1. Begins with the group singing a very slow theme, with female voices in part style, and male voices accompanying with countermelodies. This is done in a strict classical style.
2. Female soprano solo voice begins a medium tempo in a swinging two-beat, with bass and drums with brushes. This is an extended section in the solo scat jazz style.
3. Solo voice takes an abrupt cadenza break, beginning on a very high pitch and quickly ascending in a very exciting manner.
4. Tempo shifts to fast swing fours, with female and male voices in counterpoint. Also, walking bass and heavy brush accents in the rhythm.
5. Ends abruptly with a ritard and hold.

Stan Kenton

With the establishment of John Lewis' Orchestra U.S.A. on the East Coast, Stan Kenton, in 1965, reached an historic milestone by establishing the Los Angeles Neophonic Orchestra, which was devoted to contemporary music along third stream lines. Earlier, Kenton had attempted to establish modern jazz on equal footing with permanently based classical orchestras: His Innovations in Modern Music Orchestra augmented his regular 18-piece band with a miniature symphony of woodwinds, strings, and tympani. After failing in this attempt, Kenton experimented with various brass instruments and toured for several years with the Mellophonium Orchestra, which featured the music of some of the finest writers in the country like Bill Holman, Ralph Carmichael, Johnny Richards, Pete Rugolo, and Dee Barton.

Before leaving for England in 1963 Kenton thought seriously of organizing an orchestra which would be permanently based in Los Angeles. The result of this new concept was the Los Angeles Neophonic Orchestra, with a great variety of writers and musicians from the movie capital. Neophonic represented "new sounds" in contemporary mainstream music that drew upon both classical and jazz elements. The results were very imaginative, with works from writers like Hugo Montenegro, Johnny Williams, Allyn Ferguson, Jimmy Knight, and Russ Garcia. This all-star band included the likes of such former Kenton sidemen as the gifted Bud Shank on alto saxophone and Bill Perkins and Bob Cooper on tenors.

Study Guide: Stan Kenton

Recordings

"Music for an Unwritten Play"—Stan Kenton.
Stan Kenton Conducts the Los Angeles Neophonic Orchestra
(Creative World 1013). Recorded in 1965.

Personnel
Jimmy Knight—composer, Stan Kenton—conductor,
Dalton Smith, Gary Barone, Ron Ossa, Frank Higgins, Ollie Mitchell—
    trumpets,
Bud Shank—alto saxophone and woodwinds,
Bob Cooper, Don Lodice, Bill Perkins—tenor saxes/woodwinds,
Claude Williamson—piano, John Worster—bass,
Dennis Budimer—guitar, Nick Ceroli—drums,
Emil Richards—vibes, Frank Carlson—percussion,
Vince DeRosa, Bill Henshaw, Richard Perissi, John Cave, Arthur
    Maebo—French horns,
Bob Fitzpatrick, Gil Falco, Wernon Friley, Jim Amlotte—trombones,
John Bambridge—tuba.

Musical Characteristics
Jimmy Knight's musical play in three movements stresses the close relationship which exists between drama and music. Both arts depend on an interplay of emotion with personal images, once the main themes are introduced. This is a vivid example of third stream music to achieve these ends. Notice the use of classical instruments such as the xylophone and tympani. French horns and tuba are also used, with saxophone players doubling on flutes and clarinets. The music shifts back and forth between classical and jazz versions of the main theme, or motive, with brief interludes that bridge each section. This style of music is also highly programmatic and descriptive in content, reflecting the movie, television, and recording industries of the West Coast at the time. See figure 13.1 for an example.

Musical Form
1. Begins with a clarinet and flute flurry into a modern dramatic fanfare in the lower brass with bells; classical style.
2. Flutes begin the main motive and theme before giving way to the solo trumpet and brass section; clarinets take the lead.
3. Shifts to bright swing fours briefly with a walking bass; jazz style.
4. Slow dramatic fanfare of the main motive with French horns, trumpets, and alto sax solo.
5. Shifts again to swing fours, with the trumpet section playing the motive in a jazz style; piano fills and comps.

Figure 13.1: Main Motive

Source: Gene Norman, *Jimmy Knight's Music for an Unwritten Play.* Benton Publications and Neil Music, Inc. Used by Permission.

6. Sax section takes the theme, with the trumpet section playing the fills.
7. Short interlude with rhythmic breaks.
8. Alto sax solo in swinging bop style, accompanied by flutes and brass responses.
9. Piano begins the transformation of the main motive, with woodwinds, xylophone, tuba, and finally trombone fills.
10. Brass section plays the theme, with a new rhythmic treatment in swing style.
11. Brief interlude with brass, trombones, and horns fragmenting the theme.
12. Trombones begin a rhythmic section in twos, with French horns playing the motive.
13. Full band swings into the main theme with French horns in a two-beat shuffle style; woodwinds pick up the theme with brass responses.
14. Short interlude with woodwinds playing a staccato style.
15. Restatement of the opening fanfare by the brass with xylophone; all hold with a tympani roll.

Free Jazz

The term "free jazz" first appeared in 1960 with Ornette Coleman's recording *Free Jazz* by his Double Quartet. Coleman was the first to approach the harmonic freedom that had been examined by earlier classical composers. Free jazz as played by Coleman shifted the balance between composition and improvisation to the improviser. The soloist's musical emphasis was upon great spontaneity. Traditional values of predictable harmony, melody, and rhythm were intentionally discarded to provide improvisational freedom for the soloist, who became the central figure and composer. Tone color and texture became important musical elements. Coleman exaggerated traditional jazz sounds by playing a plastic saxophone, violin, and trumpet. He avoided unifying harmonic instruments such as the piano in his groups, to allow more freedom for the soloists. His was not the only approach in free style, although he was the most influential.

Cecil Taylor, the pianist, performed a free style that perhaps more closely resembled an avant garde classical approach. In creating new tonal colors Taylor would often play large clusters of notes, striking them like a percussionist. These *tone clusters* were more abstract than Coleman's technique because Taylor's more modern European classical elements differed greatly from Coleman's blues background. Taylor used classical instruments such as the oboe and bass clarinet in creating textures through collective improvisation. There is much intensity and high energy in Taylor's work, with the emphasis placed on the compositional whole rather than on individual solos, as in Coleman.

John Coltrane developed modal jazz with almost atonal melodies that became totally free-form harmonic structures. By extending the existing chordal structures, Coltrane was able to play on top of the harmonies, as in his recording of "Alabama." This application of a free improvising style is much more of a traditional approach than Coleman's and certainly Taylor's; however, this change in Coltrane was largely due to the influence of the free-form jazz movement. Coltrane's solos during this period, particularly "My Favorite Things," reveal his improvisational approach away from the roots of the chords. The soprano saxophone had become a natural doubling instrument for tenor sax players, and Coltrane was one of the first to use the instrument in modern jazz. Figure 13.2 shows the soprano saxophone, which is pitched in B♭ and is somewhat smaller than the alto saxophone, which is pitched in E♭ and is shown in figure 13.3.

Woodwind player Anthony Braxton maintained a style more closely related to Taylor's, with a balance of composition and improvisation. Braxton spent the middle '60s in Chicago, where he came under the influence of the organization formed by Richard Abrams called the Association For The Advancement of Creative Music (AACM), a highly experimental group. Braxton tends to use more compositional techniques than Taylor, and demonstrates a strong classical influence. His experimentation with various woodwinds often resulted in unorthodox and exotic sounds that produce new tonal colors and textures. His compositions vary from conventional notation to geometric diagrams and symbols, as in *Anthony Braxton: New York, Fall 1974* (Arista AL 4032). This album is a good example of his varied techniques in a free-form or avant garde style.

Free jazz, as introduced by Ornette Coleman, had a far-reaching effect on many jazz musicians who either changed course under its influence or simply were able to find their own way within this style. Coleman's music is still a strong influence for players in the '90s.

Ornette Coleman

Coleman was born in 1930 in Fort Worth, Texas and began to play alto saxophone at age fourteen. Largely self-taught, he also played tenor saxophone with groups in Texas before joining Pee Wee Crayton's band, with which he traveled to Los Angeles in 1950. There he worked in a depart-

Figure 13.2: *(left)* The Soprano Saxophone

Figure 13.3: *(right)* The Alto Saxophone

ment store and began to read theory and harmony books. His Texas blues background was reflected in an open-ended improvisational approach that shed its allegiance to chordal structures. Coleman recorded two albums for Contemporary and began to gain recognition. John Lewis of the MJQ heard Coleman and recommended him to Nesuhi Ertegun of Atlantic Records, who signed him and paid for a scholarship at the School of Jazz at Lenox, Massachusetts, in 1959. He and trumpeter Don Cherry recorded in Los Angeles before moving to New York in late 1959, with a date at the Five Spot Cafe. He became a highly controversial figure; his plastic alto saxophone and Cherry's pocket trumpet were thought to be a mockery of the jazz establishments. Among his early albums for Atlantic was *Free Jazz,* which was thirty-seven minutes of spontaneous improvisation by a double quartet.

Study Guide: Ornette Coleman

Recordings

"Free Jazz" (excerpt)—Ornette Coleman Double Quartet.
SCCJ (record side 14, cassette side J, CD V). Recorded in 1960.

Personnel
Ornette Coleman—alto sax/composer,
Don Cherry, Freddie Hubbard—trumpets,
Eric Dolph—bass clarinet,
Scott LaFaro, Charlie Haden—basses,
Billy Higgins, Ed Blackwell—drums.

Musical Characteristics
With virtually no preset harmonies, this was a daring attempt at free collective improvisation by eight men. Each had only a sketchy ensemble part that defined a brief tonal area. The rhythm was the only preset ingredient, and the soloists were left on their own with collective concepts behind Coleman's unifying solo. Many laypersons think that all jazz is generally free in this respect. It must be pointed out, however, that great imagination and creativity as well as self-discipline are necessary for the success of this music, as well as all other jazz.

Rather than trying to identify every successive phrase in this rather extended excerpt, listen for the following main elements:

1. Steady rhythm throughout most of the piece.
2. Alto sax solo, which is the thematic focal point.
3. Collective improvisation, as each instrumentalist embroiders the thematic material collectively.
4. Original theme returns played in unison, with a fadeout.

Cecil Taylor

The pianist and composer Cecil Taylor was born in 1929 in Long Island City, New York. He studied privately before attending the New England Conservatory in 1950–54. One of his first breaks occurred in 1956, when he recorded *Jazz Advance* for Transition Records, in Boston. His group with Steve Lacy on soprano sax, Buell Neidlinger on bass, and drummer Dennis Charles played at the Five Spot Cafe in New York and at the Newport Jazz Festival in 1957. His jazz influences include Dave Brubeck, Lennis Tristano, Duke Ellington, Thelonious Monk, and Horace Silver. Much controversy surrounded his attempts to fuse classical modernists like Igor Stravinsky, Bela Bartok, Karl Stockhausen, and serialists such as Arnold Schoenberg with jazz in a free style. As a result of these influences, he has been regarded as a modern experimenter in the avant garde, which sometimes characterizes his music as modern classical rather than modern jazz.

Study Guide: Cecil Taylor

Recordings

"Enter Evening"—Cecil Taylor Unit.
SCCJ (record side 13, cassette side I, CD V). Recorded in 1966.

Personnel
Cecil Taylor—arranger/piano/bells,
Eddie Gale Stevens—trumpet, Jimmy Lyons—alto sax,
Ken McIntyre—alto sax, oboe, bass clarinet,
Henry Grimes, Alan Silva—basses,
Andrew Cyrille—drums.

Musical Characteristics
Taylor's free jazz design is inspired from neoclassical experimental masters such as John Cage and Igor Stravinsky. The use of the oboe, muted trumpet, and the upper harmonics produced on string bass, with percussive tone clusters on the piano, provide an eerie sound. The music sounds more like modern European classical music than jazz during the first half of the composition, before moving to brief walking bass jazz elements. The emphasis is on creating new textures and tonal colors, rather than harmony in a traditional sense. This work's free form moves easily out and back again between the textural effects and hints of jazz rhythms or brief solos, as in the alto sax passages toward the last half of the piece.

This is a recording of well over ten minutes, challenging the listener to great patience and concentration. Again, as with the *Free Jazz* excerpt, try to identify these instruments and various elements and effects.

Instruments	Elements
oboe	textures
bells	tone colors
alto sax	tone clusters
muted trumpet	tensions
string bass bowed	jazz styles
piano effects	fragmented solos
triangle	

CHAPTER FOURTEEN

ELECTRIC JAZZ

Two important factors in the late '60s contributed to the development of a new style of jazz that became known as *fusion*. The dominance of rock as a popular form had placed a huge amount of commercial pressure on jazz musicians through their recording companies. Another important factor was the increased use of instruments such as the electric guitar, bass, and piano. These electric instruments combined with electronic effects such as the synthesized ring modulator and echoplex with increased amplification to open new possibilities.

Miles Davis—Later

Ornette Coleman had by now set the free jazz style in full gear, and its influences provided new options for musicians willing to experiment. Two men, Miles Davis and Don Ellis, were in the forefront of this experimentation, although from diverse paths. Miles Davis assembled a new band with outstanding performers such as Herbie Hancock, Chick Corea, and Josef Zawinul on electric keyboards, John McLaughlin on electric guitar, Dave Holland on bass, and Tony Williams on drums. Davis's recording *In a Silent Way* (CBS 40580), in 1969, explored new forms; his three keyboard players and guitarist broke new ground with collective improvisation behind a leading voice. The title tune "In a Silent Way" was composed by Zawinul.

Six months later, Miles' album *Bitches Brew* (CBS 40577), also produced in 1969, became one of the most important albums in the history of jazz by defining the new fusion idiom. Davis added two drummers, a bass clarinetist, a percussionist, a guitarist, and two electric keyboards to his quintet. The group with Wayne Shorter on soprano saxophone produced this follow-up to *Silent Way* that was more dynamic and emotional in scope, with denser and darker textures.

Davis's band's electric instruments and devices produced distorted reverb effects, and his musicians romped through an intense free-form style that used textures, tonal colors, and tone clusters to replace chords. John McLaughlin brought a sophisticated form of rock style to improvising which became collective and fragmented in varied lengths (see glossary: *collective improvisation*). Much of the form was conveyed by the use of *vamps*, which were repeated melodic or harmonic phrases that provided focal points. Solo and collective improvisations could be structured around vamps, a basis that was relatively simple but which placed heavy emphasis on the creative imaginations of the performers for form. It was at this time that Davis began the process of studio overdubbing, in which musicians recorded their parts individually or in small groups on separate tracks.

Don Ellis

Don Ellis, an exciting trumpet player and composer who was known for his exotic Indian-influenced mixed meters, began to experiment with the newly electrified instruments and effects. His album *Electric Bath* (CBS 9585), in 1969, was a successful big band experiment in this format. Maestro Sound Products in Lincolnwood, Illinois, had marketed many new electronic devices such as the echoplex, super fuzz, ring modulator, sustainer, and fuzz phaser which could be used on various instruments to produce amplified distortions and exciting electronic effects. On *Electric Bath* Ellis provided an exquisite example of how to use the loop delay echo chamber on his trumpet, as he played "Open Beauty." By using an echoplex Ellis was able to play highly effective solos, duets, and trios in a surrealistic manner by himself. On "Turkish Bath" the reed section tuned their instruments flat to produce distorted quarter-tones through amplifiers. Indian quarter-tones are featured by Ellis on his four-valved trumpet in "Indian Lady," which is a bluesy tune in five meter (3–2). With his big band of five trumpets, three trombones, five woodwinds, two keyboards, three basses, and four percussion, Ellis presented a highly organized compositional approach to fusion music. This was certainly one of the earliest and most successful fusions of rock and big band.

Study Guide: Miles Davis

Recordings

"Miles Runs the Voodoo Down"—Miles Davis.
Bitches Brew (Columbia 40577). Recorded in 1969.

Personnel
Miles Davis—trumpet,
Wayne Shorter—soprano sax, Lenny White—drums,

Bennie Maupin—bass clarinet, Jim Riley—percussion,
Jack DeJohnette, Charles Alias—drums,
Chick Corea, Larry Young—electric pianos,
Harvey Brook—electric bass, Dave Holland—bass,
John McLaughlin—guitar.

Musical Characteristics

This recording pointed a new direction for Miles Davis, who never looked
back. "Bitches Brew" is a very challenging experience that requires intense concentration for twenty-seven minutes. "Miles Runs the Voodoo
Down" is slightly over fourteen minutes long, with the same intensity. It
is a masterpiece of dynamic and innovative techniques. As in the *Free
Jazz* excerpt by Coleman, try to identify some of the most important elements listed below rather than trying to follow every nuance. This will
require *intense concentration.*

1. Bass clarinet with a brooding sound on the bass lines.
2. Trumpet solo—blues and chromatic extensions; smears and screams
   in phrases of varied lengths and with electronic effects.
3. Collective improvisation among the soprano sax, keyboards, and guitar.
4. Textures in thick and thin varieties.
5. Rock rhythm elements.
6. General tension levels created in the slowly-moving vamp, with all of
   its transformations.

Reading

**Ian Carr, "*Miles Davis: A Biography*
William Morrow, 1982.**
Carr brings many Miles Davis quotes to light and probably explains Miles
better than Miles does himself in his autobiography (see chapter 21).
There are some interesting anecdotes about his major recordings inter-
spersed with the discussions of Miles' life and music. Also included are a
lengthy appendix of Miles' recordings from 1945 through 1981 and nine
solo transcriptions.

Mainstream in the '60s

Although in the '60s new styles such as free jazz, third stream, and fusion
bore fruit, many artists who were becoming established stars continued
in the mainstream tradition. This is not to suggest that they were not influenced in any way by the new developments, but to show that they per-
petuated the earlier ideals of hard bop, cool, and modal jazz, with their

own individual stylings. There was much recording activity during the '60s, and many jazz historians pay little or no attention to the great mainstream activity that seemed to have been overshadowed by the newer styles. The mainstream musicians in this chapter are presented as parts of an overview of activity during the '60s. Needless to say, many other great musicians were active and influential during this period, and their work has continued to surface in recent years.

Stan Getz

Stan Getz, the great tenor sax player was born in Philadelphia in 1927, and began as a bassist and bassoonist. He began to play tenor professionally with Jack Teagarden, Bob Chester, and Dale Jones at the age of sixteen. In 1944–45 he played with Stan Kenton, and moved to California in 1947. Stan played in the new Woody Herman Second Herd from 1947 to 1949 as one of the celebrated Four Brothers. After playing in the old Birdland with Miles Davis, J.J. Johnson, Bud Powell, and Max Roach, he formed his own band and became a premier tenor soloist with his lovely vibrato during the '50s. He also began touring abroad and became one of the trendsetters, in a post-bop, cool style. Players such as Getz, Rollins, and Coltrane had moved away from the heavier tonal conceptions of Don Byas, Lucky Thompson, and Coleman Hawkins.

Stan was thirty-four years old and had been a professional musician for half of his life when he recorded *Focus* (Verbe 2071) in 1961. This amazing album featured seven compositions written and arranged by Eddie Sauter. There was no discussion of what had been written, no rewriting, and no second thoughts. Getz went into the studio and was handed a sketchy lead sheet of what had been scored for the orchestra of ten violins, four violas, two 'cellos, bass, harp, and percussion. Not one note had been scored for him, nor had any areas been left open deliberately in the compositions. The results of Stan's spontaneous improvising are an unbelievable testimony to his true talent. *Focus* had assimilated third stream string settings and free forms within the framework of a mainstream soloist. His improvised themes to the ballads "Her," "I Remember When," "Once Upon a Time," and "A Summer Afternoon" feature his characteristic lovely tenor vibrato. "I'm Late, I'm Late" and "Night Rider" are up tempo bop stylings which Getz improvised in a breathtaking, swinging manner. This album was unique in the '60s for its spontaneity within an orchestra setting and the amazing feat of Getz improvising throughout the entire album.

In the '60s, he was largely responsible for the bossa nova craze in the jazz world with his recordings of "Desafinado" and "The Girl From Ipanema." He then began to dominate all the jazz polls as an outstanding musician.

The master tenor saxophonist returned in the '90s with *Apasionado*, on A&M records, in collaboration with Herb Alpert. This album provided a natural vehicle for the beautiful melodic improvisations of Getz, in which he also improvised nearly all of the themes, as he had done in *Focus*. Getz was still regarded as a great musician with his gorgeous tone on ballads. Stan Getz died in 1991.

Herbie Mann

Flutist Herbie Mann was born in Brooklyn, New York, in 1930. He began playing clarinet at the age of nine and played later with the Army Band in Europe for three years. Mann toured with the Pete Rugolo Octet in 1954 and wrote for several television dramas which he directed. In 1956 he later toured Europe, and returned to the West Coast in 1957. He formed his Afro Jazz Sextet in New York City in 1959 with an appearance at the Newport Jazz Festival and regular appearances at the Village Gate. Mann went on a State Department tour of Africa in 1959–60, and joined other jazz stars in the summer of 1961 for a tour of South America. Herbie Mann is recognized as one of the great early flute players.

The album *Herbie Mann at the Village Gate* (Atlantic 1380), recorded in 1962, presents him at his best. Mann has been highly influenced by African instruments and styles, which he richly incorporates with his group in Gershwin's "Summertime" and in "It Ain't Necessarily So," in a 6/8-meter treatment that consumes one entire side. The latter tune features African percussion by Chief Bey, which adds exotic coloring. The bassist Ahmad Abdul-Malik also propels the extended form with Herbie's Middle Eastern solo. Also on the album is "Comin' Home Baby," which is a bop-styled tune that features a second bassist Ben Tucker, who plays a solo with double stops on two strings, reminiscent of Jimmy Blanton. Mann plays a variety of flutes, with Hagood Hardy on vibes, Ray Mantilla on percussion, and Rudy Collins on drums.

Kenny Burrell

Guitarist Kenny Burrell was born in Detroit, Michigan, in 1931. He studied classical guitar briefly in 1952–53 and received a Bachelor of Music degree at Wayne University in 1955. His early professional career included stints with the Candy Johnson Sextet in 1948, Count Belcher in 1949, Tommy Barnett in 1950, and Dizzy Gillespie in 1951. Burrell formed his own groups until 1955, when he joined the Oscar Peterson Trio. In 1955–56 he moved to New York City, where he free-lanced with his own and other groups before joining Benny Goodman in 1957. He was heard with his own trio at the 1959 Newport Jazz Festival. Burrell shows the influences of Charlie Christian, Django Reinhardt, and Oscar

Moore. He has mastered most guitar styles, including country blues, flamenco, and classical, with great versatility. Kenny is equally adept at playing in small and large groups with exquisite technique and taste.

Guitar Forms (Verve 2070), recorded in 1964–65, is a broad example
of his ability in many styles of guitar playing. The album was arranged and
conducted by Gil Evans with a large instrumentation, including French
horn, tuba, and woodwind doubling. The orchestral palette served by
Evans is reminiscent of his earlier collaborations with Miles Davis. Guitar
Forms offers a beautiful and exciting orchestral canvas in which Burrell is
free to paint his beautiful pictures with guitar. On "Downstairs" Kenny
plays a down-home blues; "Lotus Land" gives Burrell a chance to flash his
Spanish motives in flamenco style; "Terrace Theme" shows his strong
chordal style; "Moon and Sand" is a lovely bossa nova treatment with
classical guitar, on which he also plays a solo on Gershwin's Prelude No. 2
for Piano. On "Greensleeves" he begins with a pensive classical guitar
before moving to electric in the faster section. Burrell's own tunes
"Loie," a beautiful ballad, and "Breadwinner" exhibit his great versatility
as a composer. "Last Night When We Were Young" is a beautifully con-
structed piece with orchestra, and incidently one of Burrell's favorites.
This gorgeous ballad is an example of his melodic sensitivity and poign-
ancy. Be sure to listen to this haunting piece.

Wes Montgomery

Another fine guitarist of the period who enjoyed great popularity was
Wes Montgomery, born in Indianapolis, Indiana, in 1925. His brothers
Monk, a bassist, and Buddy, a vibraphonist were members of a West
Coast group, the Mastersounds. Wes played with Lionel Hampton in
1948–50. In 1959 he worked with the Mastersounds in San Francisco, and
recorded for World Pacific. His distinctive style of playing a melody in
octaves with block chords was a popular model for many young guitarists
in the mainstream bop tradition. He was a back-country legend until 1959
when he was praised by record producer Orrin Keepnews. Montgomery
had incredible right thumb speed without using a pick, and became
widely recognized as one of the great jazz guitarists in the '60s. In 1961
Montgomery and Eric Dolphy joined the John Coltrane quartet at the
Monterey Jazz Festival.

His album Goin' out of My Head (Verve 2110), 1965, was a best seller,
with music arranged and conducted by Oliver Nelson and played by an
orchestra of five trombones, three trumpets, bass, five woodwinds, two
drums, two pianos, and congas in cumulative personnel during three De-
cember recording sessions in 1965. The selections include "Goin' Out of
My Head," "O Morro," "Bass City," "Chim Chim Cheree," "Naptown
Blues," "Twisted Blues," "End of a Love Affair," "It Was a Very Good

Year," and "Golden Earrings." Wes was one of the great inspirational forces in guitar playing until his death following a heart attack in 1968, at the height of his career and popularity.

Study Guide: Wes Montgomery

Recordings

"West Coast Blues" (abridged)—Wes Montgomery Quartet. *SCCJ* (record side 12, cassette side H, CD V). Recorded in 1960.

Personnel
Wes Montgomery—guitar soloist/composer,
Tommy Flanagan—piano, Percy Heath—bass,
Albert Heath—drums.

Musical Characteristics
"West Coast Blues" is an example of Montgomery's rich earlier style that was perhaps influenced by Charlie Christian. He uses 6/4 and 4/4 meters, playing innovative single line blues with octaves in a block chord style. His fully chorded section and ability to swing also mark his stylistic tendencies.

Musical Form
Blues

1. First chorus—theme is stated by guitar solo in 6/4.
2. Second chorus—improvisations begin in 4/4 bop style, with a walking bass and swing fours in the rhythm.
3. Third chorus—continues in 4/4, exploring the single note melody with descending patterns.
4. Fourth chorus—continues in 4/4, with piano comping.
5. Fifth chorus—also in 4/4, with improvised blues inflections; the piano changes comping patterns.
6. Sixth chorus—guitar solo begins the melody in octaves.
7. Seventh chorus—remains in 4/4 with the octave treatment, begins with thumb strumming.
8. Eighth chorus—octaves continue with blues style licks, extended bop lines.
9. Ninth chorus—uses block chords in rhythmic patterns.
10. Tenth chorus—last 4/4 chorus with block chords and quick thumb strums; whole tone pattern.
11. Eleventh chorus—returns to the 6/4 theme.
12. Coda—4 bars strummed and a hold.

Bill Evans

Pianist Bill Evans was born in Plainfield, New Jersey, in 1929. He studied piano, flute, and violin, and formed his own group as a teenager with his brother. Evans attended Southwestern Louisiana College, earning a degree and playing piano with several groups before entering the Army. He left the Army in 1954 and went to New York City, gaining attention with Jerry Wald and Tony Scott. His first album was for Riverside in 1956, and he began working with composer George Russell before joining Miles Davis in 1958 as a member of the sextet that recorded *Kind of Blue*. When he left Davis he formed his own trio and developed a subtle style. Like Davis, Evans was more concerned with the quality of well-placed notes and chords rather than with technical virtuosity. After a brief year of retirement, Evans formed a second trio with bassist Eddie Gomez and drummer Marty Morell. The trio stayed together for nine years, during which Evans was involved with a drug habit; he was apparently cured in the mid-'70s. His health began to seriously decline by the late '70s, and he died in New York in 1980.

His album *Bill Evans with Symphony Orchestra*, recorded in 1965 (Verve 821983), featured classical music of J.S. Bach, Scriabin, Chopin, Fauré, and Granados, arranged and conducted by Claus Ogerman. Two compositions by Evans, "Time Remembered" and "My Bell," were also included as jazz pieces. This album thoroughly reveals Evans' controlled explorations of the keyboard. *The Bill Evans Album*, recorded in 1971 (Columbia 30855), featured him on both acoustic and electric piano with his second trio. In "Funkalero" he moves from acoustic to electric within the composition, while his classic tunes "Waltz for Debby" (his niece) and "Two Lonely People" are recorded on the acoustic piano. His great sensitivity and intellectual approach shine brightly throughout the album.

Study Guide: Bill Evans

Recordings

"Blue in Green"—Bill Evans Trio.
SCCJ (record side 13, cassette side I, CD V). Recorded in 1959.

Personnel
Bill Evans—piano/arranger,
Scott LaFaro—bass, Paul Motian—drums.

Musical Characteristics
This is an example of Evans' early work with his first trio. The composition features the interplay of the trio in a 10-measure structure. His voicing of chords, which was particularly admired by Miles Davis, is charac-

terized by playing on the top of or above the chords to release new voicing possibilities and create harmonic energy. The other lyric and introspective qualities of his playing are also quite evident.

Musical Form
Slow ballad

1. Slow theme is introduced by piano with a searching chordal style; bass plays the roots of the chords and the drummer uses light brushes on cymbals in twos.
2. Melody remains quite simple in a lyric style on piano, with occasional hints of double-time in the rhythm.
3. Chordal treatment by the piano gives space to the bass lines underneath the harmonic structure.
4. Melodic line continues in a more active rhythmic role that doubles the time in fours.
5. Drums begin more active brush work before giving way to the original slow tempo in twos.
6. Slow melodic treatment continues, with more openings for the bass.
7. Original melody slows down (ritard), with breaks in the rhythm, and the piano improvising gentle runs to the end.

Flugelhorn Masters

The flugelhorn had become a natural doubling instrument for jazz trumpet soloists during the '60s. Shorty Rogers had used the flugelhorn almost exclusively during the '50s and Miles Davis had played it on occasion. Two trumpet players who began to use the instrument more extensively were Clark Terry and Art Farmer. Pictured in figure 14.1 are the flugelhorn and the trumpet.

The trumpet and flugelhorn are both pitched in Bb because they are exactly the same length when uncurled. The trumpet has a much brighter and lighter tone because its tubing is of a smaller bore, or diameter. From the mouthpiece pipe the trumpet begins with approximately 2/3 of cylindrical boring and extends 1/3 conical boring to the bell end. The added cylindrical tubing provides a much smaller opening into which the player must blow, thus producing great resistance, or "backing up," of the air blown into the horn. On the other hand the flugelhorn produces a dark, mellow sound because its tubing is of a much larger bore. From mouthpiece pipe to bell end it is 100% conical, growing consistently larger from the very small mouthpiece bore to the very open, flared, bell. This conical pattern reduces the resistance for the player and results in a quick expansion of the air. See figure 14.2 for a comparison chart of the two instruments.

Figure 14.1: The Trumpet *(top)* and Flugelhorn

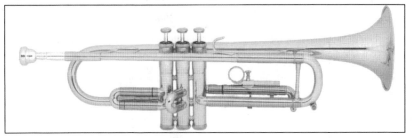

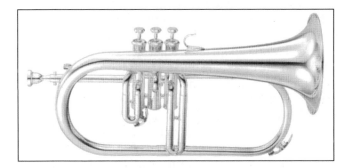

Art Farmer

Art Farmer, who was born in Council Bluffs, Iowa, in 1928, was raised in Phoenix, Arizona. He began playing trumpet and went to Los Angeles, where he worked with Horace Henderson and Floyd Ray in 1945. Coming to New York City in 1947–48, Farmer free-lanced briefly before returning to the West Coast with Benny Carter. He joined Lionel Hampton in 1952, toured Europe in 1953, and settled in New York City on his return. In 1956 Farmer joined Horace Silver, then played with Gerry Mulligan in 1958. In 1959 he and tenorman Benny Golson formed their own group, the Jazztet, and began a long association. Since switching to flugelhorn, Farmer's style has changed to a cooler West Coast sound with a very lyrical tone. A good example of his work in 1963 is the album *Interaction* (Atlantic 1412), by the Art Farmer Quartet, featuring guitarist Jim Hall. Farmer's rendition of "Days of Wine and Roses" is a true indication of his flugelhorn style.

Clark Terry

Clark Terry was born in St. Louis, Missouri, in 1920 and began as a valve-trombone player in high school. He played trumpet with the Navy Band at Great Lakes naval base, near Chicago, in 1942–45. Following the service he played with Lionel Hampton, George Hudson, Charlie Barnet, Eddie Vin-

Figure 14.2: Comparison Chart

Trumpet	Flugelhorn
1. pitched in B♭, six feet of tubing	1. pitched in B♭, six feet of tubing
2. three valves	2. three valves
3. small bore: 2/3 cylindrical; 1/3 conical	3. larger bore: 100% conical
4. produces bright tones with much resistance	4. produces darker, mellow tones with little resistance

son, and Charlie Ventura, before joining Count Basie in 1948. Beginning in 1951 he played with Duke Ellington, and left in 1959 to join Quincy Jones. In 1960 he became a member of the NBC staff band in New York City, where he was a fixture on Johnny Carson's "Tonight Show" band. Clark began to play flugelhorn more regularly as a natural doubling instrument, using a routine of trading phrases with himself, alternating playing the flugelhorn in his right hand and the trumpet in his left hand. Terry is also known for his "Mumbles" routine in which he scats the blues in a very humorous style and plays a growling plunger on the trumpet.

Unlike Farmer's, Terry's trumpet and flugelhorn playing is bop-oriented, in the style of Dizzy Gillespie and Clifford Brown. His style features a joyous sound with many ornamentations, called *turns* or *appogiaturas.* Terry's sound and improvisational style are easily recognizable and distinctive. During the '60s he teamed with valve trombonist Bobby Brookmeyer to produce two albums: *Tonight* (Mainstream 56043) and *The Power of Positive Swinging* (Mainstream 6054). On the latter album he can be heard trading solos with himself in four-bar phrases in "Green Stamps" with muted trumpet and flugelhorn. His "Ode to a Flugelhorn" on the same album is an example of his superb flugel style, with ebullient vibrato trills, and ornamentations in an up-tempo bop style. Clark Terry has been very active recently with the International Association of Jazz Educators.

Study Guide

Recording

Jazz of the '60s (Vee Jay VJS2-1008).
Features recordings and performances of many of the great jazz artists of the '60s: Art Blakey, Buddy DeFranco, Barry Harris Trio, Yusef Lateef, Lee Morgan Quintet, Eddie Harris Quintet, Wayne Shorter Quintet, Billy Taylor Trio, Buddy Collette Orchestra, Woody Herman Herd, Afro Blues Quintet, Wynton Kelly Trio, Pat Britt Quintet, Leroy Vinnegar Trio, Paul Chambers Sextet, Victor Feldman Quartet, Don Randi, Coleman Hawkins, Gene Ammons, Frank Foster, Frank Wess, Cannonball Adderley, Freddie Hubbard, and others. See figure 14.3 for a comparison chart of styles of the '60s.

Figure 14.3: Comparison Chart
Styles of the '60s

	Third Stream	Free Jazz	Fusion	Mainstream
Instruments	acoustic	acoustic, percussive	electric	acoustic
Forms	classical, jazz	free, open soloist	free, open extended	bop form tradition
Solos	classical, bop, blues	free, open collective	free, open collective	bop style tradition
Melody	original, standards	original	original	original standards
Harmony	classical and jazz tradition	modern, avant garde, experimental	textures, tonal clusters,	bop style tradition
Rhythm	classical and jazz tradition	preset, free	electronic vamps	swing style

Video

Bill Evans on the Creative Process
Rhapsody Films; 20 min.
This is a rare closeup of the great pianist Bill Evans, with an introduction by Steve Allen. The film is directed by Louis Cavrell with a mid–'60s look at the pianist in black and white. Evans demonstrates the jazz process, performing "Star Eyes" from basic melody to conclusion. He also plays several other compositions with his famous introspective style, and is assisted by his brother Harry Evans with a discussion on jazz education.

Ornette: Made in America
COD; 80 min.
Directed by Shirley Clarke, this is an award-winning film on the rhythms, images, and myths of America as seen by Ornette. The film traces his life from his beginnings with his blues background in Depression–era Texas to his triumphant return to his home town, Fort Worth. Weaving in and out of performances, this film captures the artist in a profound and provocative portrait.

PART VII

Jazz in the '70s

CHAPTER FIFTEEN

FUSION

New directions in jazz were spearheaded by extensive experimentation with new electric instruments. The 1970s produced two new styles of jazz that were termed *fusion* and *Jazz-Rock* both of which had been set in motion by the late '60s. Don Ellis, a great big band innovator and trumpet player, was one of the first musicians to use electrified instruments with great success. His constant experimentation produced numerous albums which were completely different from one another. Miles Davis began electrified musical experiments for CBS in the studio at this same time, resulting in startling effects.

The Moog synthesizer, invented by Robert Moog, caused quite a sensation in New York. The Moog synthesizer was used to reproduce music of the great Baroque masters, before being discovered by jazz musicians. Furthermore, the free jazz movement in the '60s had encouraged a more daring approach to instrumental innovations. Mainstream jazz continued on a strong path with a variety of showcase albums featuring established jazz stars such as Freddie Hubbard, Stan Getz, Kenny Burrell, and Bill Evans being highlighted by arrangements of Don Sebesky, Eddie Sauter, Gil Evans, and Claus Ogerman, to name but a few. For the mainstream community, the strong tradition of hard bop continued and the sophistication of the third stream movement produced indelible musical effects not only on individual musicians, but on composers and arrangers as well. The general trend of smaller groups continued, yet several big bands established a foothold in the '70s.

It was during this period that a diversity of opinions was created within the jazz ranks concerning instruments. The new electrified instruments offered fuzz phasers for guitars and basses, electric pianos, and clavinets, as well as ring modulators and echoplexes for wind instruments. Many established jazz musicians were firmly entrenched with the acoustic instruments, and rejected these new electrical instruments on the assumption that the electric effects had begun to supplant the natu-

ral talent inherent with acoustic instruments and musicians. The battle
that raged between players of electric and acoustic instruments during
the '70s was reminiscent of the way the third stream movement had
shocked many 1960s music audiences who were not used to hearing classical and jazz music at the same sitting. One result of the '60s controversy
was that a host of workshop leaders such as Stan Kenton began to introduce jazz as a staple in the curricula of many colleges.

Jazz musicians began to yield to the pressures of their respective recording companies, which were much like the pressures Miles Davis felt
from Columbia in the late '60s. Commercial appeals lured many musicians to cross over and compete with jazz-rock performers who were
reaching big numbers in record sales. It might be added that some musicians were tired of dwelling in the shadows of relative obscurity and poverty. There is a fine line between musicians who cannot sacrifice their
musical ideals at any cost and those who have developed an open-minded
approach to popular considerations. Although there was a wide-open gap
between these two groups in the '70s, musicians during the '80s have
closed this chasm in hopes of retaining jazz integrity in electric music.

Many of the popular forms of electric jazz have confused the public
in the '80s as to the real intention and meaning of this music. Indeed, the
term *jazz* has become increasingly confusing, and perhaps outdated.
There is a journalistic trend towards numerous classifications and trends
in an attempt to define all music. *Down Beat* magazine was once devoted
to musicians of purely jazz styles. That has changed drastically, to the dis-
may of many readers, to include reviews and advertisements of groups
and performers who have little to do with jazz. Branford Marsalis, the brilliant young saxophonist, is a case in point. His background is solidly
grounded in mainstream jazz, but he has collaborated with such pop stars
as Sting. The magazine *Jazziz* features these departments: Fission, Outside In, Traditions, Brazilian, Cosmopolitan, Contempo, Blues and
Rhythm, Academics, Video, and Radio Active. This is quite an array of
styles since 1970.

Chick Corea—The Early Years

Born in Chelsea, Massachusetts, on June 11, 1942, Anthony Armando
(Chick) Corea began playing piano at age four. His musical development
was strongly influenced and encouraged by his father. Chick grew up listening to the classical masters, and became influenced by the recordings
of Bud Powell, Charlie Parker, Lester Young, and Horace Silver. His early
work as a sideman for Willie Bobo, Cal Tjader, Herbie Mann, and Mongo
Santamarie greatly influenced his continuous love for Latin music. He
joined the Miles Davis band in 1968 and later played with the avant garde

group Circle, which reflected the strong free jazz movement of Ornette Coleman and Paul Bley.

Chick's pioneering spirit has placed him at the forefront of musical development during the '70s and '80s. Like many keyboard musicians he began his career with the acoustic piano; he switched to electric piano while with Miles Davis in 1968. The 1969 recordings *In a Silent Way* and *Bitches Brew* showcased his talent on electric keyboards. Corea went on to form Return To Forever, with bassist Stanley Clarke, and experimented successfully with the mini-Moog, which was the most technologically advanced synthesizer of the '70s. His early recordings were acoustically based music with heavy Brazilian and Spanish rhythms featuring Brazilian vocalist Flora Purim, Airto Moreira on drums, and reedman Joe Farrell. Return to Forever turned to jazz fusion with drummer Lenny White and guitarist Bill Connors. Later, with Al DiMeola replacing Connors, the band produced such award-winning albums as *Where Have I Known You Before, No Mystery,* and *Romantic Warrior.*

Study Guide: Return to Forever

Recordings

"Hymn of the Seventh Galaxy"—Return to Forever.
Hymn of the Seventh Galaxy (Polydor 825336). Recorded in 1973.

Personnel
Chick Corea—keyboards,
Stanley Clarke—electric bass,
Bill Conners—electric guitar,
Lenny White—drums, percussion

Musical Characteristics
This is one of the earliest examples of a pure fusion style by Return To Forever. The innovations of acid rock, as exhibited by Jimi Hendrix in the late '60s, are used by Bill Conners, supported by the heavy rock back-beat of Lenny White. Although Corea had not begun using the mini-Moog synthesizer, his knowledge of existing electronic keyboards on this album enabled him to demonstrate his innovative techniques, which were not dependent exclusively on electronic effects.

1. Begins with synthesized effects.
2. Guitar, bass, and electric piano play a furious rock melody in unison, to a steady rock beat.
3. Organ and rock drums begin middle section.

4. Switch to electric piano, with electric guitar playing. Hendrix free-style rock solo on top, later joined by drums.
5. Return to opening unison theme.

Video

Chick Corea
Sony; 60 min.
This tape is a reunion concert by former members of Return to Forever, with Stanley Clarke on bass, Joe Henderson on sax, Lenny White on drums, and Corea on keyboards. Selections include "L's Bop," "Why Wait," "500 Miles High," and "Guernica." Highly recommended but not currently available is the video shot in London, 1974, featuring music from Corea's Grammy Award winner *Romantic Warrior*.

Weather Report

It seems almost paradoxical that yet another great fusion band would spring up from the seeds planted by the *Bitches Brew* sessions. While Chick Corea had gone on to form Return To Forever, John McLaughlin, the gifted guitarist, assembled the Mahavishnu Orchestra. Meanwhile, Joe Zawinul and Wayne Shorter went on from the earth-shaking Miles Davis electric band to form Weather Report. Their collaboration as composers and musicians continued for fourteen years, with a top-selling album every year.

Joe Zawinul was born in 1932 in Vienna, Austria, where he studied at the Vienna Conservatory of Music from age seven. As a gifted keyboard player performing on several instruments, he was featured with Austria's leading bands. He came to the United States in 1959, where he toured with Maynard Ferguson for eight months. After leaving Ferguson, he had various club dates with Slide Hampton and Dinah Washington. His most notable tenure was with Cannonball Adderley where he composed "Mercy, Mercy, Mercy." After leaving Adderley in the late '60s, he joined Miles Davis on several sessions, including *In a Silent Way*, for which he composed the title track, and *Bitches Brew*.

Wayne Shorter, a tenor saxophone player and composer, was also weaned on early mainstream jazz. He was born in Newark, New Jersey, in 1933, and studied music education at New York University for four years. After a stint in the Army (1956–58), during which he also worked with Horace Silver, he came to New York City joining the bands of Maynard Ferguson and then Art Blakey. He received a call to play in the second great Miles Davis band in 1964, and remained with Davis throughout the *Bitches Brew* recordings. He is a very important composer of such mainstream standards as "Footprints," "E.S.P.," "Speak No Evil," "Children of the Night," and "Nefertiti," among many others.

Study Guide: Weather Report (to 1976)

Recordings

"Second Sunday in August"—Weather Report.
I Sing the Body Electric (Columbia 46107). Recorded in 1972.

Personnel
Josef Zawinul—electric and acoustic piano/composer,
Wayne Shorter—reeds,
Eric Gravatt—drums,
Dom Um Romao—percussion,
Miroslav Vitous—bass.

Musical Characteristics
This selection was chosen to serve as a comparison to Return To Forever in the development of fusion in 1972. The musical approach here is based on collective improvisation and continuous vamps. A very interesting technique is the various percussion implements which are added and subtracted throughout to preserve rhythmical interest. "Boogie Woogie Waltz," from another 1972 album, *Sweetnighter,* is yet another example of this rhythmic variation.

Musical Form
1. Begins with synthesized effects.
2. Vamp kicks in, with soprano sax freely improvising a fragmented theme above a modal keyboard and ground bass in free form that changes key almost immediately.
3. Various rhythmic instruments are freely added and subtracted throughout, with free collective interplay between the piano and soprano sax as they state melodic fragments.
4. Vamp continues throughout, and dissipates in a rhythm instrument fade-out.

Video

The Evolutionary Spiral—Weather Report
Sony; 15 min.
A dazzling multi-media montage with visuals that take the viewer on a journey through time from the birth of the universe into a vision of the future with music.

Jaco Pastorius

Born in 1951, Jaco entered Weather Report, with drummer Peter Erskine, in 1976. The young and gifted Pastorius sent fusion-style electric bass playing to new heights with his incredible technique, while impressing many of the younger bass players throughout the country. He is remembered also for his compositions "Teen Town" and the bass solo "Slang" in the Weather Report album *Heavy Weather*. His album, *Jaco Pastorius* (CBS 33949) showed that he had enhanced his abilities not only in single notes, but also on chords, textures, and other surprising nuances. Pastorius was greatly influenced by the electronic devices and techniques used by Jimi Hendrix, such as feedback and distortion. Jaco redefined the role of the bass player by expanding himself into a multi-dimensional soloist as well as timekeeper in many styles. He constantly experimented in every jazz style, carefully exploring each form. His *funk* style was a perfect complement to the early influence of guitarist John McLaughlin, who also redefined the funk-rock style into the jazz language. The successful combination of all these styles and innovative techniques helped give definition to fusion. This daring bass guitar virtuoso was able to execute incredible musical figures never thought possible on the instrument. He was the perfect musical foil for Joe Zawinul on keyboards, setting off many new unexplored musical directions.

His presence in Weather Report helped propel the group to even greater musical achievements. Unfortunately, this troubled young man who dared bare his soul was tragically murdered in 1987.

Study Guide: Weather Report (after 1976)

Recordings

"Teen Town"—Weather Report.
Heavy Weather (Columbia 34418). Recorded in 1977.

Personnel
Joe Zawinul—keyboards,
Wayne Shorter—soprano sax,
Jaco Pastorius—electric bass/composer,
Peter Erskine—drums.

Musical Characteristics
This composition by Pastorius is an excellent example not only of his melodic gifts on electric bass, but also of a more sophisticated approach to jazz fusion by the group. The interplay of solo fragments is well-placed around each theme. The extended soprano sax solo is showcased by the electric bass in the last half of the composition. Most of the piece is built

on thirteenth chords, and demonstrates the practice in fusion of using synthesized keyboards to assume the responsibilities of the bass line while the bass player becomes more melodically oriented.

Musical Forms
1. Begins with a percussion vamp.
2. Opening theme features electric bass in medium-tempo funk style, using double-time.
3. Repeat of the opening bass theme, joined by soprano sax with fragmented interplay.
4. Soprano sax introduces main theme, with bass and synthesizer using collective improvisation.
5. Vamp continues, with open soprano sax solo backed by bass and synthesizer until abrupt ending.

Video

Modern Electric Bass—Jaco Pastorius
DCI; 90 min.
This instructional video provides an excellent insight into Jaco's technique and approach to playing. Includes a twenty-minute performance with Kenwood Dennard and John Scofield. Jaco reveals his bass technique and approach to playing in an interview with Jerry Jemmott. He explains in detail his ideas about right and left hand techniques, harmonies, scales, and arpeggios. He performs his own composition "Portrait of Tracey," and plays several solos and an electric bass duet with Jemmott. A detailed book is included for those who play bass and wish to play along with the tape. Highly recommended, particularly for Jaco fans!

CHAPTER SIXTEEN

JAZZ-ROCK

In the late '60s a popular media change led to a more progressive view of rock. Many jazz musicians were drawn to this new attitude, which became commercially feasible. Musicians such as Quincy Jones, Miles Davis, Herbie Hancock, Chick Corea, Don Ellis, Maynard Ferguson, and George Benson had broken this barrier between rock and jazz, and rock was generally accepted as a creative endeavor with great public interest. Recording companies began to put much pressure on their jazz artists to reflect this new progressive view of rock, in order to sell more records. One of the most notable rock groups to use jazz horns was Blood, Sweat and Tears. Their style, which was similar to Chicago Transit Authority, or CTA, presented more of a *rock-jazz* style, which is to say that limited horn improvisations and jazz styles were used to support these primarily vocal rock groups. CTA later changed its name to Chicago. This influence on rock helped boost the musicianship of most rock musicians. Albums such as *The Child Is Father to the Man* by Blood, Sweat and Tears (Columbia 09619) employed jazz trumpeter Randy Brecker, while another jazz trumpet player, Lew Soloff, appeared on *Blood, Sweat and Tears* (Columbia 09720).

John McLaughlin, an English guitarist, began his career as a very successful jazz guitar player with Miles. After he left the Davis band he formed the Mahavishnu Orchestra, in 1972, which played several converging styles of music. McLaughlin combined powerful hard-rock rhythms on electric guitar and traditional Eastern Indian music on acoustic guitar. Compare his 1972 recording *The Inner Mounting Flame* (Columbia 31067) with a modern *New Age* group Shadowfax's 1988 album *Folk Songs for a Nuclear Village* (Capitol 7469242). Notice the use of Eastern modal melodies extended over vamps that are supported by exotic rhythm and wind instruments as well as by basic hard rock rhythms. Much of this exotic style is now being used by New Age groups in the late '80s and early '90s.

Herbie Hancock, a pianist, was another jazz musician who bridged the gap between jazz and rock with an electric funk style in his album *Headhunter* (Columbia 32731). Hancock passed through the ranks of the

second great Miles Davis band between 1963 and 1968, with great improvisational ability on both electric and acoustic keyboards. Classics
such as "Watermelon Man," "Canteloupe Island," "Maiden Voyage,"
and "Dolphin Dance" are modal pieces by Hancock that are considered
jazz standards. Yet another representative of the jazz-rock school was
Carlos Santana, who blended Latin music with rock and funk. After moving to the West Coast from Mexico, he established his reputation in the
late '60s and later joined John McLaughlin in the mid-'70s.

The effects of jazz-rock were far-reaching:

1. The influence of jazz musicians elevated the abilities of rock musicians in every aspect of music.
2. Electronic instruments came into general use.
3. The commercial value of jazz was more readily accepted by the general public, raising interest levels.

Rock and Jazz Styles

Early classic rock in the '50s drew much inspiration from *rhythm and
blues* and *country music* traditions. The Bill Haley hit, "Rock Around the
Clock," was in a blues form with a basic jazz rhythm. The drums played a
swing beat in 4/4, with a walking bass (see figure 16.1), and the vocals
were supported by lead guitar and boogie-type piano. The guitar solo in
"Rock Around the Clock" was very much like the rhythm and blues deri-
vation of boogie woogie. Harmonically, the entire form was set to the traditional blues.

Figure 16.1: Blues in C "Walking Bass"

Many of the bass lines were given to the electric bass in the early stages
of rock and roll. On the drum set, as in jazz, the left hand played snare and

left foot played hi-hat cymbals, providing beats 2 and 4. The right foot played the bass drum on beats 1 and 3, with the right hand playing the ride cymbal. This is an explanation of the most basic form of rhythm. Jazz drummers use much less bass drum on the beat, instead relying on it for accents called "bombs." Try the exercise below by tapping these various drum rhythms while sitting in a chair with your feet squarely on the floor and the palms of your hands on your knees (see figure 16.2).

Figure 16.2: Drum Set "Early Rock"

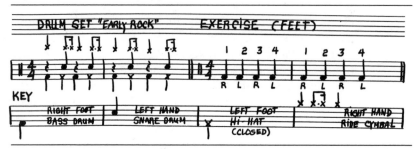

You might want to hum or scat the melody of "Rock Around the Clock" to get the initial feeling of the tempo (see figure 16.3):

Figure 16.3: "Rock Around the Clock"

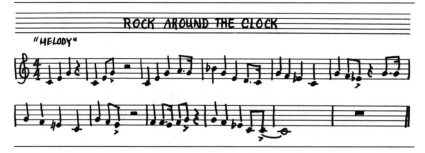

1. First, try the rhythm with your feet by tapping your right foot down on beats 1 and 3, and alternating your left foot down on beats 2 and 4.

4/4	R	L	R	L	/	R	L	R	L
	1	2	3	4		1	2	3	4

2. Next, add your left hand to the rhythm by tapping your left knee at the same time as your left foot on beats 2 and 4.

3. Last, add your right hand on your right knee for the accents on beats 1 and 3 with the ride cymbal.

By doing this simple rhythm exercise, you will have a good idea of the great amount of coordination between the hands and feet that are necessary for a good drummer. Although we are stripping this rhythm to its barest essentials, you can add fills at the end of each phrase or verse, which fall at the end of each fourth measure and particularly the final twelfth measure of each chorus. A fill is simply a short improvised rhythm or accent that serves as a musical punctuation mark to end one phrase and begin another.

Since the early '50s, rock drummers have taken on rhythmic characteristics that are now quite different from straight-ahead jazz styles. The modern rock rhythm is the style adopted by jazz drummers to play the basic jazz-rock pattern. One of the biggest changes in the modern rock rhythm is with the drummer. The modern rock drummer more or less dominates the beat with heavy accents in the bass drum. To accentuate this bass drum effect, many rock drummers began removing the front head of the bass drum or cutting a hole in the middle of the head, and placing padding inside the drum to produce a more explosive and heavy drum blow with less ring.

One of the biggest differences between modern rock and jazz is that while rock is vertically accented, jazz is more spread out in a horizontal pattern. This is one of the reasons that jazz-rock big bands didn't really sound like rock and roll bands. Rhythms of modern jazz stylists are much more complex and quick-changing, depending on musical finesse, while modern rock is a much more basic, heavy approach with less variation in rhythms.

Try the modern rock beat (see figure 16.4) as an exercise, sitting in the chair as you did earlier. Notice the dominance of the bass drum with the right foot. Figure 16.5, a comparison chart of Rock and Jazz, provides an overview of the differences between the two styles.

Figure 16.4: Drum Set "Modern Rock"

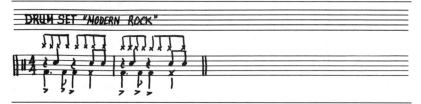

Big Band Jazz-Rock

Two big band veterans who had established their careers in jazz were Don Ellis and Maynard Ferguson. They both led big bands with albums representing the strong jazz-rock craze.

Figure 16.5: Comparison Chart
Rock and Jazz

Rock	Jazz
1. Depends on high levels of volume for effect.	1. More use of contrast levels
2. Rhythmic approach is vertical and static.	2. Rhythmic approach is varied and horizontal.
3. Melody is usually dominated by vocals.	3. Melody is usually dominated by instruments.
4. Structure is based on simple songs.	4. Structure is varied and usually expanded.
5. Chord progressions are simple.	5. Chord progressions are complex and extended.
6. Most melodic and solo material is planned.	6. Improvisation plays an important role in solos.
7. Music is intended for recreational use.	7. Music is intended more as a pure art form.
8. Much more commercial.	8. Much less commercial.

Don Ellis (1934–1978) was a creative giant who passed away at the age of forty-four as a result of a congenital heart condition. His contributions to jazz were truly enormous. The use of odd and exotic meters or time signatures go back to his days at UCLA, where he studied Indian rhythms in the early '60s and created the Hindustani Orchestra, which employed three drummers and three string basses. As a trumpet player he was one of the first to use a four-valved trumpet to play quarter tones, and ring modulator, echoplex, and phase shifter for special effects.

Don Ellis at Fillmore (Columbia G30243), 1970, was one of his follow-ups to *Electric Bath* and extended his experiments with odd meters, as in Hank Levy's chart, "Rock Odyssey," which begins in slow 7/4 meter, with the middle section in 12/8, divided 2-2-3, 2-3. The Fillmore album, which was recorded live, also expanded Ellis' use of the ring modulator and echoplex amplifying devices. His band, composed of five woodwinds, eight brass, and six rhythm, produced some hair-raising results, dipping into the rock and free form solo styles. On the contrary, Ellis's early 1971 album *Tears of Joy* (Columbia G30927) used a string quartet in addition to regular big band instrumentation, with French horn and tuba to fill out the brass voicings. The shifts of musical mood in this album vary from a very somber piece, "Tears," to a highly euphoric "Strawberry Soup."

A good example of the pure jazz-rock idiom big band style of Ellis is *Connection* (Columbia KC 31766), recorded in 1972. See figure 16.6 for a comparison chart of Jazz-Rock and Jazz-Fusion.

Ellis continued using the four valved quarter-tone trumpet that he had introduced in *Electric Bath*. His band was again expanded on *Connec-*

Figure 16.6: Comparison Chart
Jazz-Rock and Jazz-Fusion

Jazz-Rock	Jazz-Fusion
1. More commercial, using arrangements of popular music	1. More original music, less commercial
2. Use of large bands as well as small groups	2. Usually small bands
3. Limited improvisation	3. Free use of improvisation
4. Traditional use of musical elements	4. Experimentation in musical elements
5. Rhythms and forms are steady throughout	5. Rhythms and forms change frequently to extensions

tion to include a woodwind quartet that doubled on at least four instruments; a trumpet quartet that doubled on flugelhorns; a lower brass quartet; two keyboards; guitar and bass; four percussion; and an electrified string quartet. His imaginative use of all these instruments and electronic devices testify to his genius in his own "Theme from The French Connection" and the odd-metered arrangement of the popular rock tunes "Roundabout," "Superstar," "I Feel the Earth Move," "Conquistador," "Lean on Me," and "Train to Get There." Don Ellis was one of the true musical forces in the '70s.

Maynard Ferguson

Maynard Ferguson, whose background and credits have been discussed in chapter 12, began playing jazz rock in the '70s. He maintained this style until 1990, when he shifted back to a bop style. His musical preoccupation with jazz-rock styles are reflected in the CBS albums *Primal Scream, Conquistador, Carnival,* and *Chameleon.* His renderings of famous soundtrack themes such as "Gonna Fly Now" from "Rocky" and the main title theme from the television series "Star Trek" are by now legendary.

Study Guide: Maynard Ferguson

Recordings

M. F. Horn/M. F. Horn Two.
Maynard Ferguson (Columbia 33660). Recorded in 1972.

Personnel
Maynard Ferguson—trumpet, flugelhorn, valve trombone,
John Donnelly, Martin Drover, Alan Downey, Mike Bailey, Bud Parks—
    trumpets

Billy Graham, Adrian Drover, Norman Fripp, Derek Wadsworth—
    trombones
Jeff Daly, Brian Smith, Bob Sydor, Bob Watson, Stan Robinson—saxes
Randy Jones—drums
Dave Lynane—bass/bass guitar
Pete Jackson—piano/electric piano
Ray Cooper, Harold Fisher—percussion

Musical Characteristics
The *M. F. Horn Two* album is a fine example of big band jazz rock. Listen
to any of the selections, particularly the theme from "Shaft," and notice
the strong rock beats from the rhythm section that support jazz-flavored
writing for the sax and brass sections, as well as jazz improvisations on
wind solos. The rhythm section instruments usually solo in a rock format.

CHAPTER SEVENTEEN

MAINSTREAM JAZZ

The trend of mainstream jazz produced few standard big bands through-out the '70s in addition to the traditional forces led by Duke Ellington and Count Basie. Newer aggregations were led by Stan Kenton, Woody Herman, Buddy Rich, Maynard Ferguson, and Thad Jones and Mel Lewis. The great New York City-based Jones-Lewis Band began as a rehearsal band for studio musicians on Monday evenings in Greenwich Village, and developed into one of the most formidable ensembles for over twenty years. With the passing of Thad Jones and then Mel Lewis the band has maintained its reputation not only as a sit-in haven, but with many impressive performances in the U.S. and abroad. The band's tightly knit ensemble format produces an unusually clean sound that is also combo-oriented, with outstanding soloists and arrangers.

The Thad Jones/Mel Lewis album *Consummation* (Blue Note BST 84346), recorded in 1970, is a fine example of a big band in the main-stream style, with balanced contrasts of volume, texture, and tonal color. This band featured a broad base of musicians such as Marvin Stamm and Snooky Young on trumpets; Pepper Adams on baritone saxophone; Howard Johnson on tuba; and Thad Jones on flugelhorn, with Mel Lewis on drums. All of the tunes on this album were composed or arranged by Thad Jones, and show great sensitivity in straight-ahead jazz. The music ranges from the beautiful ballad "A Child Is Born," featuring Jones, to the exciting up-tempo tune "Us." This collection of compositions is definitely not intended for dancing, but for the serious jazz listener. Many school bands have used these pieces as building blocks for advanced musical conceptions in the big band arena. Their educational value was promoted by Kendor Music Publishers.

Although much of the big band tradition was declining due to the new jazz-rock idiom, Herman, Rich, Basie, and Jones/Lewis still maintained bands, each somewhat stylistically different. Buddy Rich had gone through several personnel changes in the '70s with mixed results until recording his "West Side Story Medley" live on the West Coast, which again thrust him into the spotlight of leading straight-ahead bands.

Bernard "Buddy" Rich was born in Brooklyn in 1917 and began his career as a drummer and singer as part of his parent's performances at the age of eighteen months. His jazz career began in 1938 with Joe Marsala and continued as a drummer for Bunny Berigan, Artie Shaw, Tommy Dorsey, and Benny Carter. He formed his own band and also made tours with Jazz at the Philharmonic; he appeared with small groups during the '50s and led his own group in New York City in the '60s. He was a frequent television guest on the "Johnny Carson Show." As he left the combo scene to form another big band, he became a standard-bearer of the modern swinging big band sound. Although his book (arrangements) included the works of many different arrangers, his incredible drumming was always a focal point of his band. Buddy, who died in 1987, is to be remembered as one of the most prolific drummers the jazz world has ever seen and heard. He could kick a big band with powerful explosions while executing incomparable hand speed that produced photogenic "overexposures" in live performances with quick, rudimental sticking like a machine gun.

Although Maynard Ferguson had committed himself to the more popular jazz-rock style, he occasionally featured some of his earlier *Newport* and *Birdland* straight-ahead charts. The music of Woody Herman's 1973 band from *Giant Steps* (Fantasy 9432), became available to school bands and became symbols of the great modern big band. This was true also in the case of Count Basie, whose tunes, arranged by Sammy Nestico, were served as models of good taste for teaching the elements of proper swing rhythms with the walking bass and right hand fills on the piano.

Stan Kenton's fame diminished greatly after his failure with the Los Angeles Neophonic Orchestra in 1967, and Kenton passed away in 1979. His late influence in bringing jazz to academic circles was one of his most important contributions in establishing jazz as a serious discipline. Among his credits in the early '70s are *Live at the Redlands* (Creative World 1015) in 1970, *Live at Brigham Young* (Creative World 1039) in 1971; and *Live at Butler University* (Creative World 1058) in 1972. Throughout his career Kenton stressed composition rather than improvised solos, unlike Woody Herman. Also unlike Basie or Herman, Kenton went through many musical changes with influences of Afro-Cuban, third stream, avant garde, and classical styles. Although he introduced great soloists such as Maynard Ferguson, his music was more oriented to a concert approach that featured his arrangers and composers.

Another big band that approached the sophisticated ensemble style of Jones/Lewis in the '70s was the Toshiko Akiyoshi-Lew Tabackin Band. The gifted Japanese composer Akiyoshi began writing big band charts that dwelled on subtle construction with many varied nuances. She featured her husband Lew Tabackin on tenor sax and flute, producing such

award-winning albums as *Insights* and *Kogun*. Her big band style was perhaps more appreciated in Tokyo than in New York, and reflected her
color-conscious approach to harmony and texture which was reminiscent
of Ellington.

The musical evolution that took place in the big bands during the
'70s can best be seen through the bands of Jones/Lewis and Akoyshi/Ta-
backin because of the compositional techniques provided chiefly by one
composer in each band, thus providing an individual style for each group.
The other big bands of the period used many arrangers with varied approaches, producing very general results in terms of traditional swing.
The '70s was clearly not dominated by big bands, but gave way to smaller
groups and soloists who began to assimilate the bop masters or began to
experiment with the new jazz-rock and fusion styles. In this sense two
distinct paths were taken by musicians of this period: Traditional or experimental. Musicians who reflected the jazz-rock and fusion tendencies
began to dress in a style that was influenced by rock and pop culture in
attempts to update their image. The traditionalists preferred the clean
look (suit and tie) as worn by the early beboppers.

In addition to *Giant Steps,* Woody Herman recorded *Thundering
Herds* (Columbia 44108) in 1974. Duke Ellington provided *Togo Brava
Suite* (UAR, UXS 92) in 1972 and Count Basie recorded *Prime Time* (Pablo 2310-797) in 1977. Other big band recordings included the Jones/Le-
wis *Live in Munich* (Horizon Records SP-724) in 1978.

Study Guide: Buddy Rich

Video

Mr. Drums—Buddy Rich and His Band: Channel One Set
Sony; 60 min.

Personnel
Buddy Rich—leader/drums,
Mark Pinto, Steve Marcus, Brian Sjoerdinga, Jay Craig—woodwinds,
Paul Phillips, Eric Miyashiro, Michael Lewis, Joe Kaminski—trumpets
    and flugelhorns,
Scott Bliege, Mike Davis, James Mattin—trombones,
Bill Cunliff—piano, Dave Carpenter—electric bass

Program
 1. "Machine"—soloist: Steve Marcus, tenor sax; arranger: Bill Reddie
 2. "Best Coast"—soloists: Steve Marcus, soprano sax; Scott Bliege,
    trombone; Bill Cunliffe, piano; arranger: John LaBarbero

3. "One O'Clock Jump"—soloists: Bill Cunliff, piano; Steve Marcus, tenor sax; Paul Phillips, trumpet
4. "Sophisticated Lady"—arranger: Bill Holman
5. "Norwegian Wood"—arranger: Bill Holman
6. "Love for Sale"—arranger: Pete Meyers
7. "No Exit"—arranger: Bill Cunliff
8. "Channel One Suite"—soloists: Steve Marcus, tenor sax; Buddy Rich, drums; arranger: Bill Reddie

Study Guide: Woody Herman

Recording

Giant Steps—Woody Herman.
(Fantasy 9432). Recorded in 1973

Personnel
Woody Herman—leader/clarinet and saxes,
Larry Pyatt, Gil Rathel, Walt Blanton, Bill Byrne, Bill Stapleton— trumpets,
Jim Pugh, Geoff Sharp, Harold Garrett—trombones,
Greg Herbert, Frank Tiberi, Steve Lederer, Harry Kleintank— woodwinds,
Andy Laverne—electric piano, Joe Beck—guitar, Wayne Darling—bass, Ed Soph—drums, Ray Baretto—congas

Program
1. "La Fiesta"—soloists: Greg Herbert, piccolo; Andy Laverne, piano; Frank Tiberi, tenor sax; Woody Herman, soprano sax
2. "A Song for You"—soloist: Bill Stapleton, flugelhorn
3. "Freedom Jazz Dance"—soloists: Ed Soph, drums; Steve Lederer, tenor sax
4. "The Meaning of the Blues"—soloist: Jim Pugh, trombone
5. "The First Thing I Do"—soloist: Greg Herbert, tenor sax
6. "Think on Me"—soloist: Greg Herbert, alto flute
7. "Giant Steps"—soloists: Tiberi and Herbert, tenor saxes
8. "A Child Is Born"—soloists: Woody Herman, clarinet; Herbert, tenor sax
9. "Be-bop and Roses"—soloists: Stapleton, Pugh, and Lederer

Small groups were maintained by Chuck Mangione, a flugelhorn player who found much jazz expression in Latin and rock rhythms, with great commercial success. Gary Burton, a gifted vibraharp player, began his career as a vibes sideman for the popular English jazz pianist George

Shearing. Burton then experimented in different styles, collaborating with guitar players Ralph Towner, Larry Coryell, and Pat Metheny. Listen to Burton's duets with pianist Chick Corea on *Crystal Silence* (ECM 831331), 1972. Burton's musical associations extended to violinist Stephane Grappelli and pianists Keith Jarrett and Ahmad Jamal. Another fine album is *Reunion: Gary Burton with Pat Metheny* (GRP 9598) with Mitchell Forman, Will Lee, and Peter Erskine. The versatility of Gary Burton set a very high standard of musical creativity in the '70s. His album *Alone at Last* (Atlantic 1598) won a jazz award in 1972. In 1979 he recorded new collaborations with Chick Corea on *Duet* (Warner Bros. EMC 1-1140).

Other mainstream soloists appeared in the '70s, including Jon Faddis, a young trumpet player born in 1953. He had toured with Dizzy Gillespie and became a disciple of Gillespie. Faddis featured an unbelievable *screech trumpet* style with full control that seemed effortless. He is much like Ferguson with his great strength in the upper register, and is also able to improvise in the bop tradition. Many trumpet players had gained recognition as either strong lead players like the late Conrad Gozzo or as outstanding soloists; rarely were they able to do both. Jon Faddis is an ideal lead man, featured in many albums, and has come into his own as a fine soloist with great versatility. His album *Legacy* (Concord Jazz 291), recorded in 1985, bears testimony to his rise as a soloist. In this album he pays homage to Louis Armstrong with "West End Blues," to Roy Eldridge in "Little Jazz," to Dizzy Gillespie in "Night in Tunisia," and to Thad Jones in "A Child Is Born."

Phil Woods, an alto sax player in the finest mainstream tradition, was born in 1931 and began to emerge in the '70s as a premier soloist in the style of Charlie Parker and Sonny Stitt. His perfection of the bop style is evident in his albums *Live from the Showboat* (RCA BGL 2-2202) in 1976, and *More Live* (Adelphi 5010) in 1979. Many soloists in the mainstream tradition gained wider recognition with outstanding albums in the '70s. Joe Pass, born in 1929, represents the tradition of Bird reflected through the guitar. This great bop guitarist of the '70s and '80s has appeared as a soloist and sideman with the likes of Ella Fitzgerald in *Fitzgerald and Pass* (Pablo 2310-772) in 1976 and many other fine musicians, including fellow guitarist Herb Ellis, trombonist J. J. Johnson, pianist Oscar Peterson, and violinist Stephane Grappelli. The musical maturity of pianist Bill Evans was evident during the '70s with *The Bill Evans Album* (Columbia 30855) in 1971. His style encompassed classical elements combined with modern jazz, resulting in fresh originality. Evans' tunes such as "Waltz for Debby," "Very Early," and the more introspective "Time Remembered" and "Turn Out the Stars" quickly became standards for all aspiring jazz pianists.

Oscar Peterson, born in 1925, is another fine pianist who began to play in a powerful musical style with the drive of Art Tatum and Bud Powell. He is one of the most important figures in the history of jazz on piano. Peterson has been a force in the jazz world since the early days of bop, and plays with a distinct command of the piano. In the '70s Peterson produced albums such as *The Trio* (Pablo 2310-701) in 1974, *Oscar Peterson and Dizzy Gillespie* (Pablo 2310-740) in 1975, *Montreux '77* (Pablo 2308-208), and *Jousts* (Pablo 2310-817), featuring duets with Roy Eldridge, Clark Terry, Dizzy Gillespie, Harry Edison, and Jon Faddis. Peterson recorded an impressive amount of material during his lifetime, and his style is clearly distinguishable, featuring the best qualities of swing and bop.

Just as the '80s produced innumerable artists on the saxophone, the '70s seemed to have produced many fine pianists. The pianist Keith Jarrett, born in 1945, took yet another distinct stylistic path, playing free improvisations in a classical style. As a soloist he created a unique approach to the piano with repeated vamps that were inspired by the early twentieth century French classicists like Ravel and Debussy. His quartet with Dewey Redman on tenor sax, Charlie Haden on bass, and Paul Motian on drums created a distinct approach to jazz from 1971 to 1976. The Jarrett Quartet reflected the styles of Ornette Coleman and Bill Evans. Jarrett's album *Birth* (Atlantic 1612) features his quartet, and his solo style appears on *The Koln Concert* (ECM 810067), recorded in 1975. Jarrett has played acoustic piano exclusively.

Other award-winning artists and recordings during the '70s included a group of five saxophone players called Supersax with the album *Supersax Plays Bird* (Capitol CDP7 962642) in 1973; singer Al Jarreau recorded *Look to the Rainbow* (Warner Bros. 2BZ-3052) in 1977 and *All Fly Home* (BSK-3229) in 1978. Ella Fitzgerald offered *Fine and Mellow* (Pablo 232110) in 1979.

Despite the great surge of interest in electronic instruments and the newer cross-over styles, many musicians were able to develop their art through the heritage of the bebop era. Many artists had come into wider recognition and they were finally becoming visible to the jazz public. It was a difficult period in which to maintain the level of great recordings that dominated the '60s, and certainly signalled the collision of two opposing directions in the jazz world. This collision has resulted in some sharply divided opinions on the subject of what is true jazz art. Attacks of "commercialism" often trailed those of the fusion school, while counterattacks of "antiquated traditionalism" were leveled at the opposite camp. The '70s was a time of musical divergence and retrospection as a result of the experimentation of the late '60s, and would have a clearer meaning in the '80s.

Chuck Mangione

Magione combined rock, funk, and Latin styles with great popular appeal in the '70s. As a sideman of Art Blakey early in his career, Mangione had learned the funk style and was able to dilute it with rock and Latin, thus capturing large record sales. One of his best selling albums was *Feels So Good* (A&M 3219) in 1977. *Land of Make Believe*, recorded earlier in 1973, featured the Mangione Quartet with the Hamilton Philharmonic Orchestra, featuring vocalist Esther Satterfield. With such a large musical palette, the results produced were interesting.

Study Guide: Chuck Mangione
Recordings

"Land of Make Believe"—Chuck Mangione.
Land of Make Believe (Mercury 684, CD 822539-2). Recorded in 1973.

Personnel
Chuck Mangione—leader/flugelhorn,
Gerry Niewood—soprano sax, flutes,
Al Johnson—electric bass,
Joe LaBarbera—drums,
Esther Satterfield—vocals,
The Hamilton Philharmonic Orchestra

Musical Characteristics
This piece represents jazz in one of its most popular forms during the '70s. Many musical elements are woven together to produce a colorful musical tapestry. The use of strings is largely a result of the successful third stream movement in the '60s. Interesting lyrics sung in a fine style by Satterfield reflect cultural and political amenities of the period. Mangione's quartet is successfully integrated into a big band and orchestral setting. The influence of Latin rhythms is evident, with a conga rhythm laced to a jazz style. The strings and French horn calls make for an interesting musical presentation.

The conga rhythm is played by the electric bassist after the second verse has been sung, and continues until the slow ending:

Musical Form
AABA in 4/4

1. Introduction—slow free style vocals, sustained strings.
2. First, second verses—same, accompanied by flugelhorn.
3. Conga rhythm introduced—6 bars in 4/4 by electric bass.
4. Third, fourth verses—AA, vocals continue with conga rhythm.
5. Fifth verse—B theme, or bridge; Sixth verse—A theme.
6. Instrumental chorus—orchestra and big band with flugelhorn solo, bop style.

7. Conga rhythm—returns and diminishes to slow tempo.
8. Seventh verse—vocals in slow tempo, as in the intro.
9. Eighth verse—vocals with spoken lyrics.
10. Conga rhythm—kicks in.
11. Ninth, tenth verses—vocals with conga as before.
12. Eleventh verse—vocals are very high, almost producing a falsetto.
13. Twelfth verse—same as original.
14. Solo—soprano sax with big band for one chorus.
15. Ensemble—orchestra plays fragmented melody with French horns in background; AA theme.
16. Ensemble—big band kicks in on B theme.
17. Ensemble—orchestra plays A theme with saxes background.
18. Conga rhythm—continues.
19. Last verses—sung, like the others, in conga style
20. Ensembles—orchestra and big band combine themes with French horns in background.
21. Coda—slow free style vocals over rhythm, with tag by flugelhorn and wind chimes.

Video

Sass and Brass: A Jazz Session—Sarah Vaughan
Jazzland; 60 min.

This video is a tribute to the late Sarah Vaughan, with many of the fine soloists we have discussed so far. Sarah is featured singing "I Can't Give You Anything but Love" in a scat style, "Just Friends," and her famous rendition of "Send in the Clowns." Don Cherry presents a Monk tune with his pocket trumpet, and sharing the spotlight on trumpets are Maynard Ferguson, Dizzy Gillespie, and Al Hirt, with Chuck Mangione on flugelhorn. Ferguson and Hirt team up on "I Can't Get Started," with Maynard on the vocals. Other musicians showcased are Herbie Hancock, Ron Carter, and Billy Higgins. The session was filmed at the Storyville Jazz Hall in New Orleans and presents a very interesting opportunity to study these musicians and their various styles as they contrast with each other in a rather informal setting. Ferguson and Hirt trade solos in "I Can't Get Started," and unlike the old days, this is no "carving contest." Hirt is firmly entrenched in his classic hometown New Orleans style, while Ferguson is a screamer.

Freddie Hubbard

Freddie Hubbard, born in 1938, was a great trumpet stylist from the hard bop lineage of Dizzy Gillespie, Fats Navarro, and Clifford Brown. His originality of style bore fruition in the late '60s and his influence as a trumpet player was dominating in the '70s. Hubbard's mastery of the trumpet was characterized musically by a beautifully conceived tone combined with a flawless technique. His improvisational style reflected the screaming high note entries of Gillespie and his own trademark of fast lip trills or shakes, producing a series of rapid-fire harmonics on false fingerings. The influence of ornamenting single notes or multiples, called turns, were highly characteristic of Clifford Brown.

Study Guide: Freddie Hubbard

Recordings

"Sky Dive"—Freddie Hubbard.
Sky Dive (Columbia 44171). Recorded in 1972.

Personnel
Freddie Hubbard—trumpet,
Ron Carter—bass,
Billy Cobham—drums,
George Benson—guitar,
Keith Jarrett—piano, electric piano,
Ray Baretto—percussion,
Airto—percussion,
Hubert Laws—flutes,
Alan Rubin, Marvin Stamm—trumpets, flugelhorns,
Wayne Andre, Garnett Brown, Paul Faulise—trombones,
Tony Price—tuba,
Phil Bodner, George Marge, Wally Kane, Romeo Penque—woodwinds,
Don Sebesky, arranger

Musical Characteristics
"Sky Dive" is the title song of a showcase album that featured outstanding jazz soloists highlighted by gifted composers and arrangers. This was very characteristic of mainstream jazz in the '70s and indicated despite the advent of fusion and jazz-rock, mainstream jazz had maintained a healthy tradition.

Musical Form
Medium-tempo Latin-style

1. Introduction—with guitar lead of 8 bars followed by electric piano 8 bars.
2. First chorus—AABA form, with 4-bar extensions at the end of each 16-bar A section. B theme is 16 bars.

3. Second chorus—solo trumpet; Hubbard improvises straight time through A section and double-time on last A section. B section is ornamented, and last A section shows his high-note and lip-slur trademarks.
4. Third chorus—solo guitar, Benson on both A sections, solo flute, Laws on B section, solo electric piano, Jarrett on last A
5. Last chorus—solo trumpet enters B section melody and continues to A with a fade-out vamp under flute trills.

Video

Studio Live—Freddie Hubbard
Sony; 59 min.
An exclusive studio recording session that captures his range of styles and capabilities. Selections include "Hubbard's Cupboard," "Two Moods for Freddie," "This Is It," "Birdland," "Bridgette," and "Condition Alpha."

Freddie Hubbard (*Photo courtesy of Carol Friedman*)

CHAPTER EIGHTEEN

FREE JAZZ

The free jazz movement spearheaded by Ornette Coleman in the '60s continued throughout the '70s and into the '80s. Contrary to traditional mainstream influence, free jazz produced a group of saxophonists who expanded and redefined this direction in jazz. Three tenormen demonstrated a cross-over between mainstream and free jazz that took on different approaches. Pharoah Sanders, Albert Ayler, and Archie Shepp all developed their free jazz styles within traditional African-American lines. The Association For The Advancement of Creative Musicians (AACM), which began in Chicago, was founded in 1965. It was an organization that promoted a new black awareness in modern jazz and used primarily acoustic instruments.

The Art Ensemble of Chicago

The Art Ensemble of Chicago, who were all AACM members, were Lester Bowie on trumpet, Roscoe Mitchell and Joseph Jarman on saxophones, Malachi Favors Maghostut on bass, and drummer Famoudou Don Moye. This group took some of its inspiration from Sun Ra, who is a very creative and modernistic big band leader and composer. Sun Ra's music is highly original and exotic, with on-stage extravaganzas in costume and musical presentation. Ra has used no set instrumentation, unlike other big bands, but has experimented with many instrument doublings and spontaneous improvisation. The Art Ensemble followed the unorthodox musical creations of the Sun Ra Arkestra and were also influenced by Ornette Coleman. Each member demonstrated the ability to play many different instruments, particularly percussion. Their musical approach, like Sun Ra's, was unstructured in the strictest sense, giving freedom to traditional concepts of melody, harmony, rhythm, and form.

World Saxophone Quartet

Another important free jazz group that became prominent in the late '70s was the World Saxophone Quartet. It, too, like the Art Ensemble,

evolved from a musical organization, The Black Artists Group (BAG) in
St. Louis. Unlike the AEC, the WSQ used no rhythm section, and was
made up of saxophonists Oliver Lake and Julius Hemphill on altos, David
Murray on tenor, and Hamiet Bluiett on baritone. They also drew inspiration from Coleman, and achieved a balance between written passages
and improvisation to produce a mixture of modern European classical
masters and black jazz masters. This trend has been continued more recently with Lester Bowie's Brass Fantasy.

Study Guide: World Saxophone Quartet, Sun Ra, and the Art Ensemble of Chicago

Recordings

"Steppin' "—World Saxophone Quartet.
SCCJ (record side 4, cassette side J, CD V). Recorded in 1981.

Personnel
Hamiet Bluiett—alto flute,
Julius Hemphill, Oliver Lake—soprano saxes,
David Murray—bass clarinet.

Musical Characteristics
Like many of the free jazz artists, the WSQ double on various instruments.
In this piece Bluiett plays alto flute instead of baritone sax, Hemphill and
Lake switch from altos to sopranos, and David Murray plays bass clarinet
instead of tenor. The balance between the written thematic material and
freely improvised passages exhibits an uncanny rapport within the group,
with interacting sensitivity and understanding by each member.

Try to identify the written thematic passages played by Murray on
bass clarinet and Bluiett on soprano sax, and distinguish them from the
improvised section. Notice the effect of the combined themes, producing *polyphony*, which is the use of two or more contrasting themes. The
texture produced is enhanced by the absence of a rhythm section.

Video

Sun Ra: A Joyful Noise (film by Robert Mugge).
Jazzland; 60 min.
Sun Ra's approach to the free-spirited movement in jazz is well documented in this film by Mugge. Ra's band, which he calls Ra's Intergalactic
Omniverse Arkestra, is a big band with singers and dancers in exotic costumes recalling African rituals with chants, drumming, blues, and early
swing. Unlike most musicians of the free movement, Sun Ra uses elec-

tronic devices in a highly improvised manner that sometimes results in dissonance, or noise. Ra is regarded by many as a musical cult figure owing his inspiration to Egyptian deities. This film is a very interesting portrait of the man, his music, and influences on fellow musicians.

For other examples of his music combined with mythological poetry, listen to *Astro Black* (Impulse AS-9255), 1973. A later example is *Strange Celestial Road* (Rounder 3035), recorded in 1988.

The Art Ensemble of Chicago: Live from the Showcase
Rhapsody Films; 1981
Features Lester Bowie on trumpet/ percussion, Joseph Jarman and Roscoe Mitchell on reeds, Malachi Favors Maghostut on bass/percussion, and Famoudou Don Moye on drums/percussions.

The program is: "We Bop," "Promenade," "On the Cote Bamako," "Bedouin Village," "New York Is Full of Lonely People," New Orleans," "Funky Aeco," and "Theme."

The following videos are highly recommended for a cross-section of most of the post–'50s styles studied thus far. These two videos provide excellent opportunities for identifying styles, instruments, groups and performers. It might be suggested that certain groups are more important than others in relation to the material covered in the book. Selective previews are strongly recommended, as in the four volumes of *Best of the Big Bands*:

Playboy Jazz Festival Vol. I.
BMG; 90 min.
Performers include The Great Quartet, with Freddie Hubbard on trumpet, McCoy Tyner on piano, Ron Carter on bass, and Elvin Jones on drums; a duo with Red Norvo on vibes and Tal Farlow on guitar; Willie Bobo's Latin Band; the Cal. State L.A. Band; Art Farmer on flugelhorn and Benny Golson on tenor sax; singer Nancy Wilson; the group Pieces of a Dream, with Grover Washington Jr. on tenor sax; the Maynard Ferguson Orchestra; and vibes player Lionel Hampton with an all-star big band featuring Clark Terry.

Playboy Jazz Festival Vol. II.
BMG; 90 min.
Performers include Weather Report playing "Birdland" with the vocal group Manhattan Transfer; Sarah Vaughan singing "Send in the Clowns"; Dave Brubeck on piano with his group playing "Take Five"; Milt Jackson on vibes offering "Bags Groove"; saxophonist Ornette Coleman and his group Prime Time; Dexter Gordon on tenor sax; the group Free Flight; O.C. Smith; Wild Bill Davison; and the Maynard Ferguson Orchestra.

PART VIII

Jazz in the '80s

CHAPTER NINETEEN

POP-FUSION

A strange musical phenomenon had developed during the last half of the '80s that was rooted in the '70s. The emergence of modern keyboard technology produced a fragmented style of jazz that was somewhat ambivalent, with strong mass appeal and interest. This pop-fusion style in many ways resembled the swing era in terms of popularity and shared some of the same musical characteristics. This music is a dance style, with fewer improvised solos, in simple song forms. It is a streamlined version of jazz fusion, because it offers much less variety in rhythmic and harmonic structures. Melodies remain relatively simple, with heavy emphasis on repetitive vamps that are highly dependent on studio effects.

Although pop-fusion does not maintain the musical intensity of the early jazz-fusion masters such as Miles Davis, Chick Corea, and Weather Report, much of this current style is being performed by creditable jazz musicians who have continued to cross over and back again to and from the mainstream tradition. The younger jazz musicians had, by now, been weaned on both styles.

Studio music technology, which includes overdubbing use of the MIDI process (Musical Instrument Digital Interface) with synthesizers and programmed samples from drum machines, characterize pop-fusion as in jazz-fusion. Pop-fusion is a synthesized style that is highly simplified musically with extended vamps and limited emphasis on improvisation. Vamps are used with little variation compared to fusion of the '70s; however, Latin rhythms are a major influence. The shards of sound that ripped through Davis' *Bitches Brew* are nowhere to be found in this music. Corea's highly animated mixtures of energetic Latin and funk rhythms are also absent.

The latest recordings of Miles Davis and Chick Corea, who are still accused of a commercial sell-out by the mainstream community, still maintain the highest jazz ideals in the fusion idiom and have not compromised the standard that seems to have given way to this popular version. Groups such as the Yellow Jackets, led by Russell Ferrante on keyboards,

219

Figure 19.1: Comparison Chart
Pop-Fusion and Jazz-Fusion

Pop-Fusion	Jazz-Fusion
1. Simple song forms	1. Extended forms
2. Less emphasis on improvisation	2. More emphasis on improvisation
3. More emphasis on studio effects	3. More emphasis on performers
4. More commercialized	4. Less commercialized
5. Small bands	5. Small bands and large bands

and Steps Ahead, with vibraphonist Mike Mainieri, have recorded interesting music that is rooted in traditional jazz elements, with the usual trappings of fusion.

Forerunners of pop-fusion include, among many, Spyro Gyra and The Jeff Lorber Fusion in the late '70s. Using an island style of music reflecting the West Indies, Spyro Gyra fused reggae with the basic rock beat. They became very successful, combining steel drums and marimba with rock rhythm instruments and an alto saxophone lead in simple song forms. Their 1979 hit *Morning Dance* (MCA 1650) clearly illustrates their early pop-fusion influences. George Duke emerged as one of the true masters of this techno-synthesized style that emphasized substance over form. Modern studio recordings by now had become a highly individualized effort where each performer could add his or her sound by overdubbing with other members in the band.

Check out *101 North* (Valley Vue 72945), produced by George Duke, recorded by 101 North, a group of California studio musicians in 1988. This is a good example of the production expertise of George Duke as a follow-up to his own recordings and contributions to the Miles Davis band.

The difference between pop-fusion and true jazz-fusion is sometimes a fine line (see figure 19.1). To illustrate the point we can assume that most musicians who are hired on an individual basis report to the gig (job). Many times he will be meeting the musicians he is to play with for the first time. A trained jazz musician knows the basic jazz literature or repertoire, which comes from *fake books*. With a knowledge of tunes, form, and basic chord interpretations he can play just about anything, and to the average listener the band will sound like a group that has been together for a long time. However, a standard means of operation for musicians is to often create tunes on the spot through standard progressions, like the blues form, vamps, or riffs. Many pop-fusion groups depend on their equipment for musical effects rather than on their own creativity, and thus often sound like simple jam sessions with a single repetitive vamp and standard bridge, and little variation. The harmonic progressions remain basically simple, with static melodies. There has not been much room for creativity within the infrastructure of the tune, nor does there appear to be ample opportunity for improvisation. The improvisations, like the vamps, are standard fare with cliched licks and bass lines.

Jazz-fusion, on the other hand, usually represents a much higher standard, with extremely gifted sidemen. In this kind of music there is nowhere to hide. Much planning and rehearsal are usually obvious, because of the musical dimensions of the material. The compositions are generally much more involved, with intricate harmonic schemes, subtle rhythmic changes, and fresh melodies that demand an original and creative approach to improvisation. Jazz-fusion allows true genius in musicianship to shine brightly. The "GRP Super Live in Concert" video clearly shows the difference between pop-fusion and jazz-fusion.

Study Guide: Pop-Fusion

Recordings

"The Spin"—Yellow Jackets.
The Spin (MCA 6304). Recorded in 1989.

Yellow Jackets (*Photo courtesy of Carl Studna*)

Personnel
Russell Ferrante—keyboards,
Marc Russo—saxophones,
Jimmy Haslip—bass,
William Kennedy—drums, percussion.

Musical Characteristics
The Yellow Jackets produced a Grammy award winner in 1988 with *Politics*. This album, *The Spin*, is a daring approach to pop-fusion which recrosses over to jazz-fusion. The title tune featured an up-tempo jazz beat with extended bop-style solos in a very successful manner by Marc Russo and Russell Ferrante. This performance is not typical of the Yellow Jackets.

Musical Form
1. Intro—up-tempo hard bop beat with ride cymbal
2. Main theme—three-part form stated by alto sax and acoustic piano
3. Alto sax solo extended over static bass
4. Piano vamp interlude with synthesizer overdub, sax kick
5. Piano solo extended, brief theme statement, bebop style
6. Restatement of original theme by alto and piano

In 1991 the Yellow Jackets produced *Green House* (GRP-GRC-9630). Bob Mintzer replaced Marc Russo on saxophones, and this album shows many more jazz tendencies, with extended forms and improvised solos.

Video

GRP Super Live in Concert
GRP Video; 55 min.
These performances are a mix of fusion in pop and jazz styles: Lee Ritenour performs "The Sauce" on guitar; Tom Scott performs "Target" on tenor sax; Diane Schuur sings "Deedles' Blues"; Dave Grusin plays piano on "An Actor's Life"; and The Chick Corea Elektric Band, with Corea on keyboards, Dave Weckl on drums, John Patitucci on bass, Frank Gambale on guitar, and Eric Marienthal on saxophone, play "Overture," "No Zone," "Light Years," and "Encore."

Ritenour and Scott present funk styles that follow the pop-fusion category. Both are excellent soloists on their instruments; however, the structures of the compositions are steeped in repetitive pop riffs, with closed construction for open solos.

Diane Schuur plays piano and sings the blues tune straight-ahead, in the best of jazz traditions. She is certainly one of the bright vocalists on the current scene, with an exciting voice displaying great range and the ability to scat in the classic Ella Fitzgerald style.

The Dave Grusin tune follows in the pop fusion mode, with a simple, composed-through structure and limited rhythmic variety. The solos are stereotyped riffs by Ritenour and Scott, without great improvisational depth. In this group, Tim Landers is on bass and Vinnie Colaiuta plays drums. This is a good example of the pop-fusion style, with little musical depth. There is really nothing new here!

The Chick Corea Elektric Band is quite another story. The "Overture" opens with great rhythmic variety and dramatic musical results. There is great melodic invention, with quickly changing tempos and free-wheeling intermittent solos that enhance the composition. The music is totally unpredictable, and shows great imagination under the master stroke of composer and keyboardist Corea. "No Zone" is a slow mood piece that opens with the keyboard synthesizer of Corea complemented by a Patitucci solo that is bowed on the upright acoustic bass. The interplay of the duet with percussion produces an interesting musical excursion. A classical effect is developed by the keyboards and bassist with the rhythm providing subtle Latin structures which lead to jazz improvisation in free form style by Corea. This piece is carefully developed, with great variety and sensitivity. It does not rely on electronic effects or heavy doses of rock riffs to produce the final results. Tasteful licks by saxophonist Marienthal and guitarist Gambale help solidify the piece.

"Light Years" shows the Corea band's ability to swing in an electric funk style, sustaining the vamp with scorching solos by Marienthal on alto saxophone and tight back-beat drumming by Dave Weckl. This is exciting music that represents the best of the jazz-fusion style.

Prime Cuts: Jazz and Beyond
CBS Fox.
This collection of eight videos provides an interesting review, with examples of *jazz-fusion*, *pop-fusion*, and *new age* music. The visual sequences are more creative than most of the music; however, the sound reproduction is very good. The video provides a musical contrast among these styles.

Program
1. "Decoy"—by Miles Davis opens the program with close-ups of Miles and interesting visual effects. The band plays a sustained vamp, with Miles in the opening solo followed by guitar and soprano sax. The style is *jazz-fusion*, with the rhythm vamps giving way to sequences with synthesizer and keyboard effects.
2. "Hardrock"—by Herbie Hancock presents a video in color with a subway scene accompanied by full synthesized sound effects. This

music is reminiscent of his early hit "Rockit." The excerpt features a
storyline of a chance meeting between a man (Hancock) and a
woman, with the music providing the background. This is in a *pop-
fusion* style.

3. "Diana 'D' "—Chuck Mangione's video opens with a female aerobic
dancer rearranging six TV monitors to an electric rock vamp while
Mangione plays a melody that is highly repetitive on flugelhorn. The
music uses limited vocal effects and no improvisations with the
vamp. This is in a basic *pop-fusion* style.

4. "Sequencer"—by guitarist Al DiMeola opens with a fusion theme
featuring oriental martial arts dancers over a background of visually
synthesized effects. DiMeola is shown throughout the video, and
again the improvisations are somewhat limited, with standard rock
licks that are updated through synthesizers. This is also *pop-fusion*.

5. "Pace Verde"—Andreas Vollenweider plays harp with underwater
scenes, switching to land mass formations in an homage to nature.
The video moves indoors with dancers and gymnasts, before giving
way to a scene with Vollenweider's band. The music is simple, repetitive melodic and harmonic motives with an uninhibited rhythm.
This music is a through-composed piece without improvisation, and
is typical of *new age music*.

6. "San Say"—by keyboardist Hiroshima, presents another *new age*
style, with a basic melody and bridge as a background to dancers with
his band. This seems like a Michael Jackson video in an oriental cloak.
The music is based on a theme and vamp with no solo space.

7. "Heroes"—the Clarke-Duke Project features Stanley Clarke on bass
and George Duke on keyboards. The video opens with an old time
serial throwback like the early Flash Gordon film clips. It is updated
with a storyline involving Duke and Clarke. The music is a basic pop
style with some limited vocal lyrics. This is more of a film soundtrack
approach with limited musical elements, and is *pop-fusion*.

8. "Swamp Cabbage"—Weather Report opens with a visual of the
band. A bass solo opens the structure, with the band playing interesting cross rhythms. This is followed by the main vamp theme, joined
by Wayne Shorter on tenor sax and Joe Zawinul on keyboards. A keyboard solo in the right hand closes this excerpt. The rhythmic activity
provides much interest to this example of *jazz-fusion*.

CHAPTER TWENTY

NEW AGE

One of the musical developments of the '80s has been *new age music*. Like ragtime music, new age is not considered a jazz form or style although many jazz-oriented new age musicians like Ralph Towner, a guitarist from the group Oregon, maintains strong ties with many mainstream musicians. New age music is highly programmatic and descriptive in nature, with virtually no improvisation. Artists and groups such as harpist Andreas Vollenweider, Acoustic Alchemy, and Hiroshima draw heavily upon inspirational forces such as nature for a musical agenda. Many musical elements are derived from exotic Eastern modes and folk songs that emphasize the composition.

Shadowfax

Shadowfax draws heavily upon exotic percussion and wind instruments to produce hypnotic musical effects, and sometimes uses heavy rock rhythms like the early Mahavishnu Orchestra to sustain their modal style. Synthesized effects that are overdubbed are a large part of their arsenal. Their drummer, Stuart Nevitt, is one of the more innovative new age musicians; he literally records home appliances when experimenting for synthesized samples on his drum machine. Shadowfax won a Grammy in the new age category in 1988 with *Folksongs for a Nuclear Village* (Capitol CDP 7469242). Their latest release as of this writing is *The Odd Get Even*.

Study Guide: Shadowfax

Recordings

"The Odd Get Even"—Shadowfax.
The Odd Get Even (Private Music 2065-2-P). Recorded in 1990.

Personnel
G.E. Stinson—guitars, mbira, vocal,
Chuck Greenberg—lyricon, flutes, soprano sax,

Phil Maggini—bass,
Dave Lewis—keyboards,
Charles Bisharat—electric violin,
Stuart Nevitt—acoustic and electronic percussion/composer,
Todd Yvega—synclavier and synthesizer programming

Musical Characteristics
Very heavy Indian folk-song influence, with exotic mixes of Eastern
modes and scales in the melodic material. This is largely accomplished by
programming the keyboard synthesizers with the electric violin. The
overall effect is of a high-pitched melody with string-like qualities and a
colorful timbre. See figure 20.1 for an example.

Figure 20.1: Theme A in 7/8 meter.

Source: Composed by Stuart Nevitt. Used by permission.

Musical Form
1. Opens with rock-like back beat by drums joined by keyboards. Electric violin introduces short raga-type theme.
2. Main Theme is two-part form played twice;
   A section is in 7/8, with drums in 4/4;
   B section change of key, with all in 4/4.
3. Solos: electric violin uses whole-tones in B section; synthesizer,
   acoustic and electric guitar, synclavier follow.
4. Restatement of main theme.

Video

Firewalker—Shadowfax
Choreographer: Louise Durkee; Momix Dance Troupe
Capitol Records; 4:25 min.
This video is a dance set to "Firewalker," from the *Songs for a Nuclear
Village* album, as shown on the "Grammy Awards" television program in
1988.

Mahavishnu Orchestra

An interesting comparison of the earlier Shadowfax style in 1975 to the
Mahavishnu Orchestra in 1972 shows contrasting and yet complement-

ing approaches. Shadowfax draws heavily on Eastern exotic modes and instruments with rock elements, while Mahavishnu seems to approach their style from the rock point of view with Eastern influences. Listen to "Meeting of the Spirits" from *The Mahavishnu Orchestra with John McLaughlin* (Columbia 31067) and then the Shadowfax recording of "A Song for My Brother" on *Watercourse Way* (Lost Lake Arts 0085). Many interesting musical parallels can be made and a certain evolution of New Age style can be better understood.

CHAPTER TWENTY-ONE

JAZZ-FUSION IN THE '80S

The flowering of jazz-fusion became triumphant in the '80s with the artistic success of Chick Corea and Miles Davis. Their albums retained highly personal musical statements that proved to be benchmarks in the art of jazz-fusion. The performers still dominated the synthesized proceedings without giving way to special effects or the curiosities of studio mixing as the points of departure.

Recording Terms

Here are a few basic studio recording terms:

1. *Analog*—audio signals that were used early in describing musical sounds by voltage meters rather than numbers.
2. *Digital*—audio signals that are described by numbers instead of voltage meters in recording sound.
3. *MIDI*—Musical Instrument Digital Interface; music technology that carries signals between computers and synthesizers.
4. *Multi-Tracking*—the process of overdubbing different instrumental or vocal parts on separate tracks.
5. *Sampler*—the conversion of sound through an electronic device usually played back on a synthesizer.

Miles Davis and Chick Corea—Later

After concentrating on acoustic piano for a prolonged period through the early '80s, Corea returned to the electric side in 1985 by forming his Elektric Band. This electric format continued until the 1989 release of *Chick Corea Akoustic Band*, which was a swinging set of standards that featured Chick on grand piano with the Elektric Band rhythm section of John Patitucci on upright bass and Dave Weckl on drums (*Chick Corea Akoustic Band* (GRP 9582), 1989). He returned to the electric format with

Inside Out in 1990. Miles Davis, on the other hand, was able to reach new heights with his own redefined electric music, joined by the talented composer-musician Marcus Miller, offering *Tutu* in 1986 and *Amandla* in 1989. Miller was able to capture the Miles Davis mystique with these two recordings, as Miller not only composed much of the material, but also performed on synthesizers, bass, drums, guitar, and bass clarinet and helped Davis produce the albums.

Study Guide: Miles Davis and Chick Corea

Recordings

"Tutu"—Miles Davis.
Tutu (Warner Bros. 25490). Recorded in 1986.

Personnel
Miles Davis—trumpet,
Marcus Miller—synthesizer, bass/arranger,
Paulinho da Costa—percussion

Musical Characteristics
The musical style of "Tutu" represents a bolder approach to jazz-fusion than *In a Silent Way*, which was more musically sedate. The haunting bass vamp coupled with Miles' descending blues-style, Harmon-muted licks is an uncanny example of fusing the old with the new and making it work. See figure 21.1.

Figure 21.1: Bass Vamp of "Tutu":

Source: "Tutu" Words and Music by Marcus Miller/© Copyright 1986 by Sunset Burgandy/Rights administered by MCA Music Publishing, A Division of MCA Inc., 1755 Broadway, New York, NY 10019/International Copyright Secured/All Rights Reserved.

Musical Form
  1. Introduction—bass vamp in G Dorian mode of eight bars; slow funk style with synthesizer and drums.
  2. Main theme—Harmon-muted trumpet plays melody embellished with blues licks.

3. Second chorus—synthesizer maintains vamp with fragmented trumpet improvisation.
4. Third and fourth choruses—synthesized instruments state theme as trumpet plays bop and cool style licks.
5. Vamp continues with fadeout.

"Elektric City"—Chick Corea Elektric Band.
The Chick Corea Elektric Band **(GRP 1026, CD 9535). Recorded in 1986.**

Personnel
Chick Corea—electric keyboards, including MIDI Rhodes, Latin 900, and Mini-Moog synthesizers/composer,
Dave Weckl—drums, John Patitucci—Fender jazz bass,
Carlos Rios—electric guitar

Musical Characteristics
This section shows a creative use of the fusion technique, with innovative Latin-rock rhythms tied to a vamp in the main theme. The keyboards and guitar solo creatively over the bass vamp and trade twos in the final chorus. Strong electronic effects are used by the keyboards and guitar to add a rock flavor.

Musical Form
ABA, Latin-rock fours.

1. Introduction—begins with a vamp played by the group in unison.
2. First chorus:
   A theme—stated by the bass vamp accompanied by keyboards with a Latin-rock rhythm in fours.
   B theme—guitar takes the lead in the bridge with rhythm breaks.
   A theme—returns with guitar lead.
3. Second chorus:
   A theme—keyboard solo
   B theme—as before
   A theme—guitar lead again
4. Third chorus
   A theme—guitar solo
   B theme—as before
   A theme—guitar lead again
5. Fourth chorus—keyboards trade solo twos with the guitars
6. Coda—unison vamp and tag.

Video

Miles Ahead: The Music of Miles Davis
Educational Broadcasting Corp.; Obenhaus Films, Inc. (London). Recorded in 1986. (Currently not available.)
This video captures the musical development of Miles throughout forty-five years. Highlights include the early 1959 television broadcast of "So What," the historic recordings with Gil Evans, and Davis's electric band style in 1986 with "Human Nature." Many interviews, including ones with George Benson, Bill Cosby, Gil Evans, and former sidemen. *Highly Recommended!*

Reading

Miles Davis with Quincy Troupe, *Miles: The Autobiography*.
Simon and Schuster, 1989.
Although the language is very rough indeed, many interesting and illuminating details are revealed of Miles' personal and musical life. His recollections of Charlie Parker and other fellow musicians are sometimes shocking. Very interesting account of this great jazz genius as he takes the reader through the three major periods of his musical development.

CHAPTER TWENTY-TWO

LATIN

Latin rhythms, based on songs and dances, became very influential as a stylistic vehicle during the '80s. Latin rhythms certainly have not been new in jazz—they had been used earlier, although sparingly, by Jelly Morton, with his Spanish tinge, and by the great Duke Ellington. Latin musicians have approached North American music through both jazz and classical styles. North American ideas sometimes are grossly misinterpreted by commercial versions. Cuban Salsa is a commercialized version of the Montuño style as is the Bossa Nova version of Brazilian Samba. Dizzy Gillespie and Stan Kenton used mambos and Afro-Cuban rhythms in the late '40s and '50s. Harry Belafonte, a pop singer, had spurred interest in Caribbean music with his calypso performances, and Spyro Gyra more recently explored reggae. Tenor saxaphonist Stan Getz introduced the American public to Antonio Carlos Jobim's "Desafinado" in the '60s. This Brazilian samba was tabbed as *bossa nova* in jazz clubs.

Miles Davis and Chick Corea were very much preoccupied with Spanish flamenco styles in their earlier recordings together. Since then, Corea has not altogether abandoned the flamenco style, while Miles went on to explore pure African rhythms. Latin styles of Afro-Cuban, Brazilian, and Caribbean music fused with funk to produce colorful rhythms for all forms of jazz expression.

Brazilian Styles

The Brazilian samba is usually heard in two forms today. The street or parade samba is the heavier style used in cities like Rio de Janiero in Brazil for Carnival, and can be seen and heard throughout the various samba schools in Rio. Street samba uses instruments that are generally very large with drums varying in size to produce loud effects outdoors. The other kind of samba is the jazz samba, or bossa nova, introduced to the United States during the '60s. Jazz Samba is very much a stylist staple in all of jazz today, and centers around the drummer of the band. Brazilian

strains of Latin music are by nature laid back and romantic, whereas the
Cuban strains tend to be hot and exotic. There are many Brazilian dance
styles that are used by modern composers like Chick Corea and drummers like Peter Erksine. Indeed, there is virtually no end to the Latin
styles that are being used in today's jazz, and their influences are overwhelming. It must be noted that not every drummer or composer inter-
prets or writes these rhythms in the same manner. They are widely open
to interpretation; however, there are basic rhythms in both the Brazilian
and Cuban strains.

Figure 22.1: Some examples of Brazilian rhythms.

Notice that the bass drums plays a beat similar to modern rock. This
rhythm is easily fused with Latin-rock or Latin-jazz styles. See figure 22.1
for examples of Brazilian rhythms.

Another influence on these colorful rhythms are those that are now
being used in African music. Miles Davis, in his autobiography, tells how
a touring group of African dancers influenced his thinking about rhythms
in jazz-fusion. South African township jazz is a basic kind of African popular music. The people of Africa who speak the Bantu tongue have contributed to this style. The Zulus of South Africa have many dance and
drum teams that perform regular exhibitions around Johannesburg and
its environs. Their instruments tend to be of a primitive nature, preserv-
ing the tribal rhythms. More recently, the music of Nigeria in West Africa
has been explored. It is important to remember that most Latin rhythms
are derived from West Africa and were originally brought to the New
World, South America, and the Caribbean by slaves. The slaves danced
the conga in ring shouts at Place Congo in the early 1800s in New Orleans.

The Caribbean influence, or island rhythms, seemed to have been
adopted more by pop groups than by the jazz realm, although on occasion
groups like Weather Report explored the use of reggae during the '70s.
See figure 22.2 for a comparison chart of Latin and African musics.

All of these various dances and rhythms, derived from very traditional styles within each country, are currently being explored. The traditions of Latin music have been preserved by many Latin stars in this

Figure 22.2: Comparison Chart
Latin and African Musics

1. Brazilian— rhythms such as the jazz samba style tend to be laid back, with a romantic
              flavor. Street samba tends to be heavier, danceable rhythms, with many
              drums; jazz samba uses a drum set.
2. Cuban—   rhythms such as the mambo and salsa styles tend to be characterized as
              hot and exotic, with intricate off-beat accents and patterns.
3. African— rhythms such as those used by the Zulu tribal ensembles reflect a more
              primitive approach, with instruments that are still relatively unexplored in
              jazz. These rhythms are broad-based in a heavy style and are used for
              dancing.

country, and it is still presented in the original folk-style singing and dancing settings. New patterns are constantly being introduced into modern
jazz structures that are mainstream with bop-based styles, and those that
are jazz-fusion styled.

Paquito D'Rivera has successfully shown a mastery of fusing these
various Latin rhythms into a Pan-American bop style in the '80s. Miles
Davis and Chick Corea lead the creative efforts in joining Latin styles and
jazz-fusion. One of the biggest differences between traditional Latin and
jazz Latin styles is the latter's obvious use of bop and mainstream solos
and formal structure. While traditional Latin music is presented with
singing, the jazz style is mainly instrumental with heavy emphasis on bop
influences. Many early Latin bands like those led by Perez Prado and Tito
Puente gained exposure in America during the '50s with their mambo
music. Prado's tune "Cherry Pink and Apple Blossom White" was a big
hit in the mid-'50s; Prado was greatly influenced by Kenton, and entitled
one of his pieces "Mambo a la Kenton." Tito Puente, born of Puerto Rican parents in New York City in 1925, was nicknamed "The Mambo
Kid."

Earlier, Xavier Cugat had developed a Hollywood connection after
his initial broadcasts playing rhumbas on the "Let's Dance" radio broadcasts opposite Benny Goodman. Cugat's style became very popular because it was highly simplified and attractive to American dancers. He
helped introduce Latin music to the American public during the '30s in a
highly diluted form that could best be described as "Society Latin."

Most of the real Latin music was heard in large cities with a broad
base of Latin populations. Among jazz bandleaders, Duke Ellington
hired Juan Tizol, a Puerto Rican trombonist-composer who produced
tunes such as "Caravan" and "Conga Brava." Dizzy Gillespie introduced
Afro-Cuban rhythms featuring conga player Chano Pozo with tunes such
as "Manteca," "Cubana-Be," and "Cubana-Bop." Pozo was later murdered at a bar in Harlem in 1948.

Machito led a powerful Afro-Cuban band that absorbed much of the jazz tradition in the '40s and Stan Kenton used Machito's drummers for his Latin-influenced hit "The Peanut Vendor."

Study Guide: African and Latin Rhythms

Videos

Salsa: Latin Pop in the Cities (Beats of the Heart Series)
Shanachie.
This video shows performances, interviews, and recording sessions with salsa stars Celia Cruz, Tito Puente, Reuben Blades, Charlie Palmieri, Ray Barretto, and others.

The Spirit of Samba: Black Music of Brazil (Beats of the Heart Series)
Shanachie.
The outdoor samba style is featured in street and school samba with Gilberto Gil, Milton Nascimento, Chico Braque, and other Brazilian stars in preparation for Carnival.

Konkombe: The Nigerian Pop Music Scene (Beats of the Heart Series)
Shanachie.
African rhythms are displayed through a musical kaleidoscope of Afro-Pop and Lagos street music, with many African pop artists.

Latin-American Percussion: Rhythms and Rhythm Instruments from Cuba
DCI Music Videos, 1988; 47 min.
Directed by Henrick Laier with Birger Sulsbruck, this is another instructional video that features the basic playing of Latin-American percussion instruments. Claves, congas, timbales, bongos, cow bells, maracas, and guiros are demonstrated as are proper playing techniques and notated rhythm patterns. A handbook with piano and bass lines for Cha-cha, Montuño, Guaracha, Bolero, and Rhumba is also included. Produced by ATC Video and Films.

Veteran and contemporary Latin stars such as Mongo Santamaria, Ray Baretto, Dave Valentin, Tito Puente, Eddie Palmieri, Willie Colon, Johnny Pacheco, Paquito D'Rivera, Hilton Ruiz, and Arturo Sandoval have preserved this great Pan-American heritage. With unending variety of colorfully syncopated rhythms and bass lines, Brazilian and Cuban strains continue to have a strong impact on jazz. Much of the color in Latin music results from percussion implements such as conga drums,

Hilton Ruiz (*Photo courtesy of RCA/Novus*)

timbales, cabassa, maracas, cowbells, claves, and bongo drums. See figures 22.3, 22.4, and 22.5 for examples of Cuban and Latin rhythms and
Latin instruments.

Figure 22.3: The Cow Bell

It is indeed difficult to generalize on the countless varieties of Latin
rhythms and patterns because even though some are basic, most are a
matter of interpretation by the performers. As one can see by the examples above, most patterns are off-beat and highly syncopated in different
meters (time signatures) and tempos (speeds) according to desired styles.
This is a massive undertaking and beyond the scope of this book.

Arturo Sandoval (*Photo courtesy of author*)

Figure 22.4: Some examples of Cuban rhythms and Latin instruments (*left to right*): Quinto 11 inch, Conga 11 ³/4 inch, and Tumbadora 12 ¹/2 inch.

Figure 22.5: Latin rhythms

Paquito D'Rivera

Paquito D'Rivera has emerged as one of the most exciting Latin American artists of the '80s. His alto saxophone and clarinet playing reveals a
mastery of Cuban and Brazilian rhythms throughout his recordings. He
accomplished this through a mainstream bop style, joined by a talented
Brazilian trumpet and flugelhorn player, Claudio Roditi. The result is a
collaboration of rich Pan-American styles in mainstream. D'Rivera's mastery of his instruments produces some dazzling displays of sheer energy
and technique in the Latin tradition.

Study Guide: Paquito D'Rivera

Recordings

"Guataca City"—Paquito D'Rivera.
Manhattan Burn (Columbia 40583). Recorded in 1987.

Personnel
Paquito D'Rivera—alto saxophone, clarinet;
Claudio Roditi—trumpet, flugelhorn;
Farreed Haque—acoustic, electric guitars;
Daniel Freiberg—acoustic, electric keyboards;
Sergio Brandao—electric bass;
Ignacio Berroa—drums;
Ricardo Eddy Martinez—synthesizers;
Sammy Figueroa—percussion

Musical Characteristics
"Guataca City" is a solid example of the salsa style with the montuno keyboard. This is a highly syncopated style with off-beat accents that creates
a hot sultry mixture with hard bop solos (see figure 22.6). Paquito's alto
sax technique is on display and on the front line the perfect foil is provided by the tasteful trumpet playing of Roditi.

Paquito D'Riveria

Figure 22.6: Montuño style

Musical Form

Hot salsa style with montuno or guajeo keyboards and bass.

1. Opening Theme—6 bars repeated
2. Solos: trumpet—12 bars improvised, 6-bar opening theme; guitar, piano and bass follow same pattern; alto sax—6 choruses improvised with montuno piano vamp on third chorus
3. Restatement of the theme and out in 12 bars

   The collision of free jazz and the cross-cultural explosion of Latin, Caribbean, and African rhythms is explored by Ornette Coleman and his group Prime Time in his 1988 album *Virgin Beauty* (Columbia 44301).The odd instrumentation consists of three guitars, two bass guitars, two percussionists, keyboards, and Coleman, who overdubs his alto sax playing on trumpet and violin. This odd mixture of ethnic rhythms produce some startling effects, with bass vamps that shift without warning. Coleman's overdubbing on trumpet and violin are perhaps the weakest part of the album. His music reaches primitive proportions in a free-style structure including rock beats in early rhythm-and-blues style, and also in reggae and Afro-Latin derivations. Ornette improvises in and out of these cross-cultural vamps with great freedom, playing licks that border on the abstract.

   Music based on international pop cultures, which is called *World Music*, is being readily assimilated into jazz as well as into commercial styles in the '90s. The Kool Jazz Festival of 1982 in New York reflected this union between World Music and Jazz with a concert titled "Jazz and World Music."

Study Guide: Peter Erskine

Video

Timekeeping 2—Peter Erksine
DC1; 67 min.
This is an instructional video, with accompanying booklet, that explores African, Caribbean, Brazilian, and funk rhythms in contemporary jazz through the drumming of Peter Erskine. He is accompanied by guitarist John Abercombie and bassist Marc Johnson in a variety of contemporary Latin styles. Erskine's tenure with Weather Report established him as one of the most important contemporary drummers. The last half of the video deals with Latin interpretative styles. Particularly interesting is the Baiao pattern that has come into recent vogue.

CHAPTER TWENTY-THREE

MAINSTREAM IN THE '80S

Wynton Marsalis

A truly remarkable talent that burst on the scene during the '80s was trumpet player Wynton Marsalis. At age twenty-one Wynton demonstrated his technical virtuosity in both classical and jazz fields. He began his career touring with Art Blakey and the Jazz Messengers and then with Herbie Hancock, before forming his own quintet. His classical music mastery drew rave reviews from classical trumpet virtuoso Maurice Andre, while in jazz, Marsalis won the coveted *Down Beat* award as best trumpet player at age 22. His father, Ellis, is a pianist and an important instructor and director of jazz studies in New Orleans. One of his five brothers, Branford, won recognition as a saxophone player and actor shortly after Wynton's success. Although Wynton's concept of jazz is of a strictly conservative bent, Branford occasionally ventures into the pop scene, as he did recently with another musician-actor, Sting.

Wynton Marsalis is an outspoken champion of the purist aesthetic in jazz, and regards the popular movement as exploitation in direct conflict with the earlier masters. After producing twelve successful albums for CBS and appearing in many concerts and workshops, he was named artistic director of the Classical Jazz Series presented by Lincoln Center in New York City since 1988. This jazz series is dedicated to the preservation of non-commercial jazz traditions.

Study Guide: Wynton Marsalis

Recordings

"Think of One"—Wynton Marsalis.
Think of One (Columbia 38641). Recorded in 1983.

Personnel
Wynton Marsalis—trumpet/arranger,
Branford Marsalis—tenor saxophone,
Kenny Kirkland—piano,

Jeffrey Watts—drums,
Phil Bowler—bass

Musical Characteristics
This Monk tune arranged by Wynton exhibits some of the trumpeter's
trademarks in mainstream jazz. The personalized musical effects come in
the form of refinements with tempo shifts and sharp dynamic volume
contrasts. The old call-and-response technique is evident throughout.

Musical Form
AABA, medium swing in 4/4

1. First chorus—AA with breaks in time 16 bars, B is straight swing 8
   bars, A is same.

Wynton Marsalis (*Photo courtesy of Sony Music*)

Ellis Marsalis (*Photo courtesy of Rick Oliver*)

2. Second chorus—AA sharp dynamic contrasts, B preceded by long
   trumpet gliss, A is same.
3. Third chorus—piano solo uses double-time in AA sections.
4. Fourth chorus—tenor solo also uses double-time in AA, trumpet solo
   enters B with blues licks in last A section.
5. Fifth chorus—AA in double-time, BA ends in regular time.

Video

Wynton Marsalis: Blues and Swing
CBS; 60 min.
This instructional and performance video narrated by Wynton was
filmed at Harvard University and the Duke Ellington School of Arts in
Washington, D.C. His group includes Marcus Roberts on piano, Jeff

Watts on drums, Robert Hurst on bass, and Todd Williams on tenor saxophone. His sometimes humorous demonstrations include swing-style walking bass and the groove established between drums and piano. Marsalis demonstrates his respect for traditional jazz forms with performances of tunes by Monk, Duke, and himself.

Reading

Wynton Marsalis, "What Jazz Is, and Isn't"
New York Times, Sunday July 31, 1988 (Arts and Leisure, Section 2).
This article is based on Wynton's appointment as artistic director of the Classical Jazz Series in New York and offers his opinions on the state of modern jazz.

Branford Marsalis

Branford Marsalis is one of the brightest young saxophone stars to appear on the scene during the '80s and his reputation is still growing. Although he initially followed in the footsteps of brother Wynton, he has emerged as one of the major influences in modern mainstream. He has been accused of commercialism with his pop forays, but his playing shows a distinct mastery of all the older masters of the saxophone. Another brother, Delfeayo, who is a producer and trombonist, has explained Branford's style as one full of musical content and expression, rather than of technical prowess or harmonic devices that have become commercialized. Branford's approach, like the rest of his family's is one steeped in musical tradition with respect to earlier masters like Monk, Bird, and Trane.

"The Marsalis Tapes" (*Down Beat* magazine, November, 1989) is a feature article on Branford by Dave Helland. In this interview Branford not only discusses his own approach, but makes distinctions about the area of fusion. He acknowledges some of the electric jazz artists and groups like Herbie Hancock, Mahavishnu, and Weather Report, while rejecting much of the '80s diluted fusion scene. For an interesting overview of his stylistic approaches on tenor and soprano saxes, listen to *Random Abstract* (Columbia 44055), 1987. In addition to performing Wayne Shorter's "Yes and No" and Ornette Coleman's "Lonely Woman," he features three of his own compositions: "Crescent City," "Broadway Fools," and "Steep's Theme." Branford became bandleader for the "Tonight Show" on television in May 1992. See figure 23.1 for a summary of impact musicians in the '80s and '90s.

Figure 23.1: Impact Musicians of the '80s and '90s

Trumpet	Saxophone	Flute
Wynton Marsalis	Branford Marsalis	Kent Jordan
Miles Davis	Michael Brecker	Dave Valentin
Roy Hargrove	David Sanborn	
Marlon Jordan	Courtney Pine	**Clarinet**
Tom Harrell	Christopher Hollyday	
Claudio Roditi	Paquito D'Rivera	Eddie Daniels
Wallace Roney	Greg Osby	
Jon Faddis	David Murray	
Arturo Sandoval		

Guitar	Keyboards	Percussion
Pat Metheny	Chick Corea	Peter Erskine
Stanley Jordan	Keith Jarrett	Steve Gadd
John Schofield	Joey DeFrancesco	Terri Lyne
Howard Alden	Marcus Roberts	Carrington
Frank Gambale	Kenny Kirkland	Dave Weckl
	Geri Allen	Jack DeJohnette
	Gonzalo Rubalcaba	Tony Williams
	Joey Calderazzo	Paulinho DaCosta

Groups	Composer/Arranger	Bass
Harper Brothers	Bob Mintzer	Marcus Miller
Chick Corea bands	Quincy Jones	Stanley Clarke
Miles Davis	George Duke	Charlie Haden
Sun Ra	Eliane Elias	Jaco Pastorius
Yellow Jackets	John Fedchock	John Patitucci
Steps Ahead	Frank Mantooth	
	Matt Harris	

Study Guide: Branford Marsalis

Video

Steep: The Branford Marsalis Quartet
CMV; 90 min.

Personnel
Branford Marsalis—saxophones/leader,
Kenny Kirkland—piano,
Delbert Felix—bass,
Lewis Nash—drums

Program
1. Introduction—Branford and band backstage with venue's stage manager.
2. "Swingin' at the Haven"—written by father, Ellis Marsalis; features interviews with Sting and Billy Crystal.
3. "Crescent City"—by Branford, as he instructs students at Manhattan School of Music. Interview with Herbie Hancock.
4. "Broadway Fools"—by Branford, with interviews of Herbie Hancock, Danny DeVito, Spike Lee, and Sting.
5. "Love Stone"—by Tony Williams; interviews with Sting, Herbie Hancock, and Branford.
6. "Solstice"—by Branford, with interviews of Sting and Delfeayo Marsalis.
7. "Dienda"—by Kenny Kirkland
8. "Lament"—by J. J. Johnson; interviews with Delfeayo, Branford, Kirkland, Delbert Felix, Lewis Nash, and Sting.
9. "Lon Jellis"—by Kirkland, with interviews of Sting and Hancock.
10. "Giant Steps"—by John Coltrane.

Mainstream Soloists

Eliane Elias is a Brazilian pianist-composer married to trumpeter Randy Brecker. She came to New York in 1981. Elias was born in Sao Paolo in 1960 and grew up in a musical family. She began piano lessons in the classics at twelve, and began learning jazz standards and playing in clubs at fifteen. Eliane joined the Brazilian scene, and began seriously studying the jazz piano music of Art Tatum, Bud Powell, Bill Evans, McCoy Tyner, Keith Jarrett, and Herbie Hancock. At age twenty-one she traveled around Europe, then moved to New York with her mother and began her introduction to the New York scene with bassist Eddie Gomez. She remains deeply rooted in and influenced by her Brazilian culture, in albums such as *So Far So Close* (Blue Note CDP-7914112), *Cross Currents* (Blue Note BI-48785), and *Illusions* (Blue Note BLJ-46994).

Geri Allen, born in 1958, is a pianist from Detroit who has made a recent impact on the New York jazz scene. She began piano at age seven, and was exposed to many art forms by her family. Later she received support from trumpeter Marcus Belgrave in a group called the Detroit Jazz Development Workshop before enrolling in the Howard University music department. Allen finished school in 1979 and moved to New York City, working with pianist Kenny Barron. By 1984 she began working with The Art Ensemble Of Chicago and led her own group for a brief European tour. Allen currently writes and plays keyboards for her octet, offering a multi-varied style that includes funk and modal vamps with quick changing key signatures. Two of her recent albums are *Twylight* (PGM 841-152) and *In the Year of the Dragon*.

Eliane Elias (*Photo courtesy of J. R. Duran*)

Study Guide: Mainstream Soloists 1

Recordings

In the Year of the Dragon—Geri Allen, Charlie Haden, Paul Motian.
(JMT 834-428-4). Recorded in 1989.

Personnel
Geri Allen—piano, Charlie Haden—bass, Paul Motian—drums

Musical Characteristics
1. "Oblivion"—a Bud Powell tune is up-tempo featuring the fine
   straight-ahead soloing style of Allen.
2. "For John Malachi"—an Allen original.

Geri Allen (*Photo courtesy of Shigeru Uchiyama*)

3. "Rolland"—arranged by Allen; features a bamboo flute solo by Juan
   Lazaro Mendolas.
4. "See You at Per Tutti's"—by Charlie Haden; features his fine bass
   soloing with Monk-style solo by Allen.
5. "Last Call"—by Paul Motian; a polyrhythmic abstract tune in free
   style, with the highly tonal drumming of Motian.
6. "No More Mr. Nice Guy"—by Allen; opens with a Haden bass solo in
   a slow, somber style. The group joins the medium-slow tune with
   subtle time changes. The piano solo is in free style, and almost atonal.
   A brief drum solo kicks into a fast tempo, then returns to the original.
7. "Invisible"—an Ornette Coleman tune is fast paced with a free-style
   theme. Allen's solo is again in the Monk style, followed by an interesting solo by drummer Motian.
8. "First Song"—by Haden; a slowly moving, beautiful ballad with a
   melody in a classical mode and a fine solo in the middle register of
   Haden's bass.

9. "In The Year of the Dragon"—by Motian; a slow Latin-based tune
   with melodic interplay between the piano and bass. The thematic
   material tends to be in a free style, as are the solos.

John Scofield is an electric guitarist who emerged in the '70s as a bop
modernist, and excells in blues and straight-ahead standards. His influences are pianist Jay McShann, Charles Mingus, and Miles Davis. Scofield attended The Berklee School of Music and his current trio includes
Steve Swallow on bass and drummer Adam Nussbaum. Fine representa-
tions of his work are *Flat Out* (Gramavision R215-79400) and *Loud Jazz*
(Gramavision R215-79402).

Pat Metheny, born in 1955, is another gifted guitarist who came into
his own during the '80s. His constant experimentation with electronic devices places him as one of the most popular fusion guitarists of the period.
He appeared with Ornette Coleman on *Song X* (Geffen GEF-24096) in
1985, and he worked with a host of other musical heavyweights, including
Gary Burton. Listen to his 1981 recording *Offramp* (ECM/WB L-L2L6),
and also *Still Life Talking* (Geffen-GEF-24L45) for examples of his style.

Two other musicians who came into the jazz limelight during the
'80s are saxophone players Kenny Garrett and Michael Brecker. Garrett,
born in 1961, received on-the-job training with Duke Ellington's band at
age eighteen. After playing with trumpeters Woody Shaw and Freddie
Hubbard, and drummers Mel Lewis and Art Blakey, he received great
recognition for his work with Miles Davis on *Amandla*. He has recently
diversified his musical approaches after a road trip with Sting, and has
grown considerably during the Miles fusion experience. His experiences
with Duke and Blakey had a large influence on his playing. Michael
Brecker began his career in New York City in 1970 at age eighteen and
became a favored studio musician, mastering most styles on the tenor
saxophone, and gaining most of his inspiration from John Coltrane. Michael has recently released *Now You See It, Now You Don't* and has established himself on his own terms, rather than as a sideman, since 1987. His
polyrhythmic approach to playing and writing is an attempt to go beyond
fusion and traditional mainstream in search of his musical identity.

Study Guide: Mainstream Soloists 2

Recordings

Now You See It, Now You Don't—Michael Brecker.
(GRP 9622). Recorded in 1990.
This album uses MIDI processes with synthesized programming, and is a
good example of Michael's development in jazz fusion. There is ample
use of polyphonic passages with fragmented melodic material that he

Kenny Garrett (*Photo: Atlantic Records*)

forms with traditional licks, much as Miles Davis does with his latest bands. Much of the music establishes vamps that change key and meter. Brecker's overdubbing with tenor sax and synthesized Akai EWI are skillfully honed in an interesting fusion mix. The overall result of this album is a highly eclectic approach with acoustic and electric styles that use driving, sometimes funk-based rhythms. There appear to be heavy Weather Report influences on many of the tunes.

Musical Characteristics

1. "Escher Sketch"—is a Brecker original, following the inspiration of artist M.C. Escher. Escher's highly illusionistic drawings are matched by Brecker's enigmatic rhythms.
2. "Minsk"—by Don Grolnick, like "Escher Sketch," is a musical experiment with polyrhythms and thematic vamps.
3. "Ode to the Doo Da Day"—by Jim Beard; fuses Latin music to the synthesized mixes.

4. "Never Alone"—another Brecker original; a Weather Report-style ballad.
5. "Peep"—also by Brecker; a very interesting up-tempo tune dictated by the ride cymbal with quick bop-style licks that settle into a slower straight ahead middle section before returning to the fast pace.
6. "Dogs in the Wine Shop"—by Grolnick; shows some of the *new world* influences, with rhythms in Afro-Latin styling.
7. "Quiet City"—by Beard; another Latin-based tune in a slower tempo that echoes some of the early repetitive and sequential vamps of Weather Report.
8. "The Meaning of the Blues"—a straight-ahead jazz standard which demonstrates Brecker's roots.

Video

Last Solo—Keith Jarrett
Sony; 92 min.
Jarrett performs alone in his free-wheeling improvisational style, standing at the acoustic piano. This was recorded in 1984 in Tokyo. Selections include "Tokyo '84 No. 1" "Tokyo '84 No. 2" "Over the Rainbow," and "Tokyo '84 Encore."

Standards Live '85—Keith Jarrett
Sony; 105 min.
This video features his trio with Gary Peacock on bass and Jack De-Johnette on drums. Selections include "I Wish I Knew," "If I Should Lose You," "Late Lament," "Rider," "It's Easy to Remember," "So Tender," "Priam," "Stella by Starlight," and "God Bless the Child."

Vocal Groups

Vocal groups such as Manhattan Transfer, Take 6, and New York Voices invent contemporary mainstream jazz with creative recordings utilizing bop stylings. Transfer and Voices follow the earlier traditions of the Hi-Los and Four Freshmen, while Take 6 seems to have taken the inspirational path provided by Lambert, Hendricks and Ross (later Bavan). *Another Night in Tunisia* (on Blue Note 4BT-85110), recorded in 1986, is a good example of the collaboration of Jon Hendricks, Bobby McFerrin, and the Manhattan Transfer. Transfer's recording *Vocalese* (Atlantic 7-81266-4) is one of their most successful albums. The more recent group, Take 6 has a more varied musical outlook, with a myriad of influences.

The album *New York Voices* (GRP 9589), recorded in 1989, shows great vocal versatility with modern scat and contemporary settings of

"Caravan," " 'Round Midnight," and "Dare the Moon." Their vocal improvisations, like those of Take 6, are of the highest musical standards, although with different voice textures due to the personnel of each group. Take 6 employs six male voices, while New York Voices use two male and three female voices. Take 6 has already won three Grammies and a host of other awards. Their album *So Much 2 Say* (Reprise 25892-2) is a follow-up to their gold debut album *Take 6* (Reprise 25670-2).

Study Guide: Manhattan Transfer

Video

Vocalese—Manhattan Transfer
BMG; 28 min.
Program includes "That's Killer Joe," "Blee Blop Blues," "Another Night in Tunisia," "To You," and "Ray's Rockhouse." Features the lyrics of Jon Hendricks.

Vocalists

Bobby McFerrin won three Grammies as best male vocalist in 1988, for his contribution to the " 'Round Midnight" film soundtrack, among other achievements. McFerrin was born on March 11, 1950, and his parents were professional singers. A New York City native who moved to Hollywood at age eight, he also lived in New Orleans and sang with a jazz-fusion group, Astral Project, before moving to Salt Lake City in 1977 and performing there with local groups. Discouraged, he and his wife moved again to San Francisco, and he began his jazz career with Jon Hendricks. Bobby had begun to develop a reputation for his ability to use vocal acrobatics. He began scat singing sound effects, and lists Ornette Coleman, Herbie Hancock, and Keith Jarrett as being more influential on his style than vocalists. A good example of his artistry is *Simple Pleasures* (EMI-48059), recorded in 1988.

Diane Schuur established herself as one of the leading female vocalists of the '80s. Her jazz stylings follow the earlier modern vocalists such as June Christie and Anita O'Day. She recorded with the Count Basie band in 1987 on *Diane Schuur and the Count Basie Orchestra* on GRD-9550, and her release of the *Diane Schuur Collection* (GRD-9591) is a good example of her singing style. In addition to her appearances with GRP artists, she has made several albums with tenorman, Stan Getz. She can be seen and heard on the video GRP Super Live in Concert, 1988, singing "Deedles' Blues."

Diane Schuur (*Photo courtesy of Carol Weinberg*)

Big Bands

Several big bands continued to perform with success during the '80s. With the passing of Thad Jones, Mel Lewis carried on the great Jones/Lewis band's tradition with the Mel Lewis Orchestra incorporating the same tasteful elements established with Thad in the '70s. Gil Evans had assembled a big band that reflected his innovative views of composition. This big band was unusual because of Evans' adaptation of fusion techniques to the large group. Both Thad Jones and Mel Lewis died during the '80s, leaving a highly respected ensemble that carries on in their great tradition. A younger composer, Bob Mintzer, became prominent during the '80s. This free-lance tenor saxophone player on the New York scene created highly original pieces for his band based at the Manhattan School of Music. He began writing his first compositions for the Buddy Rich Band and became popular with college and professional bands alike. His big band writing contains musical elements that are extremely refined, interlocking many styles. Many of his compositions are available in the Kendor Publishers Catalog.

Another big band to gain recognition during the '80s was the Boss Brass, led by Rob McConnell, a trombonist from Toronto. His band first appeared in the United States in 1981, and his arrangements have been nominated for Grammy awards. Outstanding Boss Brass recordings include *Big Band Jazz Vol. 1* (Pausa CD-7140) and *Big Band Jazz Vol. 2* (Pausa CD-7141).

Study Guide: The Boss Brass

Video

Rob McConnell
Sony; 25 min.
Rob is seen here with the Boss Brass. The program includes "The Waltz I Blew for You," which is an exceptional McConnell composition with very tight ensemble playing, "My Man Bill," and "Street of Dreams."

Mel Lewis

The jazz world lost another giant in the person of leader-drummer Mel Lewis on February 2, 1990. His twenty-four years of Monday night performances at the Village Vanguard in New York City, the majority of them co-led by the late Thad Jones, sustained the big band tradition with excellence and great sensitivity. Born in 1929, Mel began his career at age fourteen playing in local dance bands in Buffalo, N.Y., before moving on to bands led by Tex Benecke, Boyd Raeburn, and Ray Anthony. In 1954 he joined the Stan Kenton Band, and then moved to the West Coast with the bands of Terry Gibbs and Gerald Wilson. He came to New York in the early '60s, playing with the bands of Gerry Mulligan, Dizzy Gillespie, and Benny Goodman, before joining cornetist-arranger Thad Jones for some thirteen years. After a split with Jones in 1978 he single-handedly took over the band as the Mel Lewis Orchestra.

Starting out as a rehearsal band, the ensemble began to display amazing interaction among individual players with the ability to swing. It developed into an entourage of the finest jazz players working in New York City. Lewis pushed the band to swing in a traditional sense, relying on gifted arrangers and composers to write as he played, with a linear, smooth, and open sound. His format is often described as a band within a band because it included music in the combo style written within the larger ensemble with generous spacing for soloists. The band's vast musical legacy can still be heard at the Vanguard on Monday nights, a tribute to Mel Lewis.

Study Guide: Mel Lewis, Gil Evans, and Bob Mintzer

Videos

Mel Lewis and His Big Band
V.I.E.W., Inc.; 38 min.
This performance was filmed in 1983, in concert in Jerusalem, and features some of the finest New York studio musicians in a swinging session.

Personnel
Mel Lewis—leader/drums,
Chris Albert, Joe Mosello, Ron Tooley, Jim Powell—trumpets;

Bob Mintzer (*Photo courtesy of Trisha Yurochko*)

Joe Lavano, Billy Drewes, Ralph LaLama, Gary Smulyan, and Dick
    Oatts—saxes;
Doug Purviance, Brad McDougal, Ed Neumeister—trombones;
Sarah Larson—French horn, Lynn Roberts—vocals;
Dennis Irwin—bass, Phil Markowitz—piano

Program
1. "I'm Getting Sentimental Over You"—this Tommy Dorsey theme
   song is updated in a modern swing version with a tasteful solo by Jim
   Powell on flugelhorn playing outside the changes (outside the
   chords).
2. "Ding Dong Ding"—a good example of the ensemble in up tempo
   under Lewis's relaxed playing. Billy Drewes and Dick Oatts play extended solos on soprano saxes and then trade and team together for
   an exciting group within a group style. Phil Markowitz plays an unaccompanied piano solo with great imagination and variety in modern
   free style. Drum-and-hi-hat solo and bass kick in the band for the finale. Fine piece!
3. "I Get a Kick Out of You" and "I Want to Be Happy" are sung by
   Lynn Roberts.
4. "Little Pixie"—is a swinging, straight-ahead tune with tight ensemble playing. The sax section is featured with a Phil Markowitz piano
   solo. The sax section then play individual solos before trading
   phrases. Mel Lewis ties the piece together with a laid-back solo in a
   swinging manner. This is another fine example of the Mel Lewis big
   band style.

Gil Evans and His Orchestra
V.I.E.W., Inc.; 57 min.
Filmed in Switzerland in 1984, this group has pronounced fusion tenden-
cies in the big band style. It features the Brecker brothers, Lew Soloff,
Mike Maineri, and Billy Cobham.

Recordings

"Beyond the Limit"—Bob Mintzer.
Urban Contours (DMP 467). Recorded in 1989

Personnel
Bob Mintzer—composer, tenor sax, bass clarinet;
Marvin Stamm, Laurie Fink, Bob Millikin, Randy Brecker, Joe Mosello—
    trumpets;
Lawrence Feldman, Peter Yellin, Bob Malack, and Roger Rosenberg—
    saxophones;

Dave Bargeron, Bob Smith, Keith O'Quinn, Dave Taylor, and Jim
  Pugh—trombones

Musical Characteristics
This composition for big band is unique because it uses no rhythm section, but supplies space for modal improvisation. The main theme is built
on a single modal motive that begins in the fourth trumpet (see figure
23.2).

Figure 23.2: Main Motive "Beyond the Limit"

Source: Courtesy of Bob Mintzer

The composition moves forward in straight eighth notes in a classical
style. The brass and sax sections trade off on the motive with various rep-
etitions and new material in the bridge until Mintzer, playing the bass
clarinet, improvises a solo in a major mode, with the saxes continuing the
main motive. Several other repeated ideas are introduced before the
main motive is heard in full strength with both groups. In Mintzer's
words: "This composition is more of an orchestral style work with jazz
influences rather than an actual jazz piece." The musical form of the
piece might be characterized as a *rondo* form, much like ragtime.

Musical Form
slow fours in classical style

1. Opening section—trumpet introduces the main motive, 4 bars in 4/4
   with lower brass.
2. Opening section repeated—with theme A introduced by alto sax and
   trumpets, main motive continues.
3. Theme B—a syncopated melody, 4 bars with theme A repeated.
4. Main motive—played by the brass section; sax section plays sustained counter-theme.
5. Main motive—played by sax section with trombones playing theme
   A, while trumpets play a fragmented accompaniment, 4 bars.
6. Themes are transformed rhythmically and melodically with sax section and brass section call-and-response pattern.

7. Cut-time—The meter changes from 4/4 to 2/2, twice as fast. Brass section plays ascending figures as sax section plays response figures, 4 bars repeated or 8 bars of cut-time repeated.
8. Bridge—changes key, 8 bars of 4/4 or 16 bars of 2/2, ends with a strong statement of the main motive.
9. Solo section—in 4/4, bass clarinet (Mintzer) plays a solo in E Ionian mode with sax section followed by the trombone section playing the main motive 12 bars.
10. Transitional section—4 bars repeated played 4 times, active 16th note figures by the saxes are punctuated by short trombone figures: first 4 bars are soft, (f), second 4 bars are medium soft (mp), third 4 bars are medium loud (mf), and last 4 bars are loud (f)
11. Final section—both brass and sax sections play main motive very loud (ff), with the sharp contrast of a drop to medium soft (mp); the A theme is played by the trumpets for the last time.

For a sample of the big band writing of Bob Mintzer listen to *Spectrum* (DMP CD-461), 1988, which features both big band and small ensembles with outstanding sidemen, including Marvin Stamm and Randy Brecker on trumpet and drummer Peter Erskine.

PART IX

Jazz in the '90s

CHAPTER TWENTY-FOUR

MAINSTREAM IN THE '90S

If one can categorize jazz in the '70s as experimentation with electric technology, and jazz as fragmentation in the '80s, then the '90s seem to be producing a tendency towards retrospection, with jazz of the past masters being reviewed by younger musicians. Wynton Marsalis has been a heavy influence on young musicians of the '90s. Marcus Roberts, Marsalis's former piano player, seems to share this view by turning to an earlier era of jazz. His album *Deep in the Shed* (RCA 3078) in 1990 reflects the growing tendency to showcase the composer rather than the improviser. Roberts, born in 1965, demonstrates some of the teachings of Marsalis by paying homage to Coltrane and Ellington in this album. He is a master of the stride piano, and offered Ellington's "Black and Tan Fantasy" on solo piano at a recent May concert at the Bottom Line in New York City.

Another young musician to share this retrospective style is Marlon Jordan. This trumpet player was born in 1972; like the Marsalis family, the Jordan family is yet another influential musical force on the current jazz scene from New Orleans. His album *For You Only* (Columbia 452000), 1990, reflects his musical heritage with a highly melodic approach to improvisation rather than dazzling technical displays. Greg Osby, an alto saxophone player born in 1961, also improvises close to the melody with long lyrical lines. Other musicians that bear watching through the '90s are Courtney Pine, a Coltrane disciple on tenor saxophone from England, Joey DeFrancesco, who performs with great enthusiasm on the Hammond B-3 organ a la Jimmy Smith and the Harper Brothers who are a New York-based hard bop group nurtured by the music of Art Blakey, Horace Silver, Julian Cannonball Adderley, and Lee Morgan. Winard Harper on drums, Philip Harper on trumpet, and saxophonist Justin Robinson are all in their twenties. The Harper Brothers show remarkable poise on stage with a high energy level. Their music reflects the traditional approach to jazz that is growing as a musical forecast for the decade. Even Maynard Ferguson has returned to his bop roots with a nine-piece band, producing *Big Bop Nouveau* (Intima 7-73390-2), 1990.

Study Guide: The Harper Brothers

Recording

"Kiss Me Right"—The Harper Brothers.
Remembrance, Live at the Village Vanguard (Verve 84173). Recorded in 1990.

Personnel
Philip Harper—trumpet,
Winard Harper—drums,
Justin Robinson—alto sax,
Stephen Scott—piano,
Kiyoshi Kitagawa—bass

Musical Characteristics
The Harper brothers reflect a return to the hard bop and funk masters. This Horace Silver composition is a hard-driving funk piece in the older style. There is plenty of solo space with thunderous kicks from the drums throughout.

Musical Form
Medium hard bop in funk style, ABAB form

1. A theme funk-style with stop time 8 bars; B theme straight swing 4s, 8 bars; A and B repeated as above.
2. Piano solo—walking bass and hard drum kicks support this funky solo, A section repeated.
3. Trumpet solo—shows a conservative approach to improvisation Lee Morgan style with note bends. Climax of solo on a high sustained G with descending lick, A section repeated.
4. Alto sax solo—Cannonball Adderley-style with double-time licks and hard drum kicks.
5. Restatement of ABAB theme.

The Young Masters

The young musicians of the '90s seem to be looking from within them-selves to develop personalized styles based upon the inspiration of bop masters of the past. This might be viewed as the *second revival*, following the *first revival* of classic dixieland music in the '30s by the traditionalists. This second revival seems to flow through the late New Orleans School that has produced or inspired so much of the young talent including the Marsalis family, the Jordan family, Marcus Roberts, and Harry Connick, Jr.

Trumpet player Roy Hargrove pays his respects to Monk on *Diamond in the Rough* (RCA 3082-4-N), 1990. Appearing on the New York City scene, Hargrove has been characterized by writer Dale Fitzgerald as a kind of musical Michael Jordan, with his endless energy. Other directions in retrospect have been taken by young lions Joey DeFrancesco on organ and Christopher Hollyday on alto sax. Any attempt at defining the styles of all these young artists is unfair so early in their careers. Rather, it might be said that they have successfully emulated the past masters and are currently searching for their own identities. On most of their albums their stylistic searches are showcased with original tunes as well as with jazz classics. The young musicians appear to be redefining bop music, from dazzling technical displays to more personalized melodic approaches within the infrastructure of the music. In other words, the musical approach takes precedence over the technical approach in this revivalist mainstream music. It is difficult to speculate how successful this redefinition will be and if any originality will be found within their individual styles in terms of improvisation, tonal approach, or harmonic considerations. This is a most interesting challenge, and their progress needs close observation throughout the '90s.

This partial listing of young jazz masters is by no means meant to be exclusive. There are many fine young players currently bursting onto the jazz scene who will gain their share of recognition. The problem for the critic and serious jazz fan will be to sort out all of the talent and observe their staying power. Many of these fine young players will develop their own individual styles and will enjoy great success, if not influence. It is relatively easy to copy, but to be original is not so easy. All great artists have had distinctive styles that have thrust them into stardom. No doubt some of these young players will refine their styles, while others will revise and change direction.

It will be interesting to follow some of these players and observe their development through the stimulation and influence of others. This is an exciting aspect of the ongoing development of fine art, and jazz is exactly that. At this point there is no hint of that development. Some young performers have been purposely omitted from discussion because their musical ideals cling to commercial realization rather than artistic realization.

Christopher Hollyday

With the passing of such great jazz artists as Miles Davis, Stan Getz, Sarah Vaughan, Dexter Gordon, and Art Blakey it is indeed with more than passing interest that we look to new young talents in the '90s. A young alto saxophonist born in 1970, Christopher Hollyday is one of the youthful jazz lions who deserves serious attention. According to critic Leonard Feather, "this young man will assuredly have a significant and permanent place in the pantheon of this ever changing, ever growing art form."

Hollyday, one of the modern revivalists of the bop masters, offers evi-

Christopher Hollyday (*Photo courtesy of RCA/Novus*)

dence of influences by Jackie McLean and Charlie Parker. He has a polished, well-gleaned sound with a wide, controlled vibrato. His upper register is well under control, and seems to hearken back to the early cool sax
men of the '50s like Lee Konitz and his great tenorman of the '60s, Stan
Getz. Hollyday began his career at age fourteen when he was awarded the
Young Talent Award by the National Association of Jazz Educators.

Listen to his album, *On Course* (RCA 3087-4-N), 1990, for a sampling
of his stylistic approach. The first number, "No Second Quarter," shows
his technical approach and command of the instrument in an open-
spaced improvisation that reveals his early influences. "Westside Winds"
is a mood piece that offers another view of Hollyday's playing in the upper register. He plays some dazzling licks on the up-tempo "Hit and
Run," with chordal improvisations much like Trane's "Giant Steps." In
this piece he covers the entire register of the alto from top to bottom with
great ease and gives evidence of his remarkable talents.

Courtney Pine

One of the young emerging sax stars, by way of England, is Courtney Pine on tenor and soprano. He is also a reflection of the older masters: Pine lists Charlie Parker, Thelonius Monk, Coleman Hawkins, Wayne Shorter, Sonny Rollins, and John Coltrane as inspirations for his music.

Listen to some cuts from his album *The Vision's Tale* (Antilles 791334-4), 1989, for some of the traditionalist aspects of his style and influences. Often hailed as a Trane disciple, he pays homage to the Ben Webster tonal approach on Duke's "In a Mellotone," with the wide vibrato of Coleman Hawkins. A display of Trane's sheets of sound can be found in Pine's performance on tenor and soprano in "There Is No Greater Love." His improvisational abstractions take Coltrane's style to another dimension with great intensity. "God Bless the Child" is an excellent example of Pine's deep feeling and tonal approach on tenor in a great ballad. "Our Descendants' Descendants" reveals a multi-faceted style with shrill soprano riffs and fragmentation.

Pine was born in London in 1964 where he studied clarinet before switching to saxophone. He worked with funk and pop groups before adopting jazz as his mainstay. His first big band engagement was the Jazz Warriors debut in 1986 at a London club. Later he played briefly with Elvin Jones and the late Art Blakey, who had a profound influence on his career.

Greg Osby

Osby began with the clarinet in junior high school in St. Louis. As an alto and soprano sax player, he studied with Cannonball Adderley, Earl Bostic, and Bunky Green. He entered Berklee School of Music in 1979 and enjoyed musical associations with Branford Marsalis, Kevin Eubanks, Jeff Watts, Wallace Roney, and Terri Lyne Carrington. Greg moved to Brooklyn and joined Jon Faddis before working with Lester Bowie and with David Murray's World Saxophone Quartet. Osby's sound and approach are based on formulated principles called *shifting melodic order* in creating original material. His first album, *Eternal Spirit* (Blue Note 92051), shows his early development.

Marlon Jordan

Marlon Jordan is one of the youngest trumpet players on the jazz scene and shares with the Marsalis family his musical heritage of New Orleans. His style reflects the older master, Miles Davis, for he, too, uses few well-chosen notes to express musical ideas, as on his album *For You Only*.

The first cut, "Jepetto's Despair," reveals his minimal tonal approach, and "Cherokee" shows his great facility and technical prowess on

Greg Osby (*Photo courtesy of Masaaki Takenaka*)

his instrument. The duet with piano on "For You Only" is a moving ballad that exhibits deep musical introspection, like the style of Wynton Marsalis in an Ellington mood. Monk's tune "Monk's Point" is a straight-ahead funk tune. Another ballad, "Stardust," is a Jordan solo in the duo format. It is a classic rendition in which he stays close to the melody with beautiful tonal control before constructing some lovely improvisational lines in double-time with the Miles Davis influence before returning to the original slow tempo. There are some wonderful musicians on this album, including Branford Marsalis, Jeff Watts, and Kent Jordan.

Roy Hargrove

Another young trumpet player is Roy Hargrove, who has gained much attention through his recording *Diamond in the Rough* (RCA 3082-4-N),

1990. Hargrove's style on the horn might be termed more of a soft bop approach when compared to the likes of Lee Morgan, Clifford Brown, or Kenny Dorham. This is due to the thick, warm sound he draws from his horn, and there are virtually no hard edges in his playing.

He romps through the opening cut on the album, "Proclamation," with a funk sound that is controlled with a carefully regulated vibrato. When he turns to the tune "A New Joy" he chooses not to fill all the open spaces or rests of his Harmon-muted solo, and he is fluent throughout the entire range of the trumpet. Hargrove, although still very young, plays with a very horizontal, expansive lyrical concept to complement his rich sound. There is more emphasis on melodic structures in his solos than on technical ostentation. This might be the key to understanding these young soft bop players, compared to the hard boppers.

Roy Hargrove (*Photo courtesy of RCA/Novus*)

Hargrove was born in 1970. He went to Dallas Arts Magnet High School and later attended Berklee and the New School in New York City. His career as a sideman began with Bobby Watson and James Moody.

Terri Lyne Carrington

A child prodigy of jazz who was born in 1965 is drummer Terri Lyne Carrington. She gained much attention driving the house band on "The Arsenio Hall Show," a nationally syndicated television program from Los Angeles. Terri was born in Massachusetts and settled in New York in the mid-'80s, before moving to the west coast. Her close musical associates include Wayne Shorter, John Scofield, Grover Washington, Jr., and Carlos Santana, who appear on her first album, *Real Life Story* (Verve Forecast 837697).

Carrington's career spans rhythm and blues and various jazz stylings that are reflected in the album. She lists Jack DeJohnette, McCoy Tyner, Max Roach, and Rahsaan Roland Kirk as main influences in her early career. Her career began at age ten with piano great Oscar Peterson, and then she entered the Berklee School of Music at age twelve on a scholarship. Carrington has worked on developing discipline within her style through the practice of Buddhism.

Joey DeFrancesco

Joey DeFrancesco is a bright light as one of the new breed keyboard artists. His music reflects the organ groove style derived from such masters as Jimmy Smith and Richard "Groove" Holmes. On his album *Where Were You?* (Columbia 45443), 1990, this young musician is surrounded by a bevy of veterans like Kurt Whalum, Illinois Jacquet, Milt Hinton, Bobby Hart, and John Schofield.

On "Red Top," Joey cooks on the Hammond B3 organ and displays a deep feeling for rhythm and blues. Also featured on the album are standards "I'll Always Love You," "Teach Me Tonight," and "But Not For Me," which reveal his early influences that lead to his groove style. "Georgia on My Mind" echoes the Ray Charles down-home treatment of the blues. His original composition "Song for My Mother" is a beautiful, sensitive ballad that perhaps bares his young soul. DeFrancesco is featured on acoustic piano with "Light, Camera, Action," in which he displays a basic bop approach.

Joey, who was born in 1971, attended the High School of Creative and Performing Arts in Philadlphia. He was a sideman for Miles Davis and Houston Person.

Marcus Roberts

Marcus Roberts is a blind, Florida-born piano player who has created a sensation. He studied classical piano in St. Augustine and turned to jazz at age twelve. He won some prestigious piano competitions and joined Wynton Marsalis in 1985. His first album, *The Truth Is Spoken Here*, sold 60,000 copies. He alludes to people such as Duke Ellington and John Coltrane as his main inspirations. His piano improvisations stem from Jelly Roll Morton, Oscar Peterson, Art Tatum, McCoy Tyner, and Thelonius Monk. His album *Deep in the Shed* represents his woodshedding, or practice, on variations of the blues.

Marcus Roberts (*Photo courtesy of Gene Martin*)

Study Guide: Marcus Roberts

Video

Deep in the Shed—Marcus Roberts
BMG; 54 min.

Personnel
Marcus Roberts—piano; Herb Harris—tenor saxophone;
Todd Williams—tenor saxophone; Wessel Anderson—alto saxophone;
Scotty Barard—trumpet; Wycliffe Gordon—trombone;
Chris Thomas, Reginald Veal—bass;
Maurice Carnes, Herlin Riley—drums;
Delfeayo Marsalis—producer
　　This video was filmed at the Saenger Performing Arts Center in New
Orleans, and presents a retrospective look at the early bop masters. It is
certainly highly representative of the second revival of traditional main-
stream jazz, which was taking place during the early '90s. The music is
dedicated by Roberts to John Coltrane, Duke Ellington, Billie Holiday,
Jelly Roll Morton, and Charlie Parker.
　　The music is divided into three parts with three thematic sections:
"Young Boy" (by Jason Marsalis) deals with Marcus' spiritual awakening
and musical beginnings. The second section, "The Beautiful Woman,"
explores the mysteries of romance and relationships. "The Old Man" is
the last section, and pays homage to the jazz masters, with visuals.

Program
1. Prologue: "Blue Monk" is a piano solo by Marcus Roberts.
2. First section: Young Boy
   "Spiritual Awakening" is a slow blues with a piano solo, tenor solo,
   trombone solo with plungers, and alto solo. "Governor" features the
   group in medium swing. It opens with a piano solo followed by alto
   and tenor. The band is dressed in formal white tails a la early Ellington, which is visually very effective.
3. Second section: The Beautiful Woman
   "Mysterious Interlude" is a slow blues piano solo in the style of
   Monk. There is a tenor solo followed by a trumpet solo. The band is
   dressed in black for this section. "Nebuchadnezzar" is a medium-
   tempo Afro-Latin jazz waltz, and the group opens with the main
   theme followed by a tenor solo. The group returns with the main
   theme, which is followed this time by a trombone solo. An extended
   piano solo ensues, which is very laid back with Ellingtonian colors.
   There is an alto solo before the piano resumes to the ending.

4. Third section: Old Man

   "E. Dankworth" is a very boppish up-tempo theme. A lovely piano solo is followed by an alto sax solo, before the group returns with the main theme. This section is filmed in a blue hue. "Deep in the Shed" is a medium-tempo Afro-Latin tune featuring the group with a tenor lead. The tenor plays a solo and the group returns. Robert's piano solo helps kick in the rhythm section to straight swing fours, followed by a plunger trumpet solo. The Latin theme returns and the drummer solos with the bassist.

5. Epilogue: "Single Petal of a Rose" is by Duke Ellington and Billy Strayhorn. This is a piano solo filmed in black and white, like the Prologue. It is a slow, free-style ballad that shows off the remarkably beautiful improvisational style of Roberts.

The Old Masters

While recognizing young masters and new talent, it should be noted that many of the older jazz musicians are still very much active. The older musicians who are represented here are not meant to be exclusive of other jazz greats still recording and working but is intended to show their latest work in 1990. The musical longevity and sustaining power of these great musicians is noteworthy because they have endured for the last 30 to 40 years through all of the influences and changes in the jazz world. This ability to maintain excellence for such a long period certainly qualifies them as superstars of jazz deserving the Jazz Hall of Fame. Many of the older masters who have since passed on like John Coltrane, Duke Ellington, Thelonious Monk and Charlie Parker still exert an unbelievable influence on the younger masters. It will be interesting to see if the younger generation will be able to sustain and endure as these men have. People like Dizzy Gillespie are still in the forefront of their art in this wonderful jazz legacy.

Ornette Coleman

Coleman has again come into the limelight of the jazz world with his critically acclaimed album *Virgin Beauty*, with his group Prime Time (Columbia 44301). This album was an important step in defining the influence of multi-cultural forces on jazz in the '90s. Coleman, it must be remembered, startled the jazz world in 1960 with *Free Jazz* and influenced virtually every mainstream musician during the period. Coleman's daring exploits of the '60s led to his playing the trumpet and violin to supplement his main instrument, the alto saxophone. He formed Prime Time in the

1970s with his son, Denardo, on drums. Since his relatively obscure beginnings, Coleman has become a central figure in the history of modern jazz. His approach was still a strong inspiration for many of the younger masters of the '90s.

Quincy Jones

Composer Quincy Jones is another figure included in this brief survey because of his tremendous success during the last thirty-five years. Like George Benson, he presents some categorical problems because of his many commercial enterprises. Jones, however, had proven early in his career that he was a gifted jazz composer and arranger. His recent project *Back on the Block* (on Quest) reveals his pop and jazz influences. On the album, Birdland's theme song is set to "Jazz Corner of the World" and features Joe Zawinul, who originally penned it for Weather Report; George Benson, Ella Fitzgerald, Dizzy Gillespie, Sarah Vaughan, and James Moody also play or sing on this track. Quincy has written many soundtracks for films since 1961. His recent hits in the commercial pop vein include "The Dude" and "We Are the World." Jones has had successful arrangements for Frank Sinatra, Ray Charles, and more recently his own album *Walking in Space* for A&M. Time-Warner released a two-hour film, "Listen Up: The Lives of Quincy Jones."

Sun Ra

Sun Ra's recording *Purple Night* (A&M Records 75021) is a late example of his music, following *Blue Delight*, which was a chart-topping Billboard album. *Purple Night* features some great musicians, such as Don Cherry on pocket trumpet. This album is one of Ra's finest musical offerings presenting a band well-rehearsed in many styles of jazz. It features his classic waltz "Love in Outer Space." His mystic approach is reflected by his vocals and the twenty-one-piece Cosmic Omniversal Arkestra. Ra began his career as a piano player and arranger for Fletcher Henderson in the '40s, aka Herman "Sonny" Blount. His approach to writing over the past forty years hasn't changed much, in that he still writes in a very unorthodox manner, which sometimes leads to reading problems for his younger musicians. With Sun Ra's association with a major record company, perhaps the American public will receive better distribution of his music. He remains a spiritual person, retaining his cosmic philosophy as an "extraterrestrial" sociologist. His philosophic incantations, poetry, and songs are a strange mixture, but are an enduring influence for jazz in the modern period.

Sonny Rollins

Sonny Rollins is a master of the tenor saxophone who is approaching forty years of greatness. Rollins and John Coltrane were two of the most gifted tenormen in the '50s and '60s. Both developed along similar paths, although their playing and improvisational approaches were quite different. While Coltrane produced a rich tone with fast improvisational chordal structures, called sheets of sound, Rollins had a rougher edge on his sound and tended to develop single ideas with hard patterns that were more staccato than legato. One of Rollins' famous legendary exploits was his nightly practice excursions on one of the New York City bridges during a period of intense self-evaluation. His late release *Falling in Love with Jazz* on Milestone features Branford Marsalis, Tommy Flanagan, and Jack DeJohnette.

Gerry Mulligan

The legendary baritone saxophone player and composer Gerry Mulligan also boasts a long and successful career of over forty years. One of his most recent efforts is *Lonesome Boulevard* on A&M, which features his quartet with nine original compositions. Mulligan began his career as an important sideman on the Miles Davis *Birth of the Cool* sessions in New York City. After heading to the West Coast in the early '50s, Mulligan launched the West Coast School with trumpeter Chet Baker and a piano-less quartet. Mulligan was the seminal figure of the West Coast School, which featured mostly small groups playing laid-back arrangements highly reflecting the cool style. Subsequently, Mulligan formed his Concert Jazz Band, which made several successful recordings. He was one of the first great modern jazz baritone saxophone soloists, often improvising in the upper reaches of the alto sax register on his baritone.

Max Roach

Max Roach, the master drummer, began his career as a substitute for Sonny Greer with the great Duke Ellington Orchestra during World War II. He was also a member of the *Birth of the Cool* group, and continued his development with Clifford Brown in the mid-'50s. Max Roach has endured ever since as an outstanding soloist and jazz innovator on the drum set. His Max Roach Double Quartet features a string quartet with his regular group, and shows his gravitation toward a more free jazz style during the '90s. This is quite a departure for Roach, who has been associated with hard bop during most of his career.

Study Guide: Max Roach

Video

Max Roach: In Concert and In Session
DCI; 60 min.

In Concert—30 min.

Personnel
Max Roach—drums, chimes; Maxine Roach—viola;
Cecil Bridgewater—trumpet, flugelhorn;
Oden Pope—tenor sax, alto flute;
Calvin Hill—bass, Walter Bishop Jr.—piano;
Matilda Haywood—vocals

This performance was recorded live at the 1982 Kool Jazz Festival, featuring original compositions by Roach. This is an uncanny display, for he produces an entire concert program unaccompanied on the drum set. It is certainly a demonstration of his greatness in jazz.

Program
1. "The Smoke That Thunders"—a study in the various techniques of cymbal sonorities.
2. "African Butterfly"—a tune with mallets on the tom-toms and hi-hat time.
3. "Odd Meters"—features a drum set medley with rhythms in odd meters of 3/4, 5/4, 7/4, and 9/4.
4. "Where Is the Wind"—a sensitive brush solo.
5. "Drums Unlimited"—from an album of the same name; a furious display of technique and control.

In Session
DCI Music Video, Inc.; 30 min.
The last half of the video illustrates the Max Roach Quartet recording the album *Chattahoochie Red*. The compositions are followed from rehearsal to recording, allowing an intimate view of the leadership and guidance Max provides as a producer, composer, and improvisational genius. The program also features a stunning solo by Roach underneath an excerpt from Rev. Martin Luther King's famous "I have a dream" speech.

CHAPTER TWENTY-FIVE

JAZZ-FUSION IN THE '90s

Chick Corea

Chick Corea has once again set a new standard with his super-charged Elektric Band offering *Inside Out* (on GRP GRD-9601). This new exploration takes the band to yet another plateau. Corea's new style fusion draws on even more musical styles than in the past and are blended into a meaningful form. Classical music, flamenco, rock, bop, and funk are all integral elements contributing to the development of jazz-fusion as a serious idiom in contemporary jazz.

Study Guide: Chick Corea

Recording

"Tale of Daring"—Chick Corea.
Inside Out (GRP 9601). Recorded in 1990.

Personnel
Chick Corea—MIDI piano, synthesizers/composer;
Dave Weckl—drums;
John Patitucci—electric bass;
Eric Marienthal—alto saxophone;
Frank Gambale—guitar

Musical Characteristics
"Tale of Daring" is a four-part tour de force of jazz-fusion, with show-cased solos for each member of the band. Noteworthy is Chick's use of the MIDI grand piano, which combines the best of acoustic and synthesized possibilities.

1. "Chapter 1" is a cinematic theme serving as an overture to the suite in third-stream classical style.

Chick Corea Elektric Band (*Photo courtesy of Harrison Funk*)

2. "Chapter II" is a melodic statement featuring a strong sax solo and a six-stringed guitar solo, followed by restatement of the main theme.
3. "Chapter III" starts with a kinetic drum/piano duet and then segues to a wicked guitar solo on top of a big back beat.
4. "Chapter IV" recaps the various themes, builds to a frenzied trading of fours in classic Return to Forever style, and closes as it began, in classical style.

Video

***Inside Out*—Chick Corea**
GRP; 32 min.
This is a very interesting video with close-up shots of the Yamaha MIDI grand piano. The video features a creative use of black and white film inserts of children playing instruments and a surrealistic style of special effects on "Tale of Daring." The personnel is the same as that of the CD, with the following tunes from the album: "Inside Out," "Kicker," "Child's Play," and "Tale of Daring." Very highly recommended!

Corea's Sidemen

Frank Gambale, a fusion guitar player who hails from Australia, made his mark with the Chick Corea Elektric Band. He was influenced early by Steely Dan, Return to Forever, and the Brecker Brothers. Gambale won a jazz award on guitar in the fusion category, and his album *Frank Gambale Live* was nominated for a Grammy award. His third project, *Thunder From Down Under* (JVC JD-3321) showcases his talents as a guitar player, keyboard player, and singer. Absorbing the blues of Eric Clapton and Mike Bloomfield, he plays a rock style with a jazz interpretation. He appears to be one of the most important representatives of the modern jazz-fusion idiom, with his harmonic variety and high-voltage solos.

Dave Weckl is one of the hottest drummers in the '90s. He was first influenced by fellow drummer Steve Gadd, and made his first album as leader on *Master Plan* (GRP GRD 9619). Weckl approaches the drum set with a melodic or thematic plan, forming bass lines and grooving ideas. His hometown, like Greg Osby's, is St. Louis.

John Patitucci, born in 1960, plays the acoustic and six string electric bass. His third album for GRP, *Sketchbook*, shows him exploring a variety of jazz styles. He has appeared with pop artists as well as with jazz mainstays such as Airto Moriera, Flora Purim, and clarinetist Eddie Daniels. Patitucci grew up in Brooklyn, later moved to San Francisco in 1972, and developed a varied musical approach which attempted to master all pop and jazz styles for modern flexibility in performance. He joined Corea in 1985 and his solos tend to be high on the frets, with guitar-like sounds as the result.

Miles Davis

An important video, "Miles in Paris," released in 1990 before his passing in 1991, shows the jazz-fusion skill that Davis brought to the '90s. The music is from two of his late albums, *Tutu* and *Amandla*. It features some gifted players including Kenny Garrett on saxophone and flute, showing Miles' continuing experimentation. This video, recorded during the tenth Paris Jazz Festival on November 3, 1989, offers some brief views of Miles' personal musings. One of the most interesting aspects of the video is Miles' interaction with his players onstage. This is a critical part of his music, because he shows uncanny musical direction during the performance with minimal effort, as he guides his players by pointing his hand or nodding his head to affect important rhythmical and harmonic sequences. This live performance is not as technically effective as the studio recordings; however, the spontaneous excitement onstage makes up for the minor flaws.

Miles Davis (*Photo courtesy of Charlie Cox*)

Study Guide: Miles Davis

Video

Miles in Paris—Miles Davis
Warner Reprise Video; 60 min.

Personnel
Miles Davis—trumpet, Benjamin Rietveld—bass;
Joseph Foley McCreary—lead bass;
Ricky Wellman—drums; John Bigham—electric percussion;
Kenny Garrett—saxophone and flute;
Kei Akagi—keyboards

Program

1. "Human Nature"—standard opening theme with improvised middle section built on a single chord vamp by the bass. Miles plays fragmented, lyrical licks reminiscent of his modal period. Garrett on sax trades imitated figures with Miles before soloing over the vamp. This section uses interesting synthesized effects that feed the vamp with slight changes that are given and taken away. Miles' presence and informal format with his players is one of his innovations in this style. The vamp builds with intensity over Garret's solo and ends with two open blasts from Miles' horn.

    Interview: Miles talks about taking five years off from playing, and then trying to recover his *chops*.

2. "Amandla"—is a slow ballad featuring muted solos by Miles with synthesized backgrounds. Garrett takes the melody, with the interplay of Miles' countertheme. Miles plays the bridge without a mute, before improvising a chorus with interplay from the alto (Miles has some difficulty with his chops here). The piece breaks into an open vamp in the middle section with free-wheeling solos exchanged before returning to the original theme.

    Interview: Miles talks about South Africa and his distaste for the political situation there.

3. "Tutu"—opens with a flurry of trumpet blues before settling into the bass vamp (see chapter 21). Aside from the faster tempo, the middle section is also somewhat different from the original recording, with a brief shift to swing fours. Also, Garrett's flute playing call and response with Miles is at a faster tempo. The interview about South Africa is superimposed over a synthesizer solo, and Davis talks about indigenous African rhythms. Muted and open (without the mute), the trumpet returns with the theme on an open solo. The interview returns on the subject of his playing countermelodies over the band. Guitar returns with the live action and Miles takes the tune out, muted, while his interview continues about his electric drummer, John Bigham. Final theme is with open horn and flute.

4. "New Blues"—opens with muted trumpet playing traditional blues licks, which is Davis's original composition. Trumpet continues with open horn and alto solo. Middle section breaks into a traditional two-beat style briefly. After a flurry, the bass brings the band back to the slower opening tempo. Miles solos open horn in a more traditional style giving way to the guitar as the bass propels the form under a highly sustained fifth in the synthesized organ stop and then in the high octave root of B♭. Guitarist takes the tune out on a solo.

    Interview: Miles talks about fame.

5. "Mr. Pastorius"—is a brief, pensive ballad on trumpet with a flurry of improvisation.

CHAPTER TWENTY-SIX

LISTENER'S GUIDE

The *first key* to intelligent listening is to be able to recognize the basic musical elements used in jazz and how they are applied. Most music contains all of these elements; however, some music styles stress only several. By *studying* the elements and *listening* to recognize them, one becomes a more sophisticated listener. This is quite a different approach from listening to music in the shower or while cleaning the house. Good listening is work, and takes much practice to apply the basic elements.

The *second key* to intelligent listening is to *practice*. Of the many interviews conducted with outstanding jazz performers, the common advice is to *listen, listen, listen*. Good understanding of music requires spending at least as much time listening as learning an instrument, maybe much more. The basic definition of music as *sound passing through time* stresses the fact that the listener must *remember* what he or she has heard from beginning to end.

The Elements of Music

Rhythm

Rhythm is probably the most important of all elements in jazz because of its role in the origins of early jazz and rhythm's relation to style. *Beats* divided into measures or bars give music a pulse. *Time signatures*, or *meters*, provide the number of beats within each measure such as 4/4 or 2/4. In this case the upper number indicates how many beats are in a measure, while the lower number indicates which notes—the quarter notes, half notes, or eighth notes—receive a beat. In 4/4 meter, for example try this exercise:

Tap your foot up and down slowly four times, and observe that the tapping down motion provides four *strong* beats while the lifting up motion of the foot provides another four *weak* beats (see figure 26.1). This pulsation provides a beat with eight subdivided beats within 4/4. Another name for the strong beats is *accents*. If the downbeats and upbeats are *reversed* so that the downbeat is weak and the upbeat is strong, *syncopation* results. This can be applied in any time signature.

Figure 26.1: Time Signature

Melody

Single tones organized in a horizontal pattern which are played one after the other produce a musical thought, or melody. In terms of English grammar, a melody is like a sentence. The melody is usually the subject of the musical composition, and should be memorized for later reference to improvisation. Melodies can impart various emotions depending on length and speed with underlying harmonic structures.

   Melodies are sometimes in a form that sounds like a musical question and answer, which can be translated to call and response in jazz. For example, the melody of the Birthday Song is in a question (call) and answer (response) form:

Happy birthday to you,
Happy birthday to you (question)
Happy birthday, happy birthday,
Happy birthday to you (answer)*

Another extended example:

Oh, where have you been, Billy boy, Billy boy?
Oh, where have you been, charming Billy? (question)
I've been to see my wife, she's the pleasure of my life,
She's a young thing and cannot leave her mother (answer)

Harmony

Tones played together, simultaneously, produce *chords*, which are the basis of harmony. During the Middle Ages harmony was made by combin-

---

*"Happy Birthday to You," (Mildred J. Hill, Patty S. Hill) © 1935 (Renewed 1962) Summy-Birchard Music, a division of Summy-Birchard, Inc. All Rights Reserved. Used by Permission.

ing two tones, the first and fourth, or fifth, notes of the scale; these hollow-sounding chords were harmony to the medieval ear. The Renaissance and Classical eras produced chords of at least three tones, or triads, that removed the hollow sound and added *consonance*, or pleasant sounds, as opposed to *dissonance*, or unpleasant sounds. Modern jazz has since added to these triadic chords additional tones, called *extensions*, in which all seven notes of the scale are contained in a single chord, called a thirteenth chord. Various tones within each chord can be altered with sharps (#) or flats (♭) to lower notes of the chord (see *accidentals*, in glossary). The key signature, using sharps and flats, provides a home base for melody and harmony, as in figure 26.2:

Figure 26.2: Key of C Major and Key of G Major

The complete pattern of successive chords, or chord changes is called *progressions* in harmony.

Tone Color and Texture

Single instruments provide tone *color* and combined instruments produce *textures*. Melodic instruments of the brass and woodwind families are capable of producing bright or dark tonal characteristics, while the combination of instruments produce textures which are light and thin, or thick and heavy. Textures are important in the compositions of Duke Ellington and Gil Evans. Tone colors are an important characteristic of an individual's playing style on an instrument. A smaller instrument such as the soprano saxophone produces high pitches which result in bright colors, while the larger baritone sax produces low pitches resulting in dark colors. Individual players can change tone colors with mutes or electrical devices. Each brass or woodwind soloist is also capable of simulating various tone colors through the entire low to high registers of their instruments.

In fine art painting, colors that are used by the artist give rise to meaning. In music, by combining the tonal colors of various instruments, textures are created that have a thin or heavy quality. Modern-day synthesizers are an immediate example of varied textures in the MIDI process.

The analogy to fine art painting would be the thick or thin use of paint in the brush strokes or palette knife. By combining colors, the artist produces textures much the same as a composer or arranger.

Pitch

An individual note of a melody, chord, or scale is called a pitch. These notes can be low or high, depending on the number of vibrations per second or frequencies. Electronic devices, tuning forks, and instruments such as a tuned piano or violin are often used as pitch references, or sound checks. When a performer checks the pitch, he or she is in effect establishing correct *intonation* by attempting to play in tune. Pitch is governed by a universal measurement in Western music that establishes the pitch A, as shown below, to equal 440 vibrations per second. Any pitch below pitch A will have regressively fewer vibrations, while any pitch above pitch A will have progressively more frequent vibrations (see figure 26.3).

Figure 26.3: A = 440 Vibrations per second

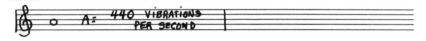

Scales

Scales are made of series of seven different pitches in order from low to high, with the repeat of the first pitch seven tones higher forming an *octave*, thus completing the scale at eight notes. The lines and spaces on which the pitches are placed is called a *staff*. Each line or space is assigned a letter name for pitch identification, as shown in the examples below. Note that the figure at the beginning of the staff, called a *clef*, establishes notation for high or low instruments. The *treble clef* is used for high instruments, while the *bass clef* is used for low instruments (see figure 26.4). Other types of clefs are used in classical music.

Figure 26.4: Treble Clef and Bass Clef

Some scales do not have a series of eight notes—for example, the pentatonic scale has five—but most scales follow a series of eight, with many possible alterations. Illustrated in figure 26.5 are some common jazz scales, or modes, with their corresponding chords, which form harmonic progressions:

Figure 26.5: F Major Scale

Note that a series of symbols called *accidentals* are used in key signatures and individual pitches. They are identified as *flats* (♭), which lower a pitch a half step, *sharps* (♯), which raise a pitch a half step, and naturals (♮), which return the note to its original pitch. Figure 26.6 is a *chromatic scale* which contains all 12 pitches used in Western music. Western music refers to music of the Western world. These are arranged a half step between each pitch:

Figure 26.6: F Chromatic Scale

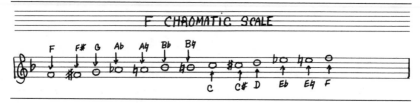

Even though the accidentals are written before the pitches they affect in actual written music, they are referred to after the pitch name when identified, e.g. F♯, A♭.

Tempo

Tempo, the speed of the beats, can be measured by a metronome, which was invented by a Bavarian named Johann Maelzel. In classical music a tempo is often suggested by, for example, M.M. = 120, or 120 beats per minute, as measured by Maelzel's metronome. In jazz scores the time indication consists of a note value followed by a number, such as ♩ = 120, which means that a quarter note is 120 beats per minute. Roughly translated, this means the music is played at the speed of two quarter notes per second. One hundred-twenty beats per minute is a medium tempo in jazz. An indication in the 200s would suggest a fast tempo, while an indication below 100 would suggest a slow ballad.

Notes

Notes are written with time and pitch indications on a staff. These notes can be changed to twice as fast or twice as slow according to the time signature. In common time, or 4/4, here are some time designations in figure 26.7:

Figure 26.7: Notes

When these values of time are mixed within the measure, their total must correspond to the time signature (see figure 26.8):

Figure 26.8: Time Signature

Form

All music is subject to some preconceived plan, like a draftsman would have to plan a building with a blueprint. Sculpture is sometimes referred to as "frozen music," and as in sculpture, the form is most important in music. There are many forms in jazz that have their origins in European music, and the jazz listener should take these into serious consideration as yet another key to understanding jazz. The listener will be readily able to follow melodies, harmonies, and rhythms as they relate to improvisation through *form*. Some of the most common song forms used in jazz are as follows:

Three-part form—AABA

A section is 8 bars that are repeated
B section is 8 bars in a different key, usually with different melodic phrases
A section is 8 bars like the first eight

Two-part form—ABAB

A section is 8 bars
B section is 8 bars in a different key, usually with different melodic
   phrases
A section is 8 bars
B section is 8 bars

Blues

The traditional blues pattern is twelve bars with the pattern of three
accents, as illustrated in chapter 2.

Playing once through the entire form is called a *chorus* in jazz terminol-
ogy. The first chorus is usually written, or played by memory, and establishes the themes; improvised solos follow in successive choruses before
restating the first chorus to round out the form. This is the favorite vehicle of post-swing jazz, and is one of the reasons that jazz is so unique as a
form. Jazz musicians can go out on a *gig*, or job, as complete strangers,
meet for the first time, and play like a well-rehearsed unit because of their
awareness of form, learned from tunes in the magic *fake book*.

Style

The history of jazz has provided us with a variety of music in its evolution. When we talk about beats or pulse in music, we are often talking
about *style*. A major difference between New Orleans and Chicago dixieland is the former's four-beat style and the latter's two-beat style. Swing
music, with its riffs and shouts, constitutes yet another style. Bebop produced highly ornate melodies and improvisations that led to further stylist developments. It is most important to understand style as it relates to
feel and the emotional process.

Jazz musicians have individual styles as they create music by using
mood swings to effect changes. Individual styles are as different as hand-
writing, and reflect the physical, mental, and spiritual makeup of every
human being. Friedrich Nietzsche, the great German philosopher, was
one of the first writers to discuss style in his book *The Birth of Tragedy*,
written in 1872. Nietzsche suggested through Greek tragedy, that two
distinct styles were evident. Apollonian spirit reflected order, repose, and
grandeur, while Dionysian spirit suggested passion, love, and intense
feeling. This brief exercise in aesthetics helps in identifying the musical
contrasting styles of tenor saxophone greats Coleman Hawkins, with his
great intensity and Lester Young, with his cool musical repose. This contrast could also be used with the West Coast School of cool music, com-

pared to emotional hard bop in the East in the '50s. The non-conformist movement of the late '40s and early '50s led by poets, painters, writers, and musicians represents yet a third type of style that is abstract in nature. This stylistic philosophy is embodied in the writing of Jack Kerouac with his book *On the Road* as he describes the free-spirited, non-conformist individual.

Style can be useful in identifying playing characteristics of individual and group performances, as well as *styles within styles,* such as the rich Latin American rhythms.

Improvisation

From the early days of the New Orleans masters to the present day, improvisation has become the hallmark of good jazz. With improvisation the soloist becomes the composer and star of jazz, unlike classical music. Jerry Coker's book *Improvising Jazz* sums up the basic elements of improvisation as *intuition, sense of pitch, emotion, habit,* and *intellect.* The great improvisers must have intuition, which is a creative instinct, and a sense of pitch, which requires musicianship. Emotion flows through great imagination, and habit is a rigid practice schedule. Intellect means that an improviser must have a rationale, logic, and a sense of reasoning.* The first great improviser of jazz, Louis Armstrong, was a creative giant because he was able to create new melodies to the existing chord structures with great instinct while most of his contemporaries paraphrased melodies.

There are basically three types of improvisation:

1. *Paraphrasing the melody*—This is the earliest type of improvisation, in which the soloist closely follows the melody. Most of the first generation New Orleans dixieland masters used this style, in which the chords were used in a vertical fashion.
2. *Inside the chords*—The bop masters developed this technique to perfection. By adding extensions of the chords they were able to play lines within the chords using scales in a horizontal fashion.
3. *Outside the chords*—Modal music provided opportunities to play notes outside of the few chord structures that were used. This style has been used with great success by soloists of the '80s and '90s as an exclusive technique. This style is sometimes referred to as "implied changes."

The freshness and spontaneity of the gifted improviser is truly one of the great thrills in jazz, separating it from all other musical art forms. In

---

*Source: Jerry Coker, *Improvising Jazz.* © 1964 by Simon & Schuster, Inc.

the most basic sense a soloist will embellish a melody that will relate to the general structure of the chord progression. By creating new melodies or ideas, he or she immediately becomes the composer.

Creativity

Much has been written about the creative act, not only in the arts, but also in the sciences, tracing great inventions and discoveries. If the creative act can be relegated to one word, it would be *genius*. Throughout the history of jazz a handful of geniuses came forth and were responsible for the evolution of the art form. To define genius, one might suggest *originality* as the main characteristic. Louis Armstrong, Duke Ellington, Charlie Parker, and Miles Davis were geniuses because of their original contributions to jazz. These contributions molded the history of jazz because their influence was so strong on their contemporaries and succeeding generations. The term "genius" should be reserved for only a select few. There are many stars and super-stars in jazz, but only a few can be considered geniuses of the creative process.

Helpful Hints

One of the best ways to listen to jazz is through headphones in the dark. Caution should be used in setting *volume control,* in order to *prevent inner ear damage.* By listening in the dark, conscious and subconscious visual distractions are eliminated, as are audible distractions when using head-phones. Above all . . . *practice listening!*

An analogy which I have used throughout this book is fine art painting. Browsing through an art gallery sharpens the same aesthetic senses visually that are desired audibly. In great paintings one can see, for example, the uses of form, color, shape, texture, style, and subject matter. Abstract painting, which is usually devoid of subject matter, can lead one to better understand abstract music devoid of melody. Creative ideas that are descriptive or programmatic, as opposed to those that are non-descriptive, without subject matter, or abstract, can be found in both painting and music.

There is no substitute for *live music performance.* CDs and videos are excellent ways to learn jazz, but attending live jazz sessions is the most rewarding activity for the true jazz experience. Attend concerts!

Finally, since most Americans now commute to and from work, tune your radio to a jazz station or take a portable cassette or CD player. The audio equipment available today—radios, compact discs and tape recorders—is a technological marvel. *Good luck on your jazz journey.*

CHAPTER TWENTY-SEVEN

JAZZ AS AN
ART FORM

The word "jazz" has again become as elusive as ever in defining a fine art form. To identify it with high cultural considerations, separating it from diluted versions, is no easy task. Throughout the history of jazz, which is at least 75 years old, this music we call jazz has been borrowed, bartered, and even stolen in its evolution. We Americans are fond of classifying everything in the scientific, economic, industrial, technological, and cultural realms, perhaps to better understand the nature and order of things. It is probably one of our greatest attributes as a free nation. In the realm of these high cultural considerations, it is universally agreed upon that jazz is a fine art form that has flourished in development through African Americans. We have traced this development from the slaves of West Africa to the modern mainstream schools of New Orleans and New York.

When we ask, what is jazz?, we discover that there is no universal definition—some contemporary jazz musicians refuse to even use the term as a classification for their craft. Much of this refusal is a result of personalized definitions. If the word "jazz" does have meaning, then we must ask what it is. Musicians and critics agree that the blues and improvisation are deeply rooted in any music we care to call "jazz," but the term has been grossly misappropriated by radio disc jockeys and commercial enterprises in general. The key to this confusion seems to be the conflict between commercial vs. cultural ideals. The modern mainstream movement that sought to revitalize the bop masters represents a purist school which holds the traditional tenets of jazz dearly. They pay homage to the bebop and hard bop masters and have little use for anything electric. This traditionalist view is good in that it helps one to discover music that is unequivocally jazz. The bad part of this view is that it discounts music which was inspired by the fusion masters.

Jazz-fusion as developed by Miles Davis and Chick Corea is an art form that can be called jazz because it does not compromise the qualities of melodic, harmonic, rhythmic, and formal considerations of the early masters, but seeks to develop them in new directions. The split between acoustic and electric instrumentation and musicians seems to be at the crux of the matter. Originality through creative genius was the master stroke of other artists like Picasso, Stravinsky, and Beethoven, who went through three periods of development in their careers. Roughly speaking, we might term these periods as imitation, realization, and abstraction. Miles Davis had certainly gone through three periods of musical evolution, and Chick Corea seems to be doing likewise. If jazz is to develop or evolve, then *originality* must be the basis of jazz musicians' art.

How does one distinguish between commercialized versions of mainstream and jazz-fusion? Which is a true art form? One can usually gain insight by evaluating the talent level of the performer or group. The content of true jazz music makes extreme artistic demands on all performers. With the development of form through melody, harmony, and rhythm there is great variety in structure. If one can guess the plots or sequences in a movie or book, the artistic effect seems lost and even boring; however one can still be thrilled by the craft of the great Dutch painters or English poets, which remain classics for all time. Attempts to dilute fine art principles result in subcultural commercialism and misrepresentation. Much of what we hear today has been stripped down to bare essentials for commercial purposes, and is devoid of artistic structure and talented performance.

A *trained* ear or eye is the path to understanding all art! This means practicing listening or viewing. We must learn to understand musical art forms, in this case jazz, and appreciate them for what they are despite personal tastes. Rejection without observation is a sign of pure ignorance. One of the most difficult tasks is to judge jazz in its own era. We have a tendency to make pronounced judgments based on the contemporary sophistication of our ears. In other words, we use subconscious criticism based on more recent experiences and expectations. There are many qualities that are evident in all fine arts. We have discussed the importance of formal structure because it is one of the most important links between representational art and abstract art. One has to sort carefully through both of these kinds of art to find continuity without deception. Recognizing formal structure is one of the important keys in judging an improvised solo as well as a composition.

It is most difficult to make any judgment, as from personal taste, on any art form—jazz, painting, poetry, or prose—without prior experience. *You must bring something to it!* The quality of structural perfection was critical to Mozart's symphonies, and the same was true of J. S. Bach's great works for clavier. These classical masters will be forever remembered because their analyzed works bore very few superficial elements. Shakespeare's works have attained a lofty position throughout history for the same reason, only with words instead of notes.

There is a definite analogy between the impressionistic jazz styles of early Miles Davis and the early impressionistic style of the early French painters like Claude Monet. Listening to the Harmon-muted improvisations of Miles Davis playing *L'ascenseur pour l'echafaud* (Elevator To The Scaffold) (Phillips 822566), 1957, as he produces tonal colors and textures that range beyond the originating songs, is a successful attempt at giving us a hazy musical impression. French composer Claude Debussy did this with classical music in *La Mer* (The Sea) and countless other pieces by using the pentatonic and whole-tone scales. The early French Impressionist painters did the same thing by using heavy brush strokes and doses of color that partially obscured their landscapes, seascapes, or skyscapes. In this style of painting one couldn't see exactly where the sky met the sea, and the viewer was left with an *impression*. Davis approached his thematic material similarly during his early modal period.

Other examples of qualities in art forms are the dramatic effects of Richard Wagner's music dramas or Paul Hindemith's symphonies or the newly-found romanticism of Beethoven, beginning with his Third Symphony (Eroica). The sheer drama of Wagner was probably best emulated by Stan Kenton in the field of jazz. Others show this dramatic quality through their religious aspirations in music like Ellington. Chet Baker's approach to jazz was passionate, with a gorgeous trumpet tone that was full of romance. In trying to understand free jazz, one can browse through abstract paintings and make some interesting analogies. For example, Jackson Pollock set the art world on its ear when he created the drip-paint method. By standing on the canvas and pouring paint he created a sensation that moved the center of the art world from Paris to New York. The New York School of abstract art in the '50s produced artists like Franz Kline, Robert Motherwell, Adolph Gottlieb, Arshile Gorky, and James Brooks, who attempted to free art from representing people, places, or events. One of these artists, William Baziotes, wrote: "What happens on the canvas is unpredictable and surprising to me . . . as I work, or when the painting is finished, the subject reveals itself."*

After viewing the works of some of these early abstract masters of painting, one can make a favorable comparison to the free jazz style of Ornette Coleman in the late '50s, for Coleman's art is based on similar principles. The musical attempt, like the painting attempt, is to draw the observer away from reality in terms of melody or image. While the artist can no longer rely on a particular subject represented on canvas, the musician can no longer rely on easily recognized musical elements. Some of the common elements that help the observer in both abstract painting and free jazz can be found in the form. Texture, color, variation, and balance are common in both of these stylistic mediums.

I have attempted to simplify some of the elementary analogies between jazz and painting by way of examples. The point of these analogies

---

*Catalogue: *The New American Painting*. The Museum of Modern Art, New York, Doubleday and Co., Inc. reprint 1959, page 15.

is to inspire the jazz enthusiast to pursue other favorite or familiar art forms, to reinforce the study of jazz. If we are calling jazz an art form, then this seems quite logical. It is hoped that some of these reflections on jazz as an art form will help listeners bring more to their musical encounters. In this way, we can demand more art for our dollar and not have it dictated by commercial enterprise.

Let us say in passing that throughout the history of fine art forms and their successful evolution, it is evident that artists we call geniuses passed through periods of imitation, realization, and abstraction. In the early '90s the young jazz musicians seem mired in imitation. Evolution in art forms is not possible without creative genius seeking originality through great imagination. The small handful of geniuses in jazz like Armstrong, Parker, Ellington, and Davis are responsible for jazz as we know it today.

Closing on a sad but truthful note, it is indeed depressing to witness the growth of jazz abroad in such cities as Tokyo, while it still lingers in the shadows as an art form in the United States. The Phillip Morris Superband, featuring Ray Charles and B. B. King, were on a world wide tour in the fall of 1990 and is a case in point. This band had a host of American all-star musicians including Harry "Sweets" Edison, Ray Brown, Kenny Burrell, Joe Morello, Urbie Green, and leader Gene Harris. A crowd of 12,000 showed up for a performance at the Olympic Natatorium in Tokyo, while 1,500 Americans were expected at the Apollo Theater in New York City for the closing of the tour. It is extremely painful that one of our pure American art forms continues to be enjoyed more abroad than it is at home.

There have been significant developments for the recognition of jazz as an original American art form, as noted by jazz critic Peter Watrous of the *New York Times* (Arts and Leisure, Section 2, January 20, 1991). Regular classic jazz performances will be presented at Lincoln Center in New York City, organized by Rob Gibson, who is setting up a jazz department on the same level as the New York Philharmonic and the Metropolitan Opera. Its million-dollar budget falls somewhat short of the appropriations for the Philharmonic; however, this new commitment to the preservation of jazz as a national musical treasure coincides with the revivalist movement by young musicians in the '90s. There is great promise that this enterprise, which will include black musical culture as well as white culture, will succeed and enter the American public domain.

The Classical Jazz Orchestra of Lincoln Center will seek to revive the repertoire of older masters such as Duke Ellington and others. The regular performance of jazz in one of America's bastions of European-based classical music, Lincoln Center, will need significant financial support and public enthusiasm to avoid a collapse similar to that of Stan Kenton's Neophonic Orchestra in Los Angeles during the mid-'60s. At least it can be said that the cultural establishment in America is ready to recognize jazz with the respect with which it has been treated throughout Europe and Japan.

GLOSSARY

Accent—A note or pitch played louder than the others.

Accidental—A sharp (♯), flat (♭) or natural (♮).

Acoustic—Instruments that have not been amplified.

Ax—Musician's slang for any instrument.

Ballad—A romantic piece in a slow tempo.

Bar—A measure; a group of beats.

Beat—Pulse and speed of a piece.

Blues—Twelve-bar form with three phrases of four bars each.

Blue Notes—Lowered third, fifth, or seventh tones of the scale, by flatting the pitches.

Bombs—Heavy accents in the bass drum of the drum set.

Break—An abrupt halt in the rhythm while the soloist usually continues to play.

Bridge—The B section of an AABA or AABB form in music.

Cadenza—A solo played without accompaniment; the soloist is free to play in any tempo.

Call and Response—A question and answer in music; can be between a soloist and group as in the early chants of leader and group.

Carving Contest—Used in early jazz when two soloists would alternate solos trying to "cut" each other.

Changes—Musicians' slang for a song's harmonic structure ("chord changes").

Chart—Any composition in jazz.

Chops—Musicians' slang for the facility necessary to play an instrument.

Chord—Usually three or more pitches played together on keyboards. Also, two pitches played together.

Chorus—Once through the entire form of a song.

Chromatic—A scale composed of twelve half-steps, rather than seven pitches in most other Western scales.

Coda—A short phrase at the end of a piece that complements the introduction; also called a tag.

Collective Improvisation—A style of improvising in which all players solo simultaneously.

Comping—The accompaniment style used to back up a soloist.

Consonance—A pleasing arrangement of sounds.

Contrapuntal—One musical idea set against another in *counterpoint*.

Dissonance—A displeasing arrangement of sounds.

Double-Time—When the rhythm or soloists proceed twice as fast.

Dynamics—Various degrees of volume control in a composition, e.g., p = soft, f = loud.

Effects—Electronic sounds produced by electronic devices.

Embouchure—The relationship of the mouth to the mouthpiece of an instrument.

Extensions—Used in melody or harmony by adding notes on top of the chords.

Fake Book—A collection of jazz and/or popular standard tunes used by musicians. Usually, the melodies are written with chord symbols to be improvised or "faked" by the musician. Lyrics are sometimes included.

Faking—Musicians' slang for improvising.

Feedback—A harsh, dissonant sound caused by overloading an amplifier.

Fills—Musical figures used to punctuate the ending of phrases.

Flat—An accidental that lowers a pitch one-half step (♭).

Flat Fours—Four beat style typical of the early New Orleans dixieland bands.

Front Line—A term in bop music to describe the horn players in front of the rhythm section.

Funky—Refers to down-home gospel style with strong blues elements. Also, the modern percussive style derived from rock as used in hard bop. The term was used in the early South to describe anything extremely distasteful or revolting.

Gig—Musicians' slang for a job.

Glissando—A rapid slide between pitches. True glissandi can only be played on the trombone and stringed instruments; however, the effect is used by most jazz instruments.

Harmony—The use of chords organized into progressions in which each chord relates to the other.

Head—The primary melody in any form, such as the A theme in AABA form. Also slang for a memorized theme.

Head Chart—A composition that is created by the musicians themselves, rather than by a composer or arranger.

Hip—Musicians' slang for a favorable reaction to another musician.

Horn—Any wind instrument played in jazz.

Improvisation—A solo which is created to a given set of chords extemporaneously. There are three basic types of improvisation:

1. Inside the changes—the player improvises on the basic scale or notes provided by the chords (traditional).
2. On top of the changes—the player improvises above the basic scale notes provided by the chords (modal).
3. Outside the changes—player improvises outside the basic scale or notes provided by the chords (free).

Interval—The distance from one pitch to the next.

Intonation—Playing "in tune" with accurate pitches.

Jam Session—An informal gathering of musicians to play for fun and learning.

Key—The key signature represents the number of sharps or flats that designate the tonal center, or "home key," of a composition.

Lay Back—One of the major differences between classical music which is on the beat and jazz which has a more relaxed melodic approach slightly behind.

Lick—A short figure or phrase used by musicians for improvising.

Melody—A series of musical notes or pitches that express a complete musical thought.

Meter—The number of beats per measure, as indicated by the meter signature. The top number indicates the number of beats per measure and the bottom number indicates which note values receive a beat. Also called *time signature*.

Mode—Refers to any kind of a variety of scales. Usually derived from the seven Greek modes such as the common Dorian or Mixolydian.

Modulation—A change of key.

Motive—A short musical phrase.

Ostinato—A short repeated rhythmic figure much like a vamp.

Pedal Point—A pitch that is sustained under chord progressions, usually in the bass.

Phrase—A musical statement; a series of phrases expresses a complete thought, or melody.

Pitch—High or low quality of a note; vibrations. A = 440 vibrations per second.

Polyphony—Two or more melodies playing simultaneously; counterpoint.

Polyrhythm—Two or more contrasting rhythms, played simultaneously.

Polytonal—Two or more simultaneous key signatures, or tonal centers.

Progression—The succession of chords as they relate to one another when used in harmony.

Quarter-Tones—Pitches that are approximately 1/4 step apart, as used in East Indian "ragas."

Rest—Silence in music for any duration.

Rhythm—The regular beats or pulses used in music.

Riff—A short melodic or rhythmic idea that is repeated, as in the music of the Swing Era.

Root—The fundamental pitch of a chord or its lowest tone.

Scat—A type of singing without words or lyrics.

Segue—A connecting passage between two sections. Also, *interlude*.

Set—A single playing session.

Sharp—An accidental that raises a pitch one-half step (♯).

Shout Chorus—The climactic finale section of a big band arrangement, in which several riffs are used in call and response, as in the Swing Era.

Sideman—Any musician who is not the leader.

Sight-Read—Playing or singing a composition from a score at first sight.

Sitting In—When a musician who is not a regular member of a group joins in a session, or jam.

Society—Musicians' slang for a commercial style.

Standard—A popular composition that is a jazz classic.

Swing—Music of the swing era featuring riffs. Also, modern jazz feeling in a laid-back style.

Syncopation—A rhythmic pattern of accenting a normally weak beat or reversing the strong and weak beat patterns.

Tag—A short ending added to the end of a piece. Coda.

Tempo—The speed of a composition. An example of universal measurement is ♩ = 120: a quarter note equals 120 beats in 60 seconds.

Texture—Generally used to describe the weight of the music as thick, heavy, or thin, light.

Tight—Musicians' slang for a well-rehearsed group.

Timbre—Tonal color of an instrument or voice.

Time Signature—See Meter.

Tone—Sound quality of a voice or instrument. Also, Pitch.

Tone Cluster—A group of unrelated notes played as a dissonant chord.

Trading Solos—Usually done between two instruments or voices, as solos with specified limits, e.g., trading fours = trading four bars.

Tutti—When the entire ensemble plays together.

Up-Tempo—A fast speed.

Vamp—A repeated melodic, rhythmic, or harmonic figure used in modern jazz and fusion.

Vibrato—The air coloring of a tone used by a singer or instrumentalist to give intensity or intimacy to the sound.

Walking Bass—A swing style in fours used by the bass player playing a pitch on each beat in a walking style ascending or descending.

Woodshed—Musicians' slang for practicing alone.

BIBLIOGRAPHY

Armstrong, Louis. *Satchmo: My Life in New Orleans.* Englewood Cliffs, N.J.: Prentice-Hall, 1954.

Carr, Ian. *Miles Davis: A Biography.* New York: William Morrow, 1982.

Coker, Jerry. *Improvising Jazz.* New York: Prentice-Hall, 1982.

Collier, James L. *Benny Goodman and the Swing Era.* New York: Oxford University Press, 1989.

Dance, Stanley. *The World of Duke Ellington.* New York: Da Capo, 1970.

Dance, Stanley. *The World of Swing.* New York: Da Capo, 1970.

Davis, Francis. *In the Moment: Jazz in the 1980s.* New York: Oxford University Press, 1986.

Davis, Miles, with Quincy Troupe. *The Autobiography.* New York: Simon and Schuster, 1989.

Ellington, Duke. *Music Is My Mistress.* New York: Da Capo, 1973.

Feather, Leonard. *The Encyclopedia of Jazz.* New York: Horizon, 1960.

Gillespie, Dizzy. *To Be or Not To Bop.* New York: Doubleday, 1979.

Goldberg, Joe. *Jazz Masters of the '50s.* New York: Da Capo, 1965.

Hodier, Andre. *Jazz: Its Evolution and Essence.* New York: Grove Press, 1980.

Hodier, Andre. *Toward Jazz.* New York: Grove Press, 1963.

Kolodin, Irving. *Benny Goodman: The Kingdom of Swing.* Harrisburg, PA: Stackpole, 1939.

Litweiler, John. *The Freedom Principle: Jazz After 1958.* New York: Da Capo Reprint, 1990.

Lomax, Alan. *Mister Jelly Roll: The Fortunes of Jelly Roll Morton, New Orleans Creole and "Inventor of Jazz."* New York: Grove Press, 1950.

Lyons, Len. *The Great Jazz Pianists.* New York: Morrow Quill, 1972.

Martin, William. *The Art of Jazz: Ragtime to Bebop.* New York: Da Capo, 1973.

Murray, Albert. *Stompin' the Blues.* New York: McGraw-Hill, 1976.

Placksin, Sally. *American Women in Jazz.* New York: Wideview Books, 1982.

Reisner, Robert. *Bird: The Legend of Charlie Parker.* New York: Da Capo, 1962.

Rose, Al. *Storyville, New Orleans.* Tuscaloosa, Ala.: The University of Alabama Press, 1974.

Schuller, Gunther. *Early Jazz.* New York: Oxford University Press, 1968.

Schuller, Gunther. *The Swing Era.* New York: Oxford University Press, 1989.

Shaw, Arnold. *The Jazz Age.* New York: Oxford University Press, 1987.

Simon, George T. *The Big Bands.* New York: Macmillan, 1974.

Stearns, Marshall. *The Story of Jazz.* New York: Oxford University Press, 1962.

Stewart, Rex. *Jazz Masters of the '30s.* New York: Da Capo, 1972.

Sudhalter, R.M., and Evans, P.R. *Bix: Man and Legend.* New York: Schirmer, 1974. (Out of print.)

Thomas, J.C. *Chasin' the Trane: The Music and Mystique of John Coltrane.* New York: Da Capo, 1975.

Williams, Martin. *Jazz Masters of New Orleans.* New York: Da Capo, 1970.

Williams, Martin. *The Jazz Tradition.* New York: Oxford University Press, 1983.

DISCOGRAPHY

The Smithsonian Collection of Classic Jazz (SCCJ), revised edition. CD edition RD 033 A5 19477. Telephone: 1-800-336-5221

Early Roots

Alan Lomax: *World Library of Folk and Primitive Music, Vol. 11*. Columbia KL-205
Follett Educational Corporation: *The Origins and Development of Jazz*. Columbia L25
Stephen Jay: *Africa. Drum, Chant and Instrumental Music, 1976*. Explorer Series, Elektra 9-72073-2

Blues

Robert Johnson: *King of the Delta Blues Singers*. Columbia 1654
Leadbelly (Huddie Leadbetter): *Leadbelly: The Last Sessions*. Folkways FP 241
Fredrick Ramsey, Jr.: *The South, Vol. I*. Folkways Records FJ 2801

Ragtime

The Greatest Ragtime of the Century. Biograph BCD-103
Joshua Rifkin: *Piano Rags by Scott Joplin*. Nonesuch H-71248
Gunther Schuller: *The Red Back Book—Scott Joplin*. Angel S36060 (out of print)

New Orleans

Louis Armstrong: *Louis Armstrong and His Hot Five, Vol. I*. Columbia 44049
Louis Armstrong: *Young Louis, the Sideman, 1924–1927*. MCA 1301
Joe King Oliver: *King Oliver's Jazz Band, 1923*. Columbia 12744
The Original Dixieland Jass Band: *The 75th Anniversary, 1992*. BMG Bluebird 61098-2

Chicago

Bix Beiderbecke: *Singing the Blues, Vol. I*. Columbia 45450
Fredrick Ramsey, Jr.: *Chicago, Vol. 6*. Folkways Records FJ 2806

Pre-Swing

Duke Ellington: *The Brunswick Era, Vol. I. 1926–29.* MCA 42325
Fletcher Henderson: *Developing an American Orchestra, 1923–1937.* Smithsonian P2-13710 (2 LPs). Tel. 1-800-336-5221
Fletcher Henderson: *Fletcher Henderson Orchestra, 1923–1927.* Biograph BLP 12039
Paul Whiteman: *Paul Whiteman, Vol. I.* RCA LPV-55

Swing

Big Band Jazz: *From the Beginnings to the Fifties.* Smithsonian. (4 CDs: 2202, 6 LPs: 2200, 3 Cassettes: 2201.) Tel. 1-800-336-5221
Duke Ellington: *Ellington at Newport.* Columbia 40587
Duke Ellington: *The Far East Suite.* Bluebird 7640
Benny Goodman: *The Carnegie Hall Jazz Concert, 1938.* Columbia 40244
Benny Goodman: *The Benny Goodman Sextet Featuring Charlie Christian, 1939–1941.* Columbia 45144

Bebop

Dizzy Gillespie: *Dizziest.* RCA 5785-4-RB
Dizzy Gillespie: *The Development of an American Artist, 1940–1946.* Smithsonian (2). Telephone 1-800-336-5221
Thelonious Monk: *Blue Monk, Vol. 2.* Prestige PR 7848
Charlie Parker: *The Savoy Original Master Takes, Vols. 1–2.* SJ ZDS 8801 (2)

Cool, West Coast, Progressive

Chet Baker: *The Complete Pacific Jazz Live and Studio Recordings of the Chet Baker Quartet with Russ Freeman.* Mosaic MR4-113, MR4-122. Mail order address: Mosaic Records/35 Melrose Place/Stamford, CT 06902. Telephone (202) 327-7111
Dave Brubeck: *Time Out.* Columbia 40585
Miles Davis: *The Complete Birth of the Cool.* Capitol CDP7-92862-2
Miles Davis: *Elevator to the Scaffold.* Phillips 822566-2
Miles Davis: *Porgy and Bess.* Columbia 40647
Miles Davis: *Kind of Blue.* Columbia 40579
Stan Kenton: *Stan Kenton Conducts the Los Angeles Neophonic Orchestra.* Creative World 1013
Stan Kenton: *Stan Kenton's Greatest Hits.* Capitol 48437, 16182
Stan Kenton: *Kenton Showcase.* Creative World 1026E
Stan Kenton: *This Modern World/City of Glass.* Creative World 1006E
Gerry Mulligan: *Gerry Mulligan and Chet Baker.* Prestige 24106 (2)

Third Stream

John Lewis: *The Art of the MJQ: The Atlantic Years*. Atlantic 2-301
John Lewis: Orchestra U.S.A.: *Sonorities*. Columbia 9195
Swingle Singers: *Jazz Sebastian Bach*. Phillips 824544

Hard Bop

Art Blakey: *One Night in Birdland, 1954*. Blue Note (2) 81521, 81552
Clifford Brown: *Study in Brown*. Emarcy 814 646-2
John Coltrane: *Giant Steps*. Atlantic 1311
Maynard Ferguson: *Message from Newport*. Roulette R-52012 (out of print)

Free Jazz, Experimentalists

Anthony Braxton: *New York, Fall 1974*. Arista AL 4032
Ornette Coleman: *Free Jazz*. Atlantic 1364
Charles Mingus: *Mingus Ah Um*. Columbia 40648
George Russell: *New York, N.Y./Jazz in the Space Age*. MCA 2-4017 (2)
Sun Ra: *Purple Delight*. A&M 75021

Jazz-Rock

Maynard Ferguson: *M. F. Horn/M. F. Horn II*. Columbia 33660
Don Ellis: *Connection*. Columbia KC 31766 (out of print)

Latin

Chick Corea: *Light as a Feather*. Polydor 5525
Paquito D'Rivera: *Manhattan Burn*. Columbia 40583
Keith Jarrett: *El Jucio*. Atlantic SD 1673
Chuck Mangione: *Land of Make Believe*. Mercury 684 CD 822539-2
Arturo Sandoval: *Flight to Freedom*. GRP-GRD-9643

Jazz-Fusion

Chick Corea: *The Chick Corea Elektric Band*. GRP 1026, CD 9535
Chick Corea: *Inside Out*. GRP 9601
Miles Davis: *Amandla*. Warner Bros. 25873
Miles Davis: *Tutu*. Warner Bros. 25490
Miles Davis: *Bitches Brew*. Columbia 40577 (2)
Don Ellis: *Electric Bath*. Columbia C30855 (out of print)
Return to Forever: *Hymn of the Seventh Galaxy*. Polydor 825336
Weather Report: *Heavy Weather*. Columbia 34418

Weather Report: *I Sing the Body Electric*. Columbia 46107
Weather Report: *Weather Report 8:30*. Columbia 36030
Yellow Jackets: *Green Horse*. GRP-GRC-9630

Pop-Fusion

101 North: *101 North*. Valley Vue 72945
Passport: *Talk Back*. Atlantic 7-81937-4
Spyro Gyra: *Morning Dance*. MCA 1650
Steps Ahead: *N.Y.C.* Capitol 4-91354
Yellow Jackets: *Politics*. MCA 6236
Yellow Jackets: *The Spin*. MCA 6304

Mainstream

Geri Allen: *In the Year of the Dragon*. JMT 834-428-4
Michael Brecker: *Now You See It, Now You Don't*. GRP 9622
Kenny Burrell: *Guitar Forms*. Verve 2070
Chick Corea: *Akoustic Band*. GRP 9582
Bill Evans: *The Bill Evans Album*. Columbia 30855
Bill Evans: *Bill Evans Trio with Symphony*. Verve 8640
Stan Getz: *Focus*. Verve 2071
Harper Brothers: *Remembrance, Live at the Village Vanguard*. Verve 841723
Woody Herman: *Giant Steps*. Fantasy 9432
Woody Herman: *The Thundering Herds*. Columbia CJT 44108
Freddie Hubbard: *Sky Dive*. Columbia 44171
Thad Jones/Mel Lewis: *Consummation*. Blue Note BST 84346
Herbie Mann: *Herbie Mann at the Village Gate*. Atlantic 1380
Manhattan Transfer: *Vocalese*. Atlantic 7-81266-4
Branford Marsalis: *Random Abstract*. Columbia 44055
Wynton Marsalis: *Think of One*. Columbia 38641
Bobby McFerrin: *Simple Pleasures*. EMI-48059
Bob Mintzer: *Urban Contours*. DMP 467
Wes Montgomery: *Goin' Out of My Head*. Verve 2110
New York Voices: *New York Voices*. GRP 9589
Marcus Roberts: *Deep in the Shed*. RCA 3078
Diane Schuur: *Diane Schuur Collection*. GRP 9591
Clark Terry/Bobby Brookmeyer: *Tonight*. Mainstream 56043

New Age

Shadowfax: *Folksongs for a Nuclear Village*. Capitol 7469242
Shadowfax: *The Odd Get Even*. Private Music 2065-2-P

VIDEOGRAPHY

The Art Ensemble of Chicago: *Live from the Showcase*. Rhapsody Films, Inc.

Toshiko Akiyoshi: *Jazz Is My Native Language*. Rhapsody Films, Inc.

Louis Armstrong: *Satchmo: Louis Armstrong*. CBS Video CMV 49024

Count Basie: *Last of the Blue Devils*. Rhapsody Films, Inc.

Chet Baker: *Let's Get Lost*. BMG Video 3090-3N

Art Blakey And The Jazz Messengers: *The Jazz Life*. Sony Video J0319

Art Blakey: *Art Blakey: The Jazz Messenger*. Rhapsody Films, Inc. 1136

Blues Like Showers of Rain: Rhapsody Films, Inc.

Ornette Coleman: *Ornette Coleman Trio*. Rhapsody Films, Inc.

Ornette Coleman: *Made in America*. COD Video

John Coltrane: *The Coltrane Legacy*. Video Artists International 69035

Chick Corea: *Chick Corea*. Sony Video J0077

Chick Corea: *Inside Out*. GRP Video GRV-9601

Prime Cuts: *Jazz and Beyond*. CBS Fox Video 7114

Miles Davis: *Miles in Paris*. Warner Reprise Video 3-38186

Duke Ellington: *Duke Ellington and His Orchestra, 1929–1941*. Jazz Classics JCVC 101

Peter Erskine: *Timekeeping 2*. DCI Music Video, Inc.

Bill Evans: *Bill Evans on the Creative Process*. Rhapsody Films, Inc.

Gil Evans: *Gil Evans and His Orchestra*. V.I.E.W., Inc.

Dizzy Gillespie: *Jivin' In Bebop, 1947*. Jazz Classics JCVC 115

GRP Super Live in Concert. GRP Video GRV-1650

Freddie Hubbard: *Freddie Hubbard*. Sony Video J0059

Keith Jarrett: *Last Solo*. Sony Video J0317

Keith Jarrett: *Standards Live*. Sony Video J0318

Konkombe: The Nigerian Pop Scene. Beats of the Heart Series, Shanachie 1201

The Ladies Sing the Blues: V.I.E.W., Inc.

Latin American Percussion: Rhythms and Rhythm Insrtuments from Cuba: DCI Music Videos

Latin American Percussion Video Session. Sony Video

Mel Lewis: *Mel Lewis and His Big Band*. V.I.E.W., Inc.

Manhattan Transfer: *Vocalese*. BMG Video

Branford Marsalis: *Steep*. CBS Video CMV 49021

Wynton Marsalis: *Blues and Swing*. CBS Video CMV 49002

Rob McConnell: *Rob McConnell*. Sony Video

Kid Punch Miller: *'Til the Butcher Cuts Him Down*. Rhapsody Films, Inc.
Charlie Parker: *The Triumph of Charlie Parker*. Sony Video J0509
Jaco Pastorius: *Modern Electric Bass*. DCI Music Video, Inc.
Playboy Jazz Festival, Vol. I. BMG Video
Playboy Jazz Festival, Vol. II. BMG Video
Buddy Rich: *Channel One Set, Live at Studio B*. Sony Video J0089
Max Roach: *In Concert/In Session*. DCI Music Video, Inc. VH0015
Marcus Roberts: *Deep in the Shed*. BMG Video 3088-3-N
Sonny Rollins: *Saxophone Colossus*. Sony Video J0583
Salsa: Latin Pop in the Cities. Beats of the Heart Series. Shanachie 1203
The Sound of Jazz. Vintage Jazz Classics VJC-2001-4
The Spirit of Samba: Black Music of Brazil. Beats of the Heart Series, Shanachie
    1207
Diane Schuur: *Diane Schuur/Count Basie Orchestra*. PI-A 2240
Shadowfax: *Firewalker*. Capitol Records
Swing: The Best of the Big Bands, Vols. I-IV. MCA Video
Weather Report: *Evolutionary Spiral*. Sony Video
Paul Whiteman: *The King of Jazz*. MCA Video
Sarah Vaughan: *Sass and Brass*. Jazzland

VIDEO DISTRIBUTORS

CMV Video
Columbia Records
Room 783
P.O. Box 4450
New York, NY 10101
(212) 445-2069

DCI Music Video, Inc.
541 Avenue of the Americas
New York, NY 10011
(212) 691-1884

GRP Records
555 West 57th St.
New York, NY 10019
(212) 245-7033

Jazz Aids
Jamey Aebersold
P.O. Box 1244C
New Albany, IN 47150
(800) 456-1388

The Jazz Store*
P.O. Box 43179, Dept. O
Upper Montclair, NJ 07043
(201) 509-8834

Jazzland
Box 366
Dayton, OH 45401
(513) 222-2413

MCA Home Video
70 Universal City Plaza
University City, CA 91608

Rhapsody Films, Inc.
P.O. Box 179
New York, NY 10014
(212) 243-0152

Sony Video Software Co.
Sony Corp. of America
1700 Broadway
New York, NY 10019

V.I.E.W., Inc.
34 East 23rd St.
New York, NY 10010
(212) 674-5550

Video Artists Inter., Inc.
P.O. Box 153
Ansonia Station
New York, NY 10023
(212) 799-7798

Zeitgeist Films, Ltd.
200 Waverly Place, Suite 1
New York, NY 10014
(212) 727-1989

---

*Highly recommended (catalog, $3.00)

INDEX